Critical Political Theory and Radical Practice

Series editor
Stephen Eric Bronner
Department of Political Science
Rutgers University
New Brunswick, NJ, USA

The series introduces new authors, unorthodox themes, critical interpretations of the classics and salient works by older and more established thinkers. A new generation of academics is becoming engaged with immanent critique, interdisciplinary work, actual political problems, and more broadly the link between theory and practice. Each in this series will, after his or her fashion, explore the ways in which political theory can enrich our understanding of the arts and social sciences. Criminal justice, psychology, sociology, theater and a host of other disciplines come into play for a critical political theory. The series also opens new avenues by engaging alternative traditions, animal rights, Islamic politics, mass movements, sovereignty, and the institutional problems of power. Critical Political Theory and Radical Practice thus fills an important niche. Innovatively blending tradition and experimentation, this intellectual enterprise with a political intent hopes to help reinvigorate what is fast becoming a petrified field of study and to perhaps provide a bit of inspiration for future scholars and activists.

More information about this series at
http://www.springer.com/series/14938

Kurt Jacobsen

International Politics and Inner Worlds

Masks of Reason under Scrutiny

Kurt Jacobsen
Department of Political Science
University of Chicago
Chicago, IL
USA

Critical Political Theory and Radical Practice
ISBN 978-3-319-85376-5   ISBN 978-3-319-54352-9 (eBook)
DOI 10.1007/978-3-319-54352-9

© The Editor(s) (if applicable) and The Author(s) 2017
Softcover reprint of the hardcover 1st edition 2017
This work is subject to copyright. All rights are solely and exclusively licensed by the Publisher, whether the whole or part of the material is concerned, specifically the rights of translation, reprinting, reuse of illustrations, recitation, broadcasting, reproduction on microfilms or in any other physical way, and transmission or information storage and retrieval, electronic adaptation, computer software, or by similar or dissimilar methodology now known or hereafter developed.
The use of general descriptive names, registered names, trademarks, service marks, etc. in this publication does not imply, even in the absence of a specific statement, that such names are exempt from the relevant protective laws and regulations and therefore free for general use.
The publisher, the authors and the editors are safe to assume that the advice and information in this book are believed to be true and accurate at the date of publication. Neither the publisher nor the authors or the editors give a warranty, express or implied, with respect to the material contained herein or for any errors or omissions that may have been made. The publisher remains neutral with regard to jurisdictional claims in published maps and institutional affiliations.

Cover Credit: CoverZoo / Alamy Stock Photo

Printed on acid-free paper

This Palgrave Macmillan imprint is published by Springer Nature
The registered company is Springer International Publishing AG
The registered company address is: Gewerbestrasse 11, 6330 Cham, Switzerland

In memory of Lloyd Rudolph and Susanne Hoeber Rudolph. Teachers, friends, and marvelous people. Paying it forward.

Contents

Introduction: Politics All the Way Down	1
Perestroika and American Political Science	17
Dueling Constructivisms: A Post-Mortem on the Ideas Debate in Mainstream IR	41
Why Do States (Bother to) Deceive? Managing Trust at Home and Abroad	73
COIN Flips: Counterinsurgency Theory and American IR	109
Why Freud Matters: Psychoanalysis and IR Revisited	149
The Mystique of Genetic Correctness	187
Loose Ends: Considerations on the Aftermaths of the Celtic Tiger and the Northern 'Troubles'	207
Conclusion: Algren, Academe and Conformity	217
Index	227

Introduction: Politics All the Way Down

Social scientists long have grappled with the influence upon their research of interest-driven or theory-derived ideas that can shape what they see and do.[1] This nettlesome plight deepens when one allows for emotional affinities between theory and theorist too.[2] 'External reality has a way,' as John Steinbeck literarily put it, 'of not being so external after all.'[3] These tricky factors may well be unintended, so much so that the researcher is blissfully unaware of them. The search for knowledge, psychologist Abraham Maslow noted, validly can be viewed as an anxiety-allaying enterprise in which science is 'considered a technique with which fallible men try to outwit their own human propensities to fear the truth, to avoid, it, and to distort it.'[4] Given that there is no such critter as immaculate perception, no matter how hard some analysts try to achieve or contrive it, state managers employ doctrines, the public resorts to 'rules of thumb,' and social scientists apply models as useful shortcuts, which do not always work. Yet there is no way to maneuver through our 'blooming, buzzing confusion' without doctrines, rules of thumb and models, at least at the outset of any venture.

When pioneering the sociology of knowledge, Karl Mannheim described how *particular* and *total* versions of ideology, arising from our skewed class and cultural experiences, affect the way we behold the wider world.[5] 'The ideas expressed by the subject are thus regarded as functions of that point of view,' Mannheim realized.[6] 'This means that opinion, statements, propositions and systems of ideas are not taken at their face value but are interpreted in the light of the life-situation of the one who expresses them.' So an ideology is not just a device for masquerading motives, as is commonly understood. Ideologies are unconscious in significant ways too, which is where psychoanalysis can help to pry them out into the sunlight. 'Orthodoxy,' Orwell pinpointed, 'is unconsciousness.'[7] Those under orthodoxy's spell don't know it and most, who feel safely nestled in a paradigmatic cocoon, wouldn't care if they did.

Examples? Christopher Lasch reproached Cold War intellectuals in the 1960s who so thoroughly 'internalized an elitist bureaucratic point of view that they were no longer aware of the way in which their writing had come to serve as rationalizations of American world power.'[8] Another searing critic chided nuclear strategists, entranced by mathematical models, for failing to detect that changes in nuclear strategy were occurring in reaction to technological innovations, rather than on the basis of circumspect political thought, as they portrayed it.[9] Philip Mirowski depicted the Nash equilibrium, a RAND gimmick stipulating economic agents are serenely rational, as the supreme mathematical expression of the 'essence of the closed world mentality of impervious rationality,' of the perfectly 'paranoid core of the Cold war fascination with axiomatics that so pervaded the social sciences in the post-war period.'[10] One can go on. Scientists, as historian E. A. Burtt attested, are no more immune against *zeitgeists*, cultural prejudices and fads as they grow up than are used-car salesmen or grammar school teachers.[11] An inquiry into the sordid history of eugenics should be enough to dispel the notion that scientists cannot wittingly or unwittingly don masks of reason.

An archetypal motive for doing so is the all too human passion for creating a precise order, one pleasingly attuned to familiar concepts and amenable to available tools. In the field of psychology a century ago John Watson's behaviorism once 'meant to many young men and women of the time a new orientation and a new hope when the old guides had become hopelessly discredited in their eyes,' Woodworth found.[12] 'It was a religion to take the place of religion.' The spread of scientism—a compulsive reduction of all forms of knowledge to the procrustean categories of natural science—became 'an evangelical gospel of salvation—promising, in its characteristic expression, escape from the irrational freedom of the human will.'[13] Scientism constantly reappears in new guises because the impulse behind it—the quest for absolute certainty—is an ineradicable human yearning. There is nothing necessarily wrong with it if you understand it and do not let it get a grip on you, but the sirens' song is eerily sweet.[14]

'Men are disturbed not by things,' Epictetus surmised, 'but by the principles and notions which they form concerning things.'[15] A realist way of saying the same thing is that the world is out there, but our perceptions of it are not. 'Inasmuch as man is a creature living primarily in history and society,' Mannheim explains, 'the "existence" that surrounds him is never "existence as such," but is always a concrete historical form of social existence.'[16] Mannheim stressed the difficulties of thinking outside of an historical context, 'outside the box' in modern parlance. Thorstein Veblen accordingly judged about a philosophical foray that this noteworthy work 'is logically consistent and convincing, but it proceeds on the ground of reasoned conduct, calculus of advantage, not on the ground of cause and effect.'[17] What worried Veblen was that the 'conclusion reached by public or class opinion is as much, or more, a matter of sentiment than of logical inference; and that the sentiment which animates men, singly or collectively, is as much, or more, an outcome of habit and native propensity as of calculated material interest.'[18] Veblen was criticizing Marxism, not rationalist theories, but his point holds for positivist renditions of both intellectual enterprises.[19]

Sound scientific theories dispel the errors of ideologies or the blind spots of superseded scientific theories, but in time can encrust into forms of ideologies themselves, Feyerabend warned.[20] Mannheim saw social science as a way of prying through ideological barriers through application of 'relationism,' which is what Perestroikans in political science (next Chapter) would call a 'methodological pluralist' device for flushing out into the open self-interests and unconscious biases.[21] Awareness, not extinction, of biases is the primary objective because for Mannheim without a personal interest, or bias, there would be no projects we would choose to undertake.[22] The Frankfurt School scholars stated explicitly that their investigations were guided by the emancipatory intent of calling into being a 'rational' society, by which they meant rationality drastically different from formal theorists.[23] Every critic could take their intent into account when assessing their studies.

Debates about paradigmatic blinders can get very touchy very fast because they strike so close to home, so close to the inner worlds of the disputants. Since Kuhn, at least, social scientists confronted the proposition, in its most radical implication, that paradigms decide for us what it is scientifically valid to perceive.[24] There is no avoiding Kuhn's bedrock conclusion that every paradigm, however useful, constructs 'for a time' an inherently limited and incomplete picture of the universe—unless we deny the conclusion.[25] For formal theorists from the Vienna Circle onward, the philosophy of science is a unitary and consensual entity that appears to the rest of us to have ceased operations, so to speak, near the turn of the nineteenth into the twentieth century.[26] Ardent positivists remain a potent presence in social sciences. Of such folks Wittgenstein reported after meeting Moritz Schlick, whose logical positivism he earlier abandoned as insupportable, 'Each of us must have thought the other was crazy.'[27]

For latter-day philosopher of science Stephen Toulmin, what is deemed universally rational may not even be sane in all situations. So universal rationality as a goal had to be 'counterbalanced with the practice of everyday reason.'[28] The triumph of modern science magnified the premium for the abstract and the general. Because positivist scholars, aggressively imitating Newtonian science, prize parsimony, they not only neglect salient details but often lose the whole plot of what is going on under their pinched gaze. Take the pronounced inclination of rational choice theorists indiscriminately to attribute rationalistic motives. 'The assumption that actors' preferences and choices are determined solely by calculations of rational self-interest is problematic,' Susanne Rudolph reproved, 'not only because it ignores the role of sentiment, passion, and commitment in behavior, not only because "rationality" itself is scarce rather than ubiquitous, but also because it is diversely defined by different cultures.'[29]

This book pries mostly at 'masks of reason' in international politics, which are of several sorts: (1) masks that political agents sport when they deceive us about their actions and their motivated misdiagnoses of 'definitions of the situation' (Chaps. "Dueling Constructivisms: A Post-Mortem on the Ideas Debate in Mainstream IR" and "Why do States (Bother to) Deceive? Managing Trust at Home and Abroad"), (2) the masks that models, uncritically or sweepingly applied, themselves can warp into (Chaps. "Perestroika and American Political Science" and "Why Freud Matters: Psychoanalysis and IR Revisited") and (3) masks covering the internal worlds of relevant players and their analysts (Chaps. "COIN Flips: Counterinsurgency Theory and American IR" , "Why Freud Matters: Psychoanalysis and IR Revisited" and "The Mystique of Genetic Correctness"). The 'masks of reason' scrutinized here are positivist methods insofar as they aspire to disciplinary dominance, constructivism of a conventional kind, realism insofar as it embraces elitism and excludes the role of the domestic realm, counterinsurgency shibboleths, crude genetic explanations of social phenomena and neoliberal developmental wisdom as exemplified in the ballyhooed Celtic Tiger.

Freud was quite right that acknowledging our inclinations, our biases and our aims frees us in the quest for knowledge and that we are likely to know the world best by knowing ourselves better.[30] Mannheim's sociology of knowledge aligns with this Freudian counsel. The sources of our attitudes, appraisals and inferences do not lie entirely with the object but as much in the beholder. Formal theorists seem to believe they operate entirely outside culture or else imagine they can erect a neat scaffolding, an Archimedean point, on which to tower above the mire.[31] The concomitant imperialistic tactic is presuming one's own culture rises above all others and even above culture itself. 'No one here but us guys in white lab coats,' as an old and much-missed teacher puckishly put it.

As always those who firmly believe they are least ideological are the most committed to skewed systems. I cannot count the seminars where I witnessed a scholar respond to fatal empirical strikes amidships on their stately formal model by taking refuge in a last ditch appeal to its 'elegance,' which editors of the professional journals, being kindred spirits, fawn over. It usually worked. The elegance of the model, for like-minded modelers, transcends many a whopping shortcoming. This one-size-fits-all craze is of course nothing new. 'The second law of thermodynamics, or the principle of natural selection, or the notion of unconscious motivation, or the organization of the means of production does not explain everything, not even everything human,' Geertz assessed, 'but it still explains something; and our attention shifts to isolating just what that something is, to disentangling ourselves from a lot of pseudoscience to which, in the first flush of its celebrity, it has also given rise.'[32] The 'first flush,' however, has yet to fade away.

RATIONALITY AND RESISTANCE

Rick: I stick my neck out for nobody.
   Captain Renault: A wise foreign policy.
   Casablanca (1942)[33]

   Rick in *Casablanca* did stick his nose into other people's business or else there would be no celebrated melodrama to which audiences respond warmly to this day. Rick was fictional, but the underlying motives, impulses and conflicts portrayed were not. Singing *La Marseillaise* in public places really was a common nationalist act of resistance in both Occupied and Vichy France.[34] It depends of course on how you define resistance, which for purposes of modeling convenience can be confined to blowing up things and shooting people. If so, resistance looks skimpy, but is that all there is to it? Do we not need to know more than the model permits?

Rational choice theory foresees no public resistance to powerful ruthless rulers because no payoff is high enough or sure enough or swift enough to offset the risk. This brutal wisdom (preceding rational choice modelers by millennia) is determined from the point of view of the managers, of the dominators who take the measure of, and try to stamp out, detectable resistance. The 'inner world' of the subjugated is banished because it is of no importance. One big catch for this dismissive strain of thought is deciphering what is rational from the resisters' point of view; yet another one is figuring how authorities go about detecting resistance. Consider briefly a crucial case, France under the Nazi occupation, as represented in a recent co-authored study on nationalism and resistance to foreign occupation, and which is much like any ambitious rationalist exercise.[35] Occupation is a matter of international politics; domestic resistance is a murkier matter of how the 'inner worlds' of a repressed population affect how they behave.

Of what is resistance, 'rational' or not, comprised? When is it reasonable to oppose malevolent rulers and why and how do rebels undertake so dangerous a task when the opponent will imprison, torture or kill not only them but associates, family and friends? (During the occupation 30,000 French were murdered in reprisals).[36] Our rationalist investigators, geared to cram oblong acts steadily into square peg categories, assume that no faintly rational person will resist, or at least not in a conspicuous way. They mount a sober-sounding argument that no causal links between nationalism and resistance actually exist.[37] So evidently the lesson for authorities contemplating future occupations is not to be deterred by mere 'affective commitments' such as anticipated nationalist reactions. French resistance was 'never a threat to German aims'; rather there was 'overwhelming compliance.'[38] Moreover, 'French patriots,' with the authors embracing the actors' self-definitions as such, 'voluntarily led Vichy France into collaboration with Germany.'[39] The authors boldly and indeed breathtakingly proclaim that the Vichy elite 'was at least as nationalistic, if not more so, than those who joined the resistance.'[40] Isn't it obvious? Were it otherwise their model would not make any sense.

French behavior is best explained by the international balance of power and domestic political competition in line with mainstream IR rationalist theories. Siding smartly with the likely winner, 'French rightwing nationalists chose collaboration with the Nazis as a means to suppress and persecute the French Left.' That point, at least, is indisputable, but by the 'French Left' don't they refer to patriots who are being persecuted? Apparently not, although they equate the Resistance with Vichy, which would have gotten them into considerable trouble in France after the Liberation when some 1500 collaborators were executed and many thousands were more killed in vigilante actions.[41] What for these scholars exactly does it take then to rate as a traitor?

Social actors who align predatorily with a foreign power in order to crush their local class inferiors, the majority of the national population, get dubbed patriots. Paxton, among others, robustly rejected the 'shield' argument that virtuous Vichy toiled to prevent France from experiencing even worse maladies.[42] The Vichy government, Ousby likewise judges, was 'more than a collaboration of common sense for survival but aimed at a rightist renaissance.'[43] Petain, that sour ascetic icon, was himself innocuously popular but the grasping Vichy regime never was and slid ever downward in public regard.[44] Jews, leftists and secularists knew they were marked men and women. Industrialists, however, sought German orders and with few exceptions 'when patriotism did not coincide with commercial interest, the latter was rarely sacrificed for the former.'[45] Jackson finds that the bureaucracy, the bourgeoisie, the Catholic hierarchy and the rich supported Vichy while workers, small farmers, small shopkeepers, and artisans opposed it from the start, and soon peasants opposed it too.[46] By late 1942, Paxton affirms, 'the Resistance became a force in the land.'[47] By late 1943, Mazower adds, 'the countryside in Vichy was mostly *maquis* controlled.'[48]

While armed resistance in many areas was virtually suicidal or mass murderous (given Nazi reprisal policy), Overy interestingly finds records that, like many continental peoples, the French, despite debacles like Dunkirk and Mers-al-Kebir, 'wanted the British to bomb collaborationist factories, despite costs and innocent casualties' and were inclined to blame Germans instead for considerable residential bombings.[49] The Allies bombed France more heavily in 1943, killing 7500 civilians and in the first 4 months of 1944 some 25,000 more.[50] De Gaulle in an October 1941 radio broadcast discouraged attacks by the sparsely armed and loosely organized Resistance until it really was in a position of some strength. His foremost concern anyway was a restoration, in his favor, of 'order and social hierarchy,' not encouraging insurrection outside his control.[51]

Must silence be construed as acquiescence? Germany siphoned 60% of French production, which fanned misery, disease, malnutrition and discontent.[52] Frank Manuel, author of a fine study of Isaac Newton as historian, cited later, served in the European Theater of Operations where he and other intelligence officers came to appreciate that 'French proletarians knew the technique of the slowdown and the acts of sabotage that could not be detected' and that their forced labor in factories 'probably did the Reich as much harm as good.'[53] Coal mining and Renault productivity was down 40% in 1942 versus 1939—some, but hardly all, attributable to wartime constraints.[54] 'All over France,' Moorehead notes, there were 'civil servants who falsified ration books, policemen who turned a blind eye, telephone operators who warned of impending raids' so that 'parallel to the map of Vichy was a map of decency.'[55] A repertoire of 'weapons of the weak' too can be availed of whereby 'thousands upon thousand of individual acts of insubordination and evasion create an economic and political barrier reef of their own.'[56] Did cumulative resistance of these least detectable kinds not matter? 'If there had been no resistance, France would still have been liberated,' Jackson concedes, but 'if there had been no resistance, the Liberation would have cost the Allies significantly higher casualties; if the Allies had more faith in the potential of the resistance, its contribution to saving allied lives would have been greater.'[57] Yet nationalism swelling up from the popular level is not a factor that need deter a major power contemplating occupation of another country. Someone in the grip of a formal rationalist framework might be forgiven for a consequent headlong dash past all these key elements toward unwarranted conclusions. Readers can count on the rest of the volume to proceed in this unrestrained critical vein.

The Chapters

The controversy surrounding rational choice theory, and its ancillary apparatus of statistical techniques, is the most educational and entertaining debate in political science and perhaps in all the social sciences, though each discipline has their own rendition of it. The Perestroika movement in political science, and how it played out, sets the stage for the remainder of the book. Rational choice theory is the application of economic methods and precepts to other fields. '[F]ormal theory involves the construction of specific mathematical models intended to represent particular real-world situations and the use of mathematics to identify the specific solutions ("equilibria") for the model(s).'[58] There is surely nothing inherently objectionable about this.[59] It has its uses. The more the merrier—except that this sentiment is hardly the aim of zealous rational choice proponents. 'It is one thing to test a fruitful line of investigation,' Mannheim cautioned, 'and another to regard it as the only path to the scientific treatment of an object.'[60]

In Chap. 1 "Perestroika and American Political Science" I perform a premature 'postmortem' on the ideas debate in mainstream international relations, which was generated by cumulative dissatisfactions with rational choice theory and also with certain tenets of realist theory. This chapter examines the shifty contours of this debate and explains how it reached its compromised limit in the form of 'conventional constructivism,' a highly bowdlerized form of critical theory and Gramscian cultural studies. 'Context' and Gramsci's 'common sense,' I argue, are sufficiently equivalent terms to enable some coherent conceptual connections to occur across a rather wide and, I suggest, ultimately unbridgeable intradisciplinary divide. The overarching obstacle remains the firm resistance of mainstream IR to integration with other social sciences.

In Chap. 2 "Dueling Constructivisms: A Post-Mortem on the Ideas Debate in Mainstream IR" asks why do democratic states bother try to deceive their own citizens as to certain unsavory foreign policies, their motives and their consequences. Surely, a population schooled in *realpolitik*, or garden-variety cynicism, would not need to be gulled, except that authorities adamantly believe that they do. This provocative question presupposes not only that states craft 'stories' to disguise activities abroad but that they do so because they are more constrained than they will admit by an audience of non-elite actors. Theories derived from *realpolitik* make little allowance for this impertinent domestic 'interference.' Yet there is plenty of evidence that in democracies the role of mass publics in driving, curbing or modifying the conduct of foreign policy is a force, and explanatory factor, to reckon with. Page and Jacobs marveled in their study regarding attitudes and awareness on policy issues that 'the general accuracy of the public's perceptions is remarkable, given the complexity of government policy, deliberate efforts to sow confusion and the wide range of topics there are to think about.'[61]

In Chap. 3 "Why do States (Bother to) Deceive? Managing Trust at Home and Abroad" examines the recent rehabilitation of counterinsurgency doctrine, especially as conducted by third-party interveners. The advent of the refurbished *US Army/Marine Corps Counter-insurgency Manual* in 2007, a volume with a painstakingly scholarly self-presentation, is the ignition point. This chapter is concerned with the shoddy yet resilient doctrinal justifications driving recent US interventions. The Vietnam War unsurprisingly persists as the crucial case for American scholars and policy makers who have strived mightily to reconstrue the history of counterinsurgency there as an unacknowledged triumph, which has become the standard account in American International relations scholarship. The chapter examines this ominous development and its implications. Regarding alleged COIN successes in Mosul in 2007, 'the Iraqis lied to the Americans, no question,' Dexter Filkins recollected.[62] 'But the worst lies were the ones Americans told themselves.' A receding of the tide of COIN enthusiasm after the US withdrawal from Iraq (but so far not Afghanistan if we count 'residual' troops) does not mean it will not, excuse the expression, surge again when elites judge it expedient to do so.

In Chap. 4 "COIN Flips: Counterinsurgency Theory and American IR" I take scholars of international relations to task for having eschewed the discipline of psychoanalysis. Here is the climactic section where I argue the case for an alternative and insightful way of approaching international politics, for incorporating the inner worlds of participants into our analyses. The fierce attacks on Freud and his fractious followers over the last generation clearly discouraged political scientists from exploring the considerable value of psychoanalytic methods. This chapter demonstrates under what kinds of circumstances psychoanalysis can prove to be a valid and enlightening interpretive approach. What is the significance in human behavior of the unconscious, that is, of motives and forces of which we are commonly unaware? The argument is that in most, if not all, cases, psychoanalytically attuned approaches yield important insights that expose masks of reason and illuminate motives guiding the way power is wielded.

In Chap. 5 "Why Freud Matters: Psychoanalysis and IR Revisited" examine the political implications of genetic research where most researchers seem to be mesmerized by a fallible model. Masks of reason are all too evident in the fast and loose way that sophisticated neo-eugenic methods and techniques are applied to serve underlying social agendas. Chapter 6 "The Mystique of Genetic Correctness" examines the social consequences of genetic hubris. Finally, Chap. 7 is a short but punchy appraisal of the follies of Irish economic development strategy, the last and only word in economic reason according to many devotees, since my book on the topic several decades back.[63] Groupthink ran ever more wild among bumptious elites in the Irish Republic right up to the great crash.

Most chapters in this volume, incidentally, first were presented, and benefitted from sharp and searching comments, at the Program on International Politics, Economics and Security (PIPES) at the University of Chicago, superbly shepherded all these years by Charles Lipson and, until a recent move to Oxford, Duncan Snidal too. Several chapters also appeared earlier in the *Review of International Studies, Cambridge Review of International Affairs, Journal of World-Systems Research, L'Economie Politique* and *International Relations*.

The latest lot of terrible simplifiers (*pace* Burckhart) do not realize that they are simplifiers, given how torturously complex their simplifications are, which, as Geertz understood, makes them more troubling because 'their errors are more sophisticated and their distortions subtler.'[64] The underlying irony is that if formalists really were interested in promoting multiple, or 'tripartite,' methods, many recruits rapidly would figure out what Green and Shapiro already did, that formal methods are oversold, under-theorized (devoid of critical self-reflection), usually trivial and often misleading.[65]

Still, in keeping with the spirit of methodological pluralism, these trenchant criticisms are no brief for abandoning the culprits, only against enthroning them. Mannheim, imperfect as his solution of 'relationism' may be, justifiably insisted that only a keen awareness of the social rootedness of thought enables us to handle distortive ideational influences. No zone free from human processing of knowledge exists in the social world. What we are dealing with all the time in political analysis is 'politics all the way down,' or 'winks upon winks upon winks' (or twitches) that require ethnographic and interpretive untangling, and always will, ever anew.

NOTES

1. See Louis Worth, 'Preface,' Karl Mannheim, *Ideology and Utopia* (New York: Harcourt, Brace Co, 1954), pp. xiii–xxxiii. Max Weber, 'Objectivity in the Social Sciences' in Edward Shils and Henry Finch, eds. *The Methodology of The Social Sciences* (New York Free Press, 1948), and John Dewey, *The Quest for Certainty* (New York: Capricorn, 1960).
2. Abraham Maslow, *The Psychology of Science: A Reconnaissance* (Chicago: Regnery Publishing, 1969), pp. 18–21.
3. John Steinbeck, *Travels with Charley* (New York, Random House, 1961), p. 139.
4. Ibid. p. 22. '[S]cientific words—prediction, control, rigor, certainty, exactness, preciseness, neatness, orderliness, lawfulness, quantification, proof, explanation, validation, reliability, rationality, organization,

etc.—are all capable of being pathologized when pushed to the extreme. All of them may be pressed into the service of the safety needs, i.e. they may become primarily anxiety-avoiding and anxiety-controlling mechanisms.'
5. Mannheim, *Ideology and Utopia*, pp. 49–50.
6. Mannheim, Ibid. p. 337. 'This then changes the task of a sociology of knowledge. We are to look not for ultimate truth, but for understanding historically situated truths, norms and modes of thought', (p. 339).
7. George Orwell, *Nineteen Eighty-Four* (London: Secker & Warburg, 1949) p. 46.
8. Christopher Lasch, 'The Cultural Cold War: A Short History of the Congress for Cultural Freedom' in Barton J. Bernstein, ed. *Towards a New Past: Dissenting Essays in American History* (New York: Vintage, 1969), p. 323. Nothing much has changed. See Bruce Kuklick, *Blind Oracles: Intellectuals and War from Kennan to Kissinger* (Princeton: Princeton University Press, 2006).
9. Carol Cohn, 'Sex and Death in the Rational world of Defense Intellectuals,' *Signs* 14, 4 (Summer 1987), p. 690. Also see Sharon Tamari-Gabrizi, *The Worlds of Herman Kahn: The Intuitive Science of Thermonuclear War* (Cambridge: Harvard University Press, 2005).
10. Philip Mirowski, *Machine Dreams: Economics Becomes a Cyborg Science* (New York: Cambridge University Press, 2002), pp. 343, 347. Mirowski quotes Evelyn Fox Keller on paranoid thinking: 'Everything must fit. The paranoid delusion suffers not from a lack of logic but from unreality. Indeed, its distortion derives, at least in part, from the very effort to make all the clues fit into a single interpretation', p. 341.
11. E. A, Burtt, *The Metaphysical Foundations of Modern Science* (New York: Doubleday Anchor, 1954), p. 17.
12. Robert S. Woodworth, *Contemporary Schools of Psychology* (New York: Ronald Press, 1948), p. 92–99.
13. Floyd Matson, *The Broken Image: Man, Science, and Society* (New York: Anchor, 1966), p. 8.
14. Domination is another motive for scientism. The Frankfurt School hint in the sirens reference is quite deliberate. See Max Horkheimer and Theodor Adorno, *The Dialectic of Enlightenment* (Stanford: Stanford University Press, 1972), pp. 26–27, 59.
15. Epictetus, *The Enchiridion* (New York: Dover, 2004), p. 4.
16. Mannheim, *Ideology and Utopia*, p. 341.
17. Thorstein Veblen, *Veblen on Marx, Race, Science, and Economics* (New York: Capricorn Books, 1969), p. 308.
18. Ibid, p. 309.

19. Turnabout being fair play, and even dialectical, Adorno in turn criticizes Veblen as a 'Pragmatist, himself regressive, [who] clings to the standpoint of those who cannot see things beyond tomorrow, beyond the next step … ' Theodor Adorno, *Prisms* (Cambridge: MIT Press, 1981), p. 93.
20. Paul Feyerabend, *Against Method* (London: Verso, 1975). pp. 25–31, 37, 233.
21. Ibid. pp. 70–71. Relationism means all 'elements of meaning in a given situation have reference to one another and derive their significance from this reciprocal inter-relationship in a given frame of thought. Such a system of meanings is possible and valid only in ä given type of historical existence, to which, for a time, it furnishes appropriate expression.' p. 76.
22. Mannheim, *Ideology and Utopia*, pp. 4–5.
23. See Martin Jay's classic introduction to the Frankfurt School *oeuvre*, *The Dialectical Imagination* (Berkeley: University of California Press, 1973) and Stuart Jeffries' popularly pitched *Grand Hotel Abyss: The Lives of The Frankfurt School* (London: Verso, 2016).
24. Thomas Kuhn, *Structure of Scientific Revolutions* (Chicago: University of Chicago Press, 1962), pp. 53, 114–115.
25. Ibid, p. 10.
26. Daniel Diermeier, 'Rational Choice and the Role of Theory in Political Science,' in Jeffrey Friedman, ed, *The Rational Choice Controversy* (New Haven: Yale University Press, 2005), p. 60.
27. Alan S. Janik and Stephen Toulmin, *Wittgenstein's Vienna* (New York: Simon & Schuster, 1973), p. 215.
28. Stephen Toulmin, *Return to Reason* (Berkeley: University of California, 2002). Stuart Schram, 'Return to Politics: Perestroika and Postparadigmtic Political Science,' *Political Theory* 1, 6 (December 200), p. 839.
29. Susanne Hoeber Rudolph, 'The Imperialism of Categories: Situating Knowledge in a Globalizing World' *Perspectives on Politics* 3, 1 (March 2005), p. 9.
30. For a recent valuable and heartening volume aiming toward that end see Amy Buzby and Matthew Bowker, eds. *D. W. Winnicott and Political Theory* (New York: Palgrave Macmillan, 2016). Also see Kurt Jacobsen, *Freud's Foes: Psychoanalysis, Science and Resistance* (Lanham, MD: Rowman and Littlefield, 2009).
31. On the totalitarian-inflected aspiration for an Archimedean point, and its alienating drawbacks, see Hannah Arendt, *The Human Condition* (Chicago: University of Chicago Press, 1958), pp. 248–289. Also see comments on Arendt's 1968 lecture on the same subject in Theresa Man Ling Lee, *Politics and Truth: Political Theory and the Postmodern Challenge* (Binghamton: SUNY Press, 1997), pp. 127–129.

32. Clifford Geertz, 'Thick Description: Toward an Interpretive Theory of Culture' in Geertz, *The Interpretation of Cultures* (New York: Basic Books, 1973), p. 4.
33. *Casablanca* Dir. Michael Curtiz. Warner Brothers. 1942. Film.
34. Richard Overy, *The Bombers and The Bombed: The Allied Air War Over Europe 1940–1945* (London: Penguin, 2015), p. 209.
35. Matthew Kocher, Aria K Lawrence and Nuno Monteiro, 'The Rabbit in The Hat: Nationalism and Resistance to Foreign Occupation.' Paper for the Annual Meeting of the American Political Science Association 2013. Available at: https://papers.ssrn.com/sol3/papers.cfm?abstract_id=2299837.
36. Mark Mazower, *Hitler's Empire: Nazi Rule in Occupied Europe* (London: Allan Lane, 2008), p. 505.
37. Kocher, et al., 'The Rabbit in the Hat,' p. 2.
38. Ibid, p. 25.
39. Ibid. p. 3.
40. Ibid. p. 2.
41. Jack Hayward, *Fragmented France: Two Centuries of Disputed Identity* (Oxford: Oxford University Press, 2007) p. 179. These execution figures double in the early estimate in Robert Aron, *Histoire de la Liberation* (Paris: Fayard, 1959), p. 655. In total, about 150,000 accused collaborators were punished in various official ways after the war. Philippe Burin, *France Under The Germans* (New York: New Press, 1993), p. 461.
42. Robert O. Paxton, *Vichy France: Old Guard and New Order, 1940–1944* (New York: Columbia University Press, 2001, orig. pub 1975), pp. x–xx. 'The fateful steps that began with the Constitutional decrees of July, 1940 were guided, it still seems to me, by partisan opportunism.' (p. xxx).
43. Ian Ousby, *Occupation* (London, John Murray, 1997), p. 86; Paxton, *Vichy France*, p. xviii.
44. Mazower, *Hitler's Empire*, p. 492. Also see Ousby, *Occupation*, pp, 274–275.
45. Julian Jackson, *France: The Dark Years 1940–1944* (Oxford: Oxford University Press, 2003, p. 295. 'A belief in the coincidence of national interest and self-interest was written onto Vichy from the start.' (p. 142).
46. Julian Jackson, *France: The Dark Years*, p. 291.
47. Paxton, *Vichy France: Old Guard and New Order*, p. xiii.
48. Mazower, *Hitler's Empire*, p. 492.
49. Overy, *The Bombers and The Bombed*, p. 365.
50. Overy, *The Bombers and The Bombed*, pp. 77, 91. Allied ground and air forces on D-Day and after were anything but unrestrained. See Anthony Beevor, *D-Day: The Battle for Normandy* (London: Penguin, 2009) and

Mary Louise Roberts, *What Soldiers Do: Sex and the American GI in World War II France* (Chicago: University of Chicago Press, 2013).
51. Robert Gildea, *Fighters in The Shadows: A New History of the French Resistance* (London: Faber & Faber, 2015), p. 410.
52. Ian Ousby, *Occupation*, p. 125. Also see Alan S. Milward, *The New Order and The French Economy* (Oxford: Oxford University Press, 1970).
53. Frank E. Manuel, *Scenes from The End: The Last Days of World War II In Europe* (South Royalton: Steerforth Press, 2000), p. 71.
54. Jackson, France, *The Dark Years,* p. 298. For an attempt to assess high- and low-level sabotage ('a deliberate strategy for the reduction of production') in the auto industry in Vichy France, which sent 85% of production to the Nazi war machine, see Martin Horn and Talbot Imlay, *The Politics of Industrial Collaboration During World War II: Ford France, Vichy and Nazi Germany* (Cambridge: Cambridge University Press, 2014).
55. Carline Moorehead, *Village of Secrets: Defying the Nazis in Vichy France* (New York: Vintage, 2014), p, 336. Also especially see John Sweets, *Choices in Vichy France* (Oxford: Oxford University Press, 1994).
56. James C. Scott, *Weapons of the Weak* (New Haven: Yale University Press, 1987), p. 36.
57. Jackson, *France: The Dark Years*, p. 557. Also see Peter Fritzsche, *An Iron Wind: Europe Under Hitler* (New York: Basic Books, 2017), pp. 246–253.
58. Stephen Walt, 'Rigor ort Rigor Mortis?' in Michael E. Brown, Owen Cote, Sean M. Lynn-Jones and Steven E. Miller, eds. *Rational Choice and Security Studies: Stephen Walt and his Critics* (Cambridge: MIT Press, 2000), p. 5.
59. Which is not to say there are none. 'The causal mechanism through which culture and institutions mould and constrain human agents remain unexplored... Essentially, there is no adequate and substantial theory of human agency at the core of the standard theory.' Geoffrey M. Hodgson, 'On The Limits of Rational Choice Theory,' *Economic Theory* 1 (2012), p. 99. He dryly advises critics not to accuse rational choice theories of failing to fit facts when, on the contrary, 'models of utility-maximizing behaviour can always be adjusted to fit the facts.' (p. 102.)
60. Mannheim, *Ideology and Utopia*, p. 160.
61. Benjamin Page and Lawrence Jacobs, *Class War?: What Americans Really Think of Inequality* (Chicago: University of Chicago Press, 2009), p. 100.
62. Dexter Filkins, *The Forever War* (New York: Knopf, 2008), p. 130.
63. Kurt Jacobsen, *Chasing Progress in The Irish Republic* (Cambridge: Cambridge University Press, 1994).
64. Geertz, 'Thick Description,' p. 12.
65. See Donald Green and Ian Shapiro, eds. *Pathologies of Rational Choice* (New Haven: Yale University Press, 1995).

Perestroika and American Political Science

Does democracy, or the lack of it, affect research methods? Philosophers of science Paul Feyerabend, and, less flamboyantly, Thomas Kuhn were among those who implied such a link. In the superpower that advertises itself as the world's greatest democracy (despite the Iraq invasion, the Patriot Act, Abu Ghraib and a panoply of voter suppression schemes), one might imagine that the American Political Science Association (APSA), which represents some 14,000 scholars and teachers of the art of politics, preached the gospel that the best system of government, despite all its faults and shortcomings, is democracy.[1] Actually, as with any group fancying itself an elite, many APSA members harbored grave doubts as to how far this unruly form of government ought to go not only in the great wide world but also especially inside their own club. The Association never considered the apparently subversive notion of conducting internal elections through a secret ballot. That is, not until the early 2000s when a rebellious bunch of political scientists explicitly connected the ascendance of a stultifying formal and quantitative view of political life to the absence of internal democracy inside the APSA.

What governed the APSA was a cozy arrangement whereby a committee chosen by the President nominates his (until the millennium, 80 times 'his' and four times 'her') successor who then picks the Governing Council who in turn pick the next President who picks the next Council, and so on and on. APSA officers were answerable to figures they themselves appointed: a splendidly regal arrangement. What did this hierarchic coziness mean for the vitality of teaching, research and democracy?

A hoary academic jest has a surly scholar grousing about a successful event: 'That's all very well in practice but how does it work in theory?'

The objection (to which I am not entirely unsympathetic) is only a slight exaggeration of the otherworldly plight afflicting American political science. For decades, it has been the icy elegance and artificial neatness of models, not their relation or relevance to real-world activities, which garnered the greatest kudos in the profession. Other kinds of scholars had gotten the unmistakable message that they need not apply. This disturbing doctrinal trend would not have come to public light except for a remarkable revolt against what disgruntled scholars complained has been the suffocating grip of mathematical models and of formal theory (rational choice, public choice, game theory) in political science, imported from economics.

Rational choice theory derives from an especially and, Perestroikans argue, excessively abstract version of neoclassical economics, which many political scientists could not help but notice win a lot of para-Nobel Prizes, though usually for no intelligible or sustainable reason and with no discernible benefit to humanity.[2] The theory deploys an arid set of assumptions about human behavior which reduce our complicated lives and societies to nothing but prioritized 'rational' choices that we supposedly make in order to maximize our materialistic 'utility' in any given situation. The theory is in deep trouble right off the bat given that utility is a notoriously circular concept.[3] In this chalkboard powder universe people are depicted in the behavioral terms of narcissistic, autistic, self-seeking 'homo economicus,' a conceptualization wherein any trace of culture, history, personality, accident, whimsy, self-reflection or other human impurity that might smudge the model is erased or ignored.[4] A heuristic concept that just might arguably be useful for some limited purposes was deemed applicable to all. In political science, the equation of 'empirical' with 'quantitative' also had become a common and, indeed, compulsory discipline-wide error, critics complained.

Although dissidents exclude statistical techniques *per se* from their critique of the careening hubris of formal theory, Professor Greg Kasza charged that it was a cohort of 'radical quantifiers' who 'popularized the study of politics outside of its historical and cultural setting, who made methodology into the core of graduate education while degrading political philosophy and foreign language study and who spawned the trend toward method-driven rather than problem-driven research.' Kasza charged that graduate students were forced to 'earn their passports to the clouds in qualifying exams that grill them on multiple regression, most-different-systems analysis, and the small-n problem' when many have yet to master the history, economics, social structure and politics of even one 'n.'[5] If you can't count it, in other words, it doesn't count.

Few Perestroikans deny that rational choice, and the statistical apparatus that often accompanies it, has some merit if employed with the ample ballast of humility, especially in studies of what rational choice proponents call 'collective action,' where groups ranging from suburban middle managers to hard bitten rural guerillas are imagined to weigh their choices according to identical incentive structures. The trouble is that formal models cannot help but dangle the tantalizing appearance of encompassing explanations for almost anything you name, although the resulting explanations, critics retort, are usually trivial, reinvent (or rephrase the invention of) the wheel, or fail to display any passing acquaintance with recognizable reality.[6]

Citizens in the UK and USA may well wonder why economic growth consistently generates a distribution upward of wealth—before and after the 2007–2008 financial crime of a crash when $40 trillion equity went poof—or why the best and brightest market economists taught the Russians in the high-spirited early days after the Soviet Union's dissolution how to send their economy, so far as the average Russian was concerned, straight to hell.[7] Might some formal analyst explain why the average tax-paying citizen rationally chose not only to bail out the bankers and brokers who sliced and diced up the financial structure a decade ago but also to be punished and plundered through imposition of austerity programs that remorselessly generate the conditions for more austerity?[8] Few mainstream economists or rational choice connoisseurs pay serious attention to such impertinent questions.[9]

'Beyond generic group death and disability insurance, discounts on other unreadable scholastic publications, cheap tickets to APSA meetings, and periodically-issued surveys of what many academics pretend is 'cutting edge research,' the APSA does very little,' Professor Tim Luke assessed. 'It no longer aspires to guide the nation's public life, it bars members from making political pronouncements in any collective manner, and it produces a fairly apolitical and largely unscientific run of self-referential literature by, for, and of college professors.'[10] Steinmo cites a survey that found more than half the APSA members had no use for the flagship journal, which virtually had become the preserve of narrow-minded quantitative and formal theorists.[11]

Like the 'post-autistic economics' movement arising in France in 2000 against the formalistic excesses of economics, the American Perestroikans advocated a 'plurality of approaches adapted to the complexity of the object studied.' American economics proved fiercely resistant and indeed oblivious to challenge and so the movement ignited instead within political science, which zealously imitated any and all fads in economics.[12] The clarion call of the US revolt came in mid-October 2000 in a circulated email by 'Mr. Perestroika'—perhaps a junior faculty member or group of them—who lashed out against 'poor game-theorists who cannot for the life of me compete with a third grade economics student' yet are able to crush the 'diversity of methodologies and areas of the world that APSA "purports" to represent.'[13]

Let us recall that Perestroika, according to its—ahem—original sponsors, promoted the 'vital creativity' of society's members, development of democracy, 'initiative and independence' and 'the widening of criticism and self-criticism in all spheres of social life.' Hence, Mr. Perestroika stated that the goals of the new movement were to 'provide a forum where people can discuss and debate methodology, politics, theory, and the world in such a manner that APSA and APSR and our discipline become more open and more diverse in gender, racial, ethnic, and methodological terms—in teaching, publishing and hiring practices.'

The Perestroikan Challenge

The anonymous email catalyzed a lively intellectual insurgency. Within a month a movement of combat-ready professors crystallized, fronted by a bevy of prominent scholars whom APSA authorities, try as some might, could not afford to ignore or deride. By January 2001 more than 200 tenured faculty members signed a toned-down version of the original reform petition, crafted by Rogers Smith, charging that formal modelers, unless strongly checked, were slowly but surely stamping out other valuable forms of research. Signatories included 24 named chairs, luminaries ranging from Yale's Ian Shapiro and political ethnographer James Scott to University of Chicago South Asian experts Susanne and Lloyd Rudolph to Penn's political semioticist Ann Norton, and Columbia University's Jan Elster.

Political science had 'been taken over by methodological parochialists who believe that the only worthwhile scholarship in political science speaks the language of mathematics,' lamented University of Chicago scholar John Mearsheimer. Only numbers and equations matter inasmuch as mathematics conveys a glittery but illusory impression of pin-it-down precision. Numbers presumably cannot lie. Just ask vote tabulators in 2000 Florida, former Enron employees or any inebriated tax accountant off the record. The dubious, indeed daft, belief that quantitative data are not an interpretation of the phenomena to which it is assigned has become sedulously institutionalized, a sad fact that forecloses many valuable insights (such as this very old one). A regrettable consequence is that economists and political scientists have less and less to say of any interest about anything that we recognize as the actual world we have to maneuver in.

Young scholars, like it or not, must bend at least outwardly to prevailing winds in order to survive in their disciplines.[14] In America rational choice modelers quickly became notorious for forming powerful coteries bent on expanding their disciplinary control. This inveterate imperializing had not gone unnoticed in Britain either. 'The governing principle in most sensible political science departments is that rational choice theorists should be on tap but not on top,' the chair of a top UK politics department, who preferred anonymity, told me. 'They should exist, be permitted to flourish, but never be permitted dominance. Once dominant, they are incapable of appointing other than their own; the more vulgar they are the more this is true.'[15] Dissidents found that rational choice/mathematical modelers cannot bring themselves to concede that their phantasmagoric terms are just as much metaphors as any literary image deployed by supposedly 'soft' social scientists.[16] Professor Giandomenico Majone believes the fault for this doctrinaire behavior lies not with formal models in themselves but with the excesses of undereducated disciples: 'You should know more than the tool you use,' he observed. That state of affairs, unfortunately, is not the norm.

A side benefit of hyperspecialization—what Thorstein Veblen labeled 'trained incompetence'—for acolytes (or those lacking a sense of intellectual adventure) is that when they encounter flak from more broadly (multi-disciplinary) educated people, they retreat along a trail of numerological platitudes into the APSA fortress where number crunchers rule the roost. Other social science fields, except of course economics, are off-limits. The result is that blithe positivists tend to penalize, whenever they can, anyone who knows more than they do as a result of wandering off the reservation into realms they do not deem frigidly scientific. For all the positivists' protestations of superiority in skills over qualitative scholars, it is child's play for area specialists to puncture big-N study balloons, to unravel the strained assumptions, motley mistakes and vapid generalizations on which such work is usually built.[17]

Formal modelers too often take a framework derived from a Western context and apply it indiscriminately.[18] A typical example I witnessed at the height of the initial Perestroika controversy was a paper by two academics who imposed a one-size-fits-all rational choice framework upon Northern Ireland where, among other howlers, they argued that the Irish Republic could pressure Ian Paisley to endorse the fitful peace process, which was akin to asserting the Pope could make Osama bin Laden do his bidding. A tenured rising star Ivy League professor studying guerrilla wars (including Vietnam) with the finest of quantitative precision tools turned out not to even have heard of Daniel Ellsburg ('How do you spell that?'), let alone his contributions on the subject.[19] A graduate student on the perestroika listserv recalled a faculty modeler incorporating India into his data set without any grasp of its history or cultures. 'Isn't Delhi the national language of India?' the undaunted scholar asked. Everything looks like easy prey if you never tried to capture it or just need to look as if you did. Practitioners plummet headlong into the blinkered touristic assumption that American values and practices are universal, even after posting ritualized disclaimers. They get away with it by assuming that putative neutral theories and procedures automatically make anything they do impeccably scientific.

The Perestroika movement, which subsided in the late 2000s, had two main prongs. One was opposition to the non-competitive process by which political scientists in the world's second largest democracy organized themselves. The second was resistance to the hegemony of formal and quantitative work in the journals and forums of the Association. Opposition took several forms. The severest criticisms regarding narrowness in quantitative approaches homed in on the American Political Science Review, flagship journal of the Association. 'Homogenous, narrow journals,' Susanne Rudolph stated, 'reduce the space in which political scientists can ask questions, pursue questions, find and retain jobs, and get promoted.'[20] Journals of several regional associations also came under scrutiny. These prized official organs were selected by many departments as shortcut certifications for faculty recruitment, promotion and tenure, which are useful as 'easy markers' for harried search committees and provost offices who wish to relieve themselves of the burden of reading and evaluating the work of prospective candidates.[21]

In riposte to Perestroikan upstarts, Ada Finifter, then APSR journal editor, opined that nothing more than sheer professional ambition was at stake in the insolent uproar. This dismissiveness ideally suited the rational choice *weltanshauung*, where self-interested gain is all that comes into play. All else is at best mere marginalia. She remained puzzled then as to why prominent dissenters were so upset inasmuch as they were twice as deft as anyone else at inserting their work into the main journals. Finifter's reaction, widespread among positivists, nicely exemplified the trusty defense mechanism of projection, the first resort among dominant groups facing challenge. Finifter was oblivious to the slippery ambiguity of claiming that all's well in the discipline so long as scholars deliver 'high-quality work using methods appropriate to the research problem'—as if the definition of those 'appropriate' methods was not the crux of the matter.

Still, a conciliatory APSA selected as its next President a Perestroika-backed candidate, Harvard's Theda Skocpol. Even this emollient move was greeted with suspicions that crafty APSA honchos reckoned that Skocpol, although renowned as no pushover, could likely be co-opted into the 'East coast Brahmin' network and so opt to preserve undemocratic mechanisms. Everyone assiduously had read their Machiavelli, in which case it is a bit more difficult to be a wily Machiavellian. Most dissidents were pleased that, as Mr. Perestroika put it, there was a prospect of a 'dismantling of the Orwellian system that we have in the APSA.'

Yet it still spoke volumes that junior scholars feared to reveal Perestroikan sympathies in a profession that purported to prize vigorous and open exchange. When lifelong students of the way power works express surprise, and in some cases indignation, that some Perestroikans must conceal identities for fear of reprisals, one gets a whiff of apparatchik or inexcusably naive mentalities at work—even among a few Perestroika adherents. 'One does not need to be a rocket scientist—or a political scientist—to see that transparency does not always serve insurgency well,' replied Anne Norton to those Perestroikans who righteously demanded Mr. Perestroika disclose his/their identity. Imagine what would become of Mr. Perestroika's career if a Department superior like Daniel Diermeier (more below) or David Laitan, who disparaged Mr. Perestroika as a Luddite intent on sabotaging science altogether, got hold of him.[22]

'If P "came out of the closet" and turned out to be a graduate student at Michigan State, a junior faculty member at Los Angeles Community College, a recent Ph.D. with no job and no book contract, a recent Ph.D. from Chicago with a visiting post at a small college, or some senior scholar somewhere, how many of us would give their collective opinions equal weight with those of Anne Norton, Rogers Smith, or Joanna, Dvora, and Sandy? Sure we all would,' snarkily but accurately estimated Michael Bosia. 'But talk to graduate students and recent Ph.D.s (and many scholars) about why they don't post on Perestroika, and you might learn that we don't weigh all voices equally. The group P, then, equalizes the discussion. Perestroika or P is a disembodied voice with no more power than the ability to remind and recall.'

During the early 2000s the network underwent two 'constitutional crises': one over whether to become a formalized institution with officers (rejected) and the other whether to become a forum for general political criticism (mostly rejected). The e-mail network did become semi-institutionalized and gave rise to a coherent collaboration by colleagues who in many cases had never seen each other. In 2003, a committee of major scholars formed to oversee listserv traffic. Listservs are never free from foibles and often get diverted for spells to the hobbyhorse concerns of a few garrulous members. The perestroika listserv seemed in danger of occupation by arch-conservatives who, in an era spanning Presidents Reagan, Bush I and II and an interim Southern Democrat who scuttled the welfare system and played enabler for Wall Street predation, asserted that they too are discriminated against within the Academy. Russell Jacoby, elsewhere, mooted the instructive notion of a trade of left/liberal influence in humanities and some social science programs for the loot available to business schools and other professional schools firmly in conservative safekeeping—not mention the Pentagon and Wall Street.[23]

Theda Skocpol was followed as President in 2003 by avowed Perestroikan Susanne Hoeber Rudolph. Rudolph, Skocpol and predecessor Robert Putnam appointed Perestroikans to APSA decision bodies. An initiative set in motion by in-house critics of the APSR to launch a journal as an alternative to the methodological parochialism of the APSR, accelerated during the Perestroika movement. Jennifer Hochschild ran the first 2 years of the new *Perspective on Politics*. A new APSR editor issued a welcome statement recognizing the accumulating grievances about absence of diversity in the journal. The issues of the APSR under Lee Siegelman's watch showed improvement though, by some accounts, it tailed off quickly.[24] From the September 2002 to the February 2004 APSR issues, a Perestroikan found twice as many purely qualitative articles (10–14%) appeared as in the previous decade. A self-nominated committee on reform of Association governance would formulate proposals for competitive elections, which, however, did not get very far.

Not all can be sweetness and light in methodological fights, which burrow right down to the roots of practitioners' beings. A 'Mr. Pravda' interjected, like Finifter, that Perestroikans patently were motivated by sheer careerism, even though open association with Perestroika scarcely was calculated to garner merit points with most hiring committees. As Chris Hedges notes of the upper ranks of journalism, the political science profession too has been packed over the years (as tuitions escalated) with people who spent their lives since kindergarten single-mindedly promoting their career interests *uber alles* and so cannot comprehend or must denigrate anyone who does otherwise.[25] In office Skocpol, ironically, chided Perestroika for itself being unrepresentative within the APSA—spectacularly missing the whole point of the movement—while APSA nominating committee member Joan Scott testily claimed that reforms were in the pipeline anyway so what was all the fuss about? Hence, on becoming APSA President in 2003, Susanne Rudolph received numerous letters warning her about cooptation, expressing fears that the Perestroikan agenda would be thwarted by a blend of inertia, divide-and-conquer tactics, and outright obstruction. The Perestroikans knew their politics and their colleagues all too well. A prominent Perestroikan even warned of Thermidore. Dissidents at the time fretted that the new journal launched to broaden the Association's appeal was fated to become a steerage class organ, though that clearly hasn't been the case, except in the eyes of hardcore 'qaunts.'[26] Nonetheless, studies of the key regional journals—AJPS, JOP, PRQ—showed they 'continue to represent a narrow section of the scholarship and a small section of the membership in our profession.'

Another problem that Perestroikans did not solve is how to ensure 'diversity of methods' in departmental hiring processes, which are usually steered by hegemonic formalists. Cyberspace discussions suggested an informal process to rank departments on degree of diversity, relying on the information process itself as a form of critique and consciousness raising. That discussion became mired in questions of, you guessed it, methodology, which shades and infiltrates everything in this fray. Getting it exactly backwards, Sidney Tarrow, ordinarily one of the fairer minded eminences in the field, therefore wrote in a retrospective on Perestroikans that they 'strove mightily to sharpen boundaries between themselves and mainstream political scientists, but in the end failed,' although the movement plainly arose in response to the frustrating positivist barriers they increasingly encountered.[27] Finding a Perestroikan who derides quantitative methods as a part of any repertoire is difficult; not so, finding formal theorists and quantitative practitioners who regard anyone lacking their overrated skill sets as a species of charlatan. Perestroikans never opposed formal methods or mathematical models, as the late Susanne Rudolph stressed, but rather opposed their consecration as sacred and sufficient devices of investigation, thereby squeezing out cultural, historical and psychological approaches. Rudolph stated that the objective is 'high-quality work using methods appropriate to the research problem,' and aligned with fellow dissident Margaret Keck in advising that 'the problem dictates the method,' not the other way around.

Like much else in American politics, the Perestroika movement was convolutedly many-stranded, which was both its initial strength and an eventual cause of dissolution. The objectives of demographic groups within the Association happened to overlap with those of Perestroika. Skocpol was supported by the women's caucus while Rudolph was supported by the women's caucus, the black caucus, the lesbian and gay caucus and the Hispanic caucus. Indeed, after Perestroika, four of the next six APSA Presidents were women, and seven of the last 15 up to 2016. Nearly all those Presidents were sympathetic or else made their peace with Perestroikans as an APSA faction whose influence wasn't going away even if the titular organization would.

When the September 11 attacks occurred an acrimonious political debate erupted which was shunted rapidly to other Web sites. Perestroikans had to be wary of provoking splits in their volatile melange of methodological approaches and political colorings. By contrast, Chris Howell protested that overreliance on quantitative methods were only a symptom and that the 'real goal is a critical and engaged political science that does not readily conform to what the powers that be want of it.' Stuart Schram proposed a Perestroikan-inspired political science 'open to allowing ongoing political struggle to serve as the context for deciding which methods will be used in what ways to address which problems' and so 'enable people on the bottom working in dialogue with social researchers to challenge power.'[28] That didn't go over big. Brian Caterino lamented the loss of an opportunity to bring political science more squarely into political life.[29] Both had their supporters. Certainly, a key 'purpose of education is precisely to promote reflection on preferences,' Mark Graber contended. Tim Luke noted, however, that 'formally inclined rational choicers look down on others as story tellers and journalists.'

No epithet—except maybe plagiarist—is more damning. A political science department in North Carolina a few decades ago discarded a young academic as a mere journalist—just months before he was awarded a Pulitzer Prize for a political biography. One doubts that those who did it harbored the slightest regret afterward. This ingrained conceit is concisely expressed in a 2011 post discussing Perestroika—treated by then as almost ancient—on the PolSciRumors Web site: 'The Perestroika people were just bothered by the fact that there were people who knew more than they did ... the best advice is actually 'Tool up!''[30] Likewise, Laitin's seemingly conciliatory suggestion that political scientists train in a skewed tripartite mode—narrative, statistics, formal modeling—was just a disingenuous way of disregarding anyone not entranced by the latter pair of methods.[31] That certain highly treasured 'tools' can be dubious ones for examining given problems, or operate to distort or prevent understanding of any subject matter, are possibilities that do not compute for scholars of this stern mindset.

Mr. Perestroika summarized the insurgency's aim as retaining 'the amorphous character of this movement and list group. However, we will form working groups in Democracy, publishing, future initiatives to broaden intellectual base. In the same vein, perestroika as it stands needs to make a real effort to draw in people of color and other oft-marginalized communities if it is to make any valid claims to representativeness.' There was always danger of rifts among a delicately constructed coalition who are up against a set of opponents who are cohesive to a fault. While Fiorina disarmingly avers that he suspected 'the only thing that all RC [rational choice] people would agree upon is that their explanations presume that individuals behave purposively,' the other thing that the vast majority of rational choice modelers do agree on is that non-practitioners really aren't doing anything scientific, according to their shriveled definition of science.[32] They are of course entitled and welcome to explore this single groove of desiccated inquiry for all it is worth (which is matter of perpetual dispute), but not entitled to impose it as a standard on everyone else.

How to Look like a Science

Examples proliferate of this stale and obstructive rendition of science at mischievous work. The acrid exchanges especially between Laitin and Shapiro are a must read on this score, but let's hone in for the sake of illustration on Daniel Diermeier's stab at a refutation of Green and

Shapiro's wrecking ball of a book *Pathologies of Rational Choice*.[33] This he attempts by invoking what he calls 'the philosophy of science,' which phrase is itself a dead giveaway, employed as it is in a manner indicating that 'the philosophy of science' is a single-minded enterprise which ultimately yields correct method, and there can only be one. Stephen Toulmin in the 1970s wisely warned we seminar members that the word 'the' preceding any concept was a red alert signal as to dogmatic dangers within, and even way back then Diermeier's unduly restrictive idea of 'the philosophy of science' (which stalls out with saint Carl Hempel) was a nineteenth-century relic barely worth the trouble of ridiculing anymore.[34]

Diermieier strives to execute a table-turning exercise—the favorite tactic of rational choice defenders who unsurprisingly behave as though they have a listserv too. Cursorily citing Thomas Kuhn's work, Diermeier nevertheless lauds Newtonian science, whose overdue overturn Kuhn charts, as an ideal that needs to be emulated in political science. (This presumably is the Newton who in his turn as historian a biographer discerns that 'everything human is alien to him—at least insofar as he expressed himself on Mankind').[35] A little knowledge of philosophy of science is a dangerous thing, as Green and Shapiro remark.[36] Diermeier gripes that Green and Shapiro "do not point to paradigmatic cases of good theorizing," as if one is required to do so first in order to criticize rational choice, which is a conveniently conservative restriction. For people in Diermeier's camp, it's inconceivable that social sciences proceeded as other than an ardent collective quest ultimately for a unitary science in the sense of 'what is fated to be agreed by all who investigate,' as Charles Sanders Pierce long ago yearningly phrased it.[37] Diermeier therefore must reckon that it is Green and Shapiro's criteria, and not innocent rational choice methods, that 'would hinder scientific progress in political science' despite the obvious embarrassing fact that Green and Shapiro pointedly applied criteria that rational choice proponents themselves champion! Green and Shapiro accomplished this task so well that many rational choicers mistook the pair for paid-up, purse-lipped positivists. Hoisted high by their own petard, rational choice theorists could only lamely point fingers the other way.

Progress, according to Diermeier and his comrades, entails generating a mathematized and positivist brand of inquiry that refashions by fiat all realms of phenomena in its own image.[38] This familiar quest is a deeply romantic one, a determined hunt for coveted certainty even if one must force a predesignated template on a recalcitrant world.[39] Yet the studiously ignored lessons of Kuhn's work for most readers are that this quest is both undesirable (because it restricts forms of inquiry) and impossible (because no single model ever accounts for all relevant explanatory factors). Kuhn did make a highly hedged case for 'methodological conservativism'as one way forward, but only as one such way and as a matter of preference, not principle.[40] Imre Lakatos went much further, thereby gaining favor with positivists, opining jaw-droppingly that 'dogmatism in normal science does not prevent growth.'[41] Popper, Feyerabend and other scruffy philosophers of science milling around outside of 'the philosophy of science' respectfully but emphatically disagreed.[42]

Diermeier deflects attention from Green and Shapiro's charge of 'post hoc theory development'—meaning rational choice theorists work only from past cases—by excusing the practice as providing legitimate grist for 'puzzle-solving,' as if that is the sole aim of scientific inquiry.[43] Kuhn famously distinguished between solving a puzzle (or 'mopping up') within the terms of a dominant paradigm and the crisis situation arising from accumulated anomalies throwing a paradigm into radical doubt, the latter of which Deiermeier can't conceive might befall his favorite explanatory apparatus. His purpose rather is to work out 'puzzles' according to an abstruse instruction manual laced with positivist homilies. Science thereby becomes a staunchly conservative enterprise wherein, as Green and Shapiro noted, the preservation of the model supersedes all other concerns. A recipe for dogmatism is disguised as a plea for rigor.

Diermeier, otherwise quite the stickler, avers that 'puzzle-solving—the explanation of a known but unexplained fact by means of a theory—should not cause any methodological concern.'[44] The problem with this stance is his solution, which is the application of a single model, or a severely skewed 'family' of models, to explain phenomena according to inadequately examined assumptions. The theory, and the practices by which it is tested, are held sacrosanct. There is no appeal. There is no alternative—in science as in Maggie Thatcher's Britain. Sophisticates like Diermeier know that what is really tested anyway is not assumptions but a conjuncture between sets of statements (which are deemed uncontaminated by assumptions) and sets of initial conditions (also supposedly uncontaminated) so that it's fine to proceed with rational choice excursions even if several conditions underpinning and predicted by them admittedly do not apply because otherwise one would 'hinder science,' by which he means the stately ascension of rational choice theory to status of dominant paradigm. Political science should aspire to become nothing less than a subset of a theory of Newtonian particle mechanics. What is striking is the cool calm extremism underlying the scientific patina of this argument.

Any entity, Diermeier acknowledges, 'is T-theoretic if its measurement presupposes the validity of Theory T.'[45] Why, yes. Angels are T-theoretic. So are phlogistons. Luminiferous ether too, which Lord Kelvin thought of as a sure bet.[46] Prosperity might be said to be T-theoretic during expansionary phases of property bubbles. 'At this stage one may be tempted to argue that the presence of T-theoretic terms would be a fatal blow to any theory,' he admits, but this 'would be a serious misconception' because all theories contain T-theoretic terms.'[47] This revelation, which is anything but, is conjured to gain *carte blanche* to simplify and promote a favored paradigm. In 1911, by contrast, Hans Vaihinger too argued that conscious fictions can be useful to scientific inquiry but was roundly spurned by Diermeier's predecessors, the logical positivists, for it.[48] Karl Popper tolerated the role of fictions as hypothesis generators in the 'context of discovery', phase so long as hypotheses were subjected to the testing ground of the 'context of verification,' insofar as these contexts are distinct.[49] Popper's rebel pupil Paul Feyerabend, who would seem anathema to Diermeier, heartily agreed that obsolete theories and even fantasy can generate useful hypotheses except that playing with such fictions only made sense to him in the realm of a proliferation of theories by which to test what theory as well as what hypothesis worked.[50]

One might well confuse some of these preceding stances with stark relativism.[51] 'The confusion stems from the belief that theories in some sense determine their domain,' asserts Diermeier, who thereby proves to be confused about this confusion inasmuch as Kuhn indicated that theories do exactly that, though the *extent* of it, not *whether* it happens, has been a matter of vigorous debate.[52] Diermeier takes refuge in Sneed's ordered pairs of a core C which expresses the mathematical core of a theory, and a set of intended applications which 'are common procedures in the empirical sciences.'[53] The future of research consists of 'strengthening C or extending I,' as if dumping or demoting Sneed is not an option for reasonable investigators. 'By a reasonable position, I mean one that does not declare typical scientific behavior, *such as that exemplified by Newtonian physics*, to be unscientific or bad science' (italics mine).[54] The catechism stays intact. Normal science reigns undisturbed.[55]

The question whether Newtonian physics really is applicable outside its proper domain goes resolutely unasked. Defenders plead the case for rational choice as if it were an endangered marginal species rather than the ubiquitous doctrine that hordes of practitioners implacably are set on spreading. Diermeier ends by insinuating the standards Green and Shapiro use to evaluate rational choice theory are 'deeply questionable' and inconsistent with, according to his bowdlerized rendition of 'the philosophy of science,' 'established practices in the most successful empirical science,' by which he means nineteenth-century physics and chemistry. The kind of stringent coherence that rational choicers seek 'cannot be the major test of validity for a cultural description,' Geertz argued in his actual thick description essay.[56] 'Cultural systems must have a minimal degree of coherence, else we would not call them systems; and, by observation, they normally have a great deal more. But there is nothing so coherent as a paranoid's delusion or a swindler's story.'

Rational choice academics, such as Diermeier (now a Provost), are notable enough for seeking out administrative power—and why wouldn't seekers of pat answers not pursue the power to enforce their preferences, which they portray as unassailable? One cannot 'limit a problem by reason of a method of attack,' Alfred North Whitehead long ago protested against similar methodological antics.[57] While Kelly opines that any fault with rational choice, formal theory or quantitative methods lies with theorists and not the theory, there clearly is an underlying elective and even emotional affinity between any theory and an adherent of it. Every social scientist can divide their grad students into those who crave certainty and precision at all costs, and those interested in exploring open-ended approaches, and it is clear which sort of students filed onto either side of the perestroika chasm.[58] When certainty seekers slip into positions of power, they cannot help but enforce their myopic vision upon everyone else. And that is why Perestroika arose.

In response to mounting critiques rational choice theorists claim they have evolved since such that there now is 'thin' theory and a richer 'thick' one, thereby feinting toward Clifford Geertz's use of 'thick description' (via Gilbert Ryle) though in its execution more often approaching the colloquial Irish sense of 'thick.'[59] Yet these excursions plainly are *ad hoc* maneuvers. However many layers are added, and caveats acknowledged, the result usually winds up exhibiting one of two tendencies, or both. First, that of incorporating sundry aspects into rational choice so that everything seems rational and therefore 'the boundaries become so murky that it becomes difficult, if not impossible, to assess when rational choice theories succeed and when they fail.'[60] Second, and not by any means secondary, the vaunted 'family of approaches,' 'analytic narratives' and anything else are only integrated into the degree that they serves the original purpose of the enterprise, customized to sustain the model, and so affirm the critics' charge about the handling of evidence all along. 'It is in the interest,' Susanne Rudolph glumly noted, 'of a conversionary project—and much modernization theory, as well as its generational successors [such as rational choice] was a conversionary project—not to attend sympathetically to alternative worldviews.'[61] A third tendency that formal theory proponents do not care to reckon with is that people equipped with all the skills they cherish will recognize the intrinsic limitations and oversold nature of these ballyhooed methods, just as Green and Shapiro did.

That said, there should be room for humility all around. 'I rarely encounter any political scientist,' attests Rogers Smith, 'who is 100% versatile in all the methods that are employed within political science'—though clearly a very large and influential swarm of rational choice proponents believe they attained exactly that exalted status and do not take kindly to anyone who tugs at their flimsy masks of reason. A discipline that is 'methodologically dexterous is bound to advance more effectively,' Skocpol wisely stated, 'than one becoming overly specialized in narrow or fixed techniques.'

The rebels agreed that diversity of methods needs encouragement also looked into NSF and SSRC funding practices, which, in opponents' hands, shore up a quantitative hegemony. Attention also was drawn to the permanent non-elected, bureaucracy of the APSA who had some interesting historical links to the national security establishment.[62] Yet the overarching challenge remains hiring and promotion criteria, which are controlled by individual departments, and a long struggle has ensued on hundreds of fronts. Dissidents, or many of them, still aimed to improve democracy outside as well as inside their profession. The increasingly otherworldly methods of 'the social sciences make it difficult to communicate with and make our work relevant to the wider public,' argued the late Lloyd Rudolph. 'We have to know and live with differences within our profession as well as in the world.'

CONCLUSION

What did the Perestroikans accomplish? Plenty. The movement undid the shiny masks of reason that so many opponents delightedly had donned, behind which was the unkillable conceit that a single unitary 'neutral' language or set of technical procedures can bypass human interests and foibles so as to establish scientific reality for once and for all. The qualitative studies branch of the APSA is a welcome institutionalized breakwater.[63] Green and Shapiro, among others, wielded both the complement of skills and the temerity to call the bluff and—*lese-majeste* on wheels—helped to beat back the latest attempt at disciplinary hegemony, at least for a while. If Lowi is right in his impish but serious observation that 'the APSA follows Leviathan' (state funding shapes research priorities), then it is possible that upon a receding of the neoliberal tide, if ever, nationally that rational choice fancies will subside with it.[64] All the foregoing conflicts have arisen before in political science (in the 1960s uproar over the 'behavioral revolution'), and no scientific field, as will be seen in Chap. 7 "The Mystique of Genetic Correctness", is proof against them, nor need they be. Conflicts, civilly conducted, can illuminate; consensus, if imposed, terminates routes to invaluable insights.

The Perestroikan movement 'never sought to have a unified program or agenda or any formal organizational existence,' as Rogers Smith later assessed.[65] 'It has instead provided venues—public letters, conference panels and receptions, and especially a list serve—through which political scientists could air and debate their dissatisfactions with and their aspirations for the profession.' That suffices. In my long lapsed Catholic youth, priests (with, as always, some exceptions) were pretty imperious characters, and why not? The Church could damn you by mumbling a few hermetic words. Yet from the 1960s onward, one could not help but notice that as Church deference faded (and scandals erupted), and they no longer commanded obedience, most priests transformed into genial gents.[66] They could not afford to behave otherwise. One would like rational choice theorists, who tend to take on the mien of a religious order when they acquire power, to remain genial colleagues too. There is something about being the bearer of the one true faith, or science, that brings out the unapologetic or unwitting authoritarian. This is 'Newton's sleep' from which William Blake wanted to wake us. In the service of what such formalist scholars believe is scientific rigor they want to snuff out other fertile means of inquiry. Parsimony has a lot to answer for.

Notes

1. On voter suppression see Greg Palast, 'The GOP's Stealth War Against Voters,' *Rolling Stone* 24 August 2016 and his *The Best Democracy Money can Buy* (New York: Seven Stories Press, 2016, 2nd ed).
2. The Nobel Prize in economics, bestowed by Sweden's Central Bank, has nothing to do with the original Nobel Prizes. The economics profession made it up, the media sold it, and the public, hearing nothing to the contrary, bought it. See Avner Offer and Gabriel Soderburg, *The Nobel Effect: The Prize in Economics, Social Democracy and the Market Turn* (Princeton: Princeton University Press, 2016) and Philip Mirowski, *Never Let a Serious Crisis Go To Waste: How* Neoliberalism *Survived the Financial Meltdown* (London: Verso: 2013).
3. Utility, Robinson pointed out, is determined by people wanting to buy the particular commodity while we reckon people will want a given commodity because of its, well, utility. Joan Robinson, *Economic Philosophy* (Hammondsworth: Penguin, 1964), p. 46.
4. For critiques of the concept see Amartya Sen, 'Rational Fools: A Critique of the Behavioral Foundations of Economic Theory,' *Philosophy & Public Affairs* 6, 4 (Summer 1977 as well as the early insightful appraisal of Adam Smith's 'egoism' by Hans Vaihinger in *The Philosophy of As-If* (London: Routledge & Kegan Paul, 1924).
5. Greg Casza, Perestroika listserv, 30 June 2004. A key critique that just preceded the onset of the Perestroika movement is Jan Elster, 'Rational Choice Theory: A Case of Excessive Ambition,' *American Political Science Review* 94 (2000).
6. See Donald Green and Ian Shapiro, eds. *Pathologies of Rational Choice* (New Haven: Yale University Press, 1995) and Steve Walt, 'Rigor or Rigor Mortis?' in Michael E. Brown, Owen Cote, Sean M. Lynn-Jones, and Steven E. Miller, eds. *Rational Choice and Security Studies: Stephen Walt and his Critics* (Cambridge: MIT Press, 2000). The firestorm over Walt's piece, first appearing in *International Security*, got this volume out within a year, which is head-spinningly swift for academia.
7. See Peter Gowan, 'Neoliberal Theory and Practice in Eastern Europe,' *New Left Review* 213 (January–February 1996) and Naomi Klein, *The Shock Doctrine* (London: Penguin, 2008), pp. 246–262.
8. See Michael Hudson, *Killing The Host* (Dresden: Islet, 2015), Wolfgang Streeck, *Buying Time: The Delayed Crisis of Democratic Capitalism*, (London: Verso, 2014), Yanis Vaourfakis, *The Global Minotaur: America, Europe and the Future of the Global Economy* (New York: Zed Books, 2015) and Michael Lewis, *The Big Short* (London: Penguin, 2011).
9. Lloyd Rudolph and Susanne Rudolph, 'Economics' Fall from Grace', *PS: Political Science and Politics* October 2010. p. 747.

10. Tim Luke, 'Caught between Confused Critics and Careerist Co-Conspirators: Perestroika in (American) Political Science' in Kristen Renwick Monroe, ed, *Perestroika!: The Raucous Rebellion in Political Science* (New Haven: Yale University Press, 2006), p. 469.
11. Sven Steinmo, The Emperor Had No Clothes", in Monroe, *Perestroika!* p. 296.
12. Still, there have been inroads and there are 'heretics.' Note the formation of the World Economics Association consisting of well over a thousand dissident economists in the USA and the world over.
13. The clarion call is reprinted in Monroe, Perestroika!: *The Raucous Rebellion in Political Science, pp. 9–11.*
14. Peter Loewenberg's essays on psychological conflicts arising in graduate school and in university departments remain relevant. See his *Decoding the Past: The Psycho-historical Approach* (New York: Knopf, 1983).
15. Cited in Kurt Jacobsen, 'Unreal, Man' *The Guardian* 3 April 2001 and in Kurt Jacobsen, 'Perestroika dans la science politique Americain.' *L'Economie Politique* Winter 2004–2005. One gets a strong dose in Daniel Diermeyer, 'Rational Choice and the Role of Theory in Political Science,' in Jeffrey Friedman, ed, *The Rational Choice Controversy* (New Haven: Yale University Press, 2005), a volume marshalled in riposte to Donald Green and Ian Shapiro's *Pathologies of Rational Choice.*
16. Kurt Jacobsen and Donald MacLeod, "Fired Up For Battle: Economic Traditionalists and Their Critics." The Guardian 9 September 2003. 'What rarely is grasped is that these economic theories are themselves metaphors; *homo oeconomicus* is a particle, the commodity-space is a force field, utility is energy, disutility is work, force and marginal utility are vectors energy and utility are scalars …. ' James Bernard Murphy, 'Rational Choice Theory as Social Physics,' in Friedman, *The Rational Choice Controversy*, p. 157.
17. Chalmers Johnson, 'Preconception Versus Observation, or the Contributions of Rational Choice Theory and Area Studies to Contemporary Political Science' *PS: Political Science and Politics* 30, 2 (June 1997).
18. 'At its extreme, area scholars regard any methodology that does not recognize specificity and context as immoral; they condemn as the gas pump strategy of research scholarship that takes a purely utilitarian stance toward area knowledge, exploiting it as the 'raw material' of hypothesis testing.' Rudolph, 'Situated Knowledge', p. 11.
19. See Daniel Ellsberg's *Papers on The War* (New York: Simon & Schuster, 1972) and his *Secrets: A Memoir of Vietnam and The Pentagon Papers* (London: Penguin, 2003).
20. Susanne Rudolph, 'Perestroika and the Other' in Monroe, *Perestroika!* p. 14.
21. Sven Steinmo, 'The Emperor Had No Clothes: The Politics of Taking Back the APSR' in Monroe, *Perestroika!*, p. 295.

22. David Laitin, 'The Perestroikan Challenge to Social Science,' *Politics & Society* 31 (200), p. 163. Reprinted in Monroe, *Perestroika!*
23. Russell Jacoby, 'The New PC: They Claim that Liberals are Victimizing Them' *The Nation* 18 March 2005.
24. Greg Kasza, 'Perestroika and The Journals,' *PS: Political Science and Politics* 43, 4 (October 2010). Kasza's article is a contribution to a symposium entitled 'Perestroika in Political Science: Past, Present and Future' in this issue edited by Tim Luke and Patrick McGovern. Also see David Pion-Berlin and Dan Cleary, 'Methodological Bias in The APSR,' in Monroe, *Perestroika!*
25. Chris Hedges interview 2013. www.herealnews.com/t2/index.php?option=com_content&task=view&id=31&Itemid=74&jumival=10449.
26. See Jeffrey C. Isaac, 'Perestroika and the Journals?: A Brief Reply to My Friend Gregory Kasza,' *PS: Political Science and Politics* 4, 4 (October 2010).
27. Sidney Tarrow, 'Polarization and Convergence in Academic Controversies,' *Theory and Society* 37, 6 (December 2008), p. 517.
28. Stuart Schram, 'Return to Politics: Perestroika and Postparadigmatic Political Science,' *Political Theory* 1, 6 December 2003, p. 838.
29. See Brian Caterino, 'The Practical Import of Political Inquiry: Perestroika's Last Stand' *Logos: A Journal of Modern Society & Culture* 14, 1–2 (2015) and his contribution in Monroe, *Perestroika!*
30. www.polscirumors.com/topic/perestroika-movementin-polsci/page/2.
31. Laitin, 'The Perestroikan Challenge to Social Sciences.' p. 165.
32. Morris Fiorina, 'Rational Choice, Empirical Contributions, and the Scientific Enterprise' in Friedman, *The Rational Choice Controversy: Economic Models of Politics Reconsidered* (New Haven: Yale University Press, 1996), p. 87.
33. See David Laitin, 'The Perestroika Challenge' and Ian Shapiro, *The Flight from Reality in The Human Sciences* (Princeton: Princeton University Press, 2005) as well as Shapiro's essay in Monroe, *Perestroika!*
34. For a 1970s philosophy of science volume whose implications entirely elude or are disregarded by Diermeier and most RC enthusiasts see the rich combative essays in Richard Musgrave and Imre Lakatos, *Criticism and the Growth of Knowledge* (New York: Cambridge University Press, 1970).
35. Frank Edward Manuel, Isaac Newton, *Historian* (Cambridge: Harvard University Press, 1963), pp. 17–18.
36. Green and Shapiro, 'Revisiting Rational Choice,' in Shapiro, *The Flight from Reality in The Human Sciences*, p. 78.
37. A pertinent critique of Peirce's project is found in Jurgen Habermas, *Knowledge and Human Interests* (Boston: Beacon Press, 1971).
38. Diermeier, 'Rational Choice', p. 61.

39. See Floyd Matson, *The Broken Image* (New York: Anchor, 1966) and Stephen Toulmin, *Return to Reason* (Berkeley: University of California Press, 2002).
40. See Thomas Kuhn, 'Logic of Discovery or Psychology of Research?' in Lakatos and Musgrave, *Criticism and the Growth of Knowledge,* and his *The Essential Tension: Selected Essay in Scientific Tradition and Change* (University of Chicago Press, 1997), pp. 225–239. See also Steve Fuller's controversial biography, *Thomas Kuhn: A Philosophical History for Our Time* (Chicago: University of Chicago Press, 2000).
41. Imre Lakatos, 'Falsification and the Methodology of Scientific Research Programmes,' in Lakatos and Musgrave, *Criticism and The Growth of Knowledge*, p. 177.
42. On Lakatos' conservative affinity to conventional political science see Thomas C. Walker, 'The Perils of Paradigm Mentalities: Revisiting Kuhn, Lakatos and Popper,' *Perspectives on Politics* 8, 2 (June 2010). Like virtually all IR scholars Walker has taken the disciplinary hint that he should shun Feyerabend. The plea for pluralism goes only so far. See, then, Jacobsen and Gilman, 'Paul Feyerabend's Philosophy of Science,' in Kurt Jacobsen, *Dead Reckonings: Ideas, Interests and Politics in the 'information Age'* (Atlantic Highlands, NJ: Humanities Press, 1997).
43. Diermeier, 'Rational Choice,' p. 61.
44. Diermeier, 'Rational Choice,' p. 62.
45. Diermeier, 'Rational Choice,' p. 64.
46. Matson, *The Broken Image*, p. 243.
47. Diermeier, 'Rational Choice,' p. 62.
48. Vaihinger, *The Philosophy of As-If.* Vaihinger has attracted a renewal of interest. See Mauricio Suarez, *Fiction in Science: Philosophical Essays on Modeling and Idealisation* (London: Routledge, 2009). '[T]he impact of Vaihinger's work then was not unlike the impact of Thomas Kuhn's work in our own time,' Pine reckons. 'In the 1960s and 1970s most philosophers of science reacted to Kuhn with strident criticism.' Arthur Pine, 'Fictionalism' *Midwest Studies in Philosophy* XVIII (1993). pp. 3, 4. That seems to be the cut-off period when Diermeier and a good many other positivist social scientists formed and finished their idea of 'the philosophy of science.'
49. Karl Popper, *The Logic of Scientific Discovery* (London: Hutchinson & Co, 1959, 1935). Kuhn wrote how 'extraordinarily problematic' he found the discovery/justification distinction such that, while 'circularity does not at all invalidate them ... it does make them parts of a theory and, by doing so, subjects them to the same scrutiny regularly applied to theories in other fields.' Thomas Kuhn, *The Structure of Scientific Revolutions* (Chicago: University of Chicago, 1962), pp. 8–9. See Paul Hoyningen-Heune, 'Context of Discovery Versus Context of Justification and Thomas Kuhn' in Jutta Schikore and Fruedrich Steinle, eds. *Revisiting*

Discovery and Justification (Springer, 2006). Also see Herbert Butterfield, *The Origins of Modern Science* (New York: Free Press, 1957) and Norwood Hansen, *Patterns of Discovery: An Inquiry into the Conceptual Foundations of Science* (New York: Cambridge University Press, 1958), p. 18.
50. Paul Feyerabend, *Against Method* (London: Verso, 1975).
51. See Jacobsen and Gilman, 'Paul Feyerabend's Philosophy of Science'.
52. '[S]omething like a paradigm is prerequisite to perception itself.' Hence, '[d]ebate over theory-choice cannot be cast in a form that fully resembles logical or mathematical proof.' Kuhn, *The Structure of Scientific Revolutions*, pp. 113, 199. See William Brewer and Bruce Lambert, 'The Theory-Ladeness of Observation: Evidence from Cognitive Psychology' in *Proceedings of the Fifteenth Annual Conference of the Cognitive Science Society* (Hillsdale, NJ: Lawrence Erlbaum Associates, 1993) and the intermediary approach in Peter Galison, *Image and Logic: A Material Culture of Microphysics* (Chicago: University of Chicago Press, 1997), pp. 787–796.
53. Diermeier, 'Rational Choice,' p. 66.
54. Diermeier, 'Rational Choice,' p. 68.
55. 'Normal science does not aim at novelties of fact or theory and, when successful, finds none.' Kuhn, *The Structure of Scientific Revolutions*, p. 52.
56. Geertz, 'Thick Description: Toward an Interpretive Theory of Culture' in Geertz, *The Interpretation of Cultures* (New York: Basic Books, 1973), p. 26.
57. 'There is clear evidence that certain operations of certain animal bodies depend upon the foresight of an end and the purpose to attain it. It is no solution to the problem to ignore this evidence because other operations have been explained in terms of physical and chemical laws. The existence of a problem is not even acknowledged. It is vehemently denied.' Whitehead, cited in Matson, *The Broken Image*, pp. 147–148.
58. Stanley Kelly, 'Promises and Limitations of Rational Choice,' in Friedman, *The Rational Choice Controversy*, p. 87.
59. Clifford Geertz, 'Thick Description: Toward an Interpretive Theory of Culture,' p. 32.
60. Shapiro, *The Flight from Reality in the Human Sciences*, p. 78.
61. Susanne Hoeber Rudolph, 'The Imperialism of Categories: Situating Knowledge in a Globalizing World' *Perspectives on Politics* 3, 1 (March 2005), p. 12.
62. Ido Oren, *Our Enemies and Us: America's Rivalries and the Making of Political Science* (Ithaca: Cornell University Press, 2002).
63. See the issue on Qualitative methods in the *Newsletter of the American Political Science* Association, 5, 1 (Spring 2007).

64. Theodore Lowi, 'Every Poet His own Aristotle,' in Monroe, Perestroika!, p. 51.
65. Rogers Smith, 'Systmatizing the Ineffable: A Perestroikan's Methods for Finding a Good Research Topic,' *Newsletter of the American Political Science Association*, p. 6. For other reflections on the movement see Andrew Hindmoor, 'Review Article: 'Major Combat Operations have Ended'? Arguing about Rational Choice' *Perspectives on Political Science* 41, 1 January 2011, Simon Hug, 'Further Twenty Years of Pathologies?: Is Rational Choice Better Than It Used to Be?' *Swiss Political Science Review* 20, 3 (September 2014), and John Gunnell, 'Pluralism and The Fate of Perestroika: A Historical Reflection' *Perspectives on Politics* 13, 2 (June 2015).
66. Here I belatedly realize I also am echoing Mannheim. See Mannheim, *Ideology and Utopia*, p. 11.

Dueling Constructivisms: A Post-Mortem on the Ideas Debate in Mainstream IR

The experience of a critic putting one's ideas 'into context' often rankles and sometimes with good reason. Except in the rare circumstances of equal status, good will and an unstinting search for common ground, as expressed perhaps in Habermas' ideal speech situation, the exercise can be a subtly negating one that simply fits an adversary's argument inside one's own framework in order to tell them what they meant to say if only they had sufficient rigor and wit to do so.[1]

This tactic commonly is wielded by mainstream scholars against those on the disciplinary fringes—and, whenever possible, vice versa. The rationales are, for the mainstream, that fringe frameworks such as critical theory and Gramscian cultural studies are of interest only to the degree that one converts these analytical modes into positivist and measurable terms by which means alone they are to be deemed scientific, and, for scholars outside the mainstream, that positivism—which holds no known patent on testable propositions—frequently functions as a device by which to exclude forms of analysis that challenge the scholarly status quo.[2]

Scholars at the fringes argue that, as in the classic relation of colonizer and colonized, they have every incentive to study the dominant discourse while the reverse phenomenon is rarely the case.[3] Marginal modes of inquiry accordingly gain admittance to center stage debates only if they are presented in compatible terms and can be absorbed into reigning research agendas with minimal disturbance. I examine this subtle filtration process at work in the recent ideas debate in American—virtually synonymous with 'mainstream'—international relations and consider whether the ascent of 'conventional constructivism' forms a new barrier or a boon to alternative frameworks.

If 'historicising IPE,' a central goal of non-mainstream scholars, means to promulgate transdisciplinary, non-state-centered and reflexive frames of thinking, then this aim remains dismayingly low on the mainstream agenda.[4] Despite all the attention lavished on a single form of constructivism, one detects little evidence that countertrends such as critical theory or Gramscian cultural studies have made any inroads in the debates that preoccupy American IR journals. In fact, it is unusual even for self-described constructivists to display any awareness of debates in the alternative (and mostly British or, even, continental) journals.[5] There are exceptions, but they tend to prove the rule.

The constructivist 'turn,' if it is one, is an enterprise explicitly devoted to 'seizing the middle ground' and succeeds to the degree it has largely by appropriating or approximating alternative critical constructs and concerns.[6] The 'new' research agenda it posits already existed in radical European traditions but could be imported into the mainstream only when palatably rendered, a not unprecedented phenomenon.[7] In any field it is difficult to offer fresh or unfamiliar perspectives in forms other than ones 'readily acceptable to the profession.'[8] (Whether critical theory, in the form it takes in British studies, lives up to its avowed standards is an interesting but separate question).[9] Scanning American IR journals for signs of dialogue with alternative schemas, one finds Robert Cox occasionally cited but hardly anyone else who works in a critical theory or Gramscian tradition is ever noticed. This 'silence,' as social historians might term it, should be no surprise. Mainstream scholarship, as a recent survey soberly reminds, is not in the business of promoting the 'emancipatory interests' that motivate some other scholars.[10] This pertinent point about purposes has major implications for the ways in which mainstream and non-mainstream scholars grapple with the nature of contexts in political analysis.

In the aftermath of the ideas debate two key questions arise: (1) Has mainstream IR fixed its limit of permissible debate at the border of 'conventional constructivism,' as rendered by Wendt, Checkel, Adler and others? And (2) is there any prospect for a productive dialogue not only between mainstream IR and critical theory but also between the different kinds of constructivism?[11] Pessimism is not unwarranted, yet one potential bridge is to explore the theme of context-sensitivity, an admitted weak spot in mainstream analyses. The influence that contexts exert upon the interpretation that individuals and collectivities make of their interests and, consequently, their choices has been underplayed in IR because of realist axioms regarding the immutability of systemic imperatives and of national interests. Realists today are more attentive to the influence of contexts upon state behavior but according to a strictly managerial orientation 'fixing the realm of the possible in terms of permissible social and political actions.'[12] Realists, neorealists and even liberal institutionalists tend to embrace the given distribution of interests and capabilities with the same impatient panache with which Samuel Johnson allegedly refuted Bishop Berkeley's nominalist fancies by giving the nearest stone a swift kick.[13]

By contrast, critical theorists, harking to the 1930s heyday of the Institute for Social Research headed by Max Horkheimer, held that what today are called 'discursive formations' always fashioned our knowledge of the world within a range of possibilities set by the context of historically specific structures of power—a context of which we scholars and citizens are, at best, only partially aware. The project of the Frankfurt School was to devise an 'interdisciplinary materialism' geared to 'pursue philosophical questions with the most refined scientific methods, to reformulate and sharpen these questions in the course of the work, to devise new methods, and yet not lose sight of the larger context.'[14] This larger context—explicitly encompassing those engaged in analyzing it—was understood primarily through an unorthodox but fertile blend of Marxism and psychoanalysis.

The critical theorists stressed that a valid macroconceptualization of political life required rigorous multidisciplinary research in order to illuminate the effects of a given political-economic structure upon institutions and individuals—which have different degrees of autonomy and reflective capacity—and, in turn, their cumulative effects upon that structure. This approach was, so far as critical theorists saw it, kindergarten dialectics. Contemporary constructivists are approaching what critical theorists long have taken as their research starting point. For the latter, however, the willingness to understand the importance of context must be infused with the will to change or resist it.[15] Critical theory took pains to distinguish itself from 'traditional theory' which the Frankfurt school argued had obscured the underlying interests and purposes of societal actors.

Critical theory, Horkheimer writes, 'was incompatible with the idealist belief that any theory is independent of men or has a growth of its own.'[16] No less than for Karl Korsch or Georg Lukacs in the Western

Marxist tradition, philosophy for Antonio Gramsci was never 'purely contemplative, theory itself engenders practice' and it exerted 'practical, even political consequences, even if it is avowedly non-political.'[17] Habermas characterized the Frankfurt project as pursuing 'philosophy by other means, namely the social sciences,' and with no inhibitions about crossing disciplinary boundaries in order to create an appropriate analytical synthesis for the study of societies.[18] Critical theory, thus understood, forms a key component in the analytical arsenal of many scholars on the margins of the discipline, as odd as it seems to describe as 'fringe' a theoretical mode that is considered a major player in international studies outside the USA.[19]

Any scholar who spends significant time in the USA and the UK cannot help but be struck by the virtually parallel universes inhabited by American and British IR scholars (for whom neo-Marxist influences long have been part of the post-imperial mainstream).[20] The conservative slant of American IR studies preceded congressional witch-hunts but McCarthyism certainly quieted what few dissident voices there were.[21] A slowly waning legacy of the latter in the social sciences is discouragement not only of radical scholarship but even of any questioning of state-defined managerial imperatives in the American sphere of influence. Today this cross-Atlantic schism in IR studies may stem more so from disciplinary boundary maintenance. Every lively debate in British international studies also appears in American academe, though usually in the adjacent fields of comparative politics, historical sociology and public policy where American IR specialists traditionally have been reluctant to tread.

Still, at the brink of the 1990s, mainstream scholars significantly conceded that ideas, under certain circumstances, do matter, and this concession opened up opportunities for multidisciplinary explorations and cross-fertilizations.[22] A spate of ideas-oriented arguments quickly emerged or, in some cases, resurrected. Here I assess why neither a critical theory nor Gramscian-based approach, despite high visibility elsewhere in the profession, made a direct or acknowledged impact in the debate at a time when so many attempts were made to integrate an ideational dimension. In ensuing sections I introduce pertinent insights from psychologically trained analysts, examine the American debate about ideas, assess prospects of a 'theory of contexts' as a bridge and conclude with an assessment of the relation of constructivism to critical theory, and of both to mainstream (mainly American) scholarship. My central argument is that 'conventional constructivism,' as now inducted into the mainstream, poses severe limitations for IR studies and that engagement with (if not wholehearted acceptance of) the 'critical' variant of constructivism improves analytical sensitivity to the intricate interaction of ideas and interests, the 'mutual constitution' of agent and structure, and the role of the investigators in whatever they are investigating.

Rationality and Contexts

The first task is definitional. Context is 'that which environs the object of our interest and helps by its relevance to explain it.'[23] In standard usage a context is the background against which we pose pertinent facts. Contextualizing is assumed to be unproblematic; one merely brings to light salient features of the environment, like silhouettes.[24] In a second and quantitative sense 'contextual analysis' comes into play when examining 'the way the relationship between two variables (e.g., two individual-level variables, or perhaps an individual and a context variable) may change systematically, for individuals, across groups which are set up to differ in a systematic way on a group-level variable.'[25]

Finally, in a critical—not just critical theory—tradition, a context, when brought into what an interested agent portrays as its proper focus, imbues data with a new meaning. One reconfigures the context—the very sinews of everyday common sense—and sees a larger or different picture, incorporates new factors and shifts the relative importance of various explanatory factors according to one's training, interests, ideational inclinations and unconscious predilections. What is desirable in one context—privatizing public transport, capital punishment, an international anti-drug war—may appear perfectly pernicious when placed convincingly in another.[26] Only the way the world is viewed changes but this activity triggers actions that can alter the physical world.

Whether globalization or whatever the third way is are viewed as desirable things hinges on how cultural notions of justice inflect one's experience when interpreting events or evaluating arguments. Results often depend on the capacities of competing elites to attach or align their particular agenda to public norms, beliefs and values. Hence, corporate CEOs 'do not talk about escaping from the law (it sounds unpatriotic). Instead they promote the goal of greater efficiency—a 'harmonization of national laws that will remove barriers and encourage greater trade.'[27] A congressional bill designed to slash aid to the poor was dubbed the 'Personal Responsibility and Job Opportunity Act.' The political world doesn't turn, it spins, and it is hard for the nimblest to keep their footing in this slippery interpretative milieu.

Few participants in the ideas debate aimed at anything more ambitious than expanding the conceptual base of reigning models. Ideas usually were seen as factors to be plugged into dominant frameworks or else as ad hoc devices. There was no intention that an ideas-oriented model, however well grounded, could become a rival to realism/neo-realism, liberal institutionalism or the rational choice methods that increasingly suffuse them. It seems all the more extraordinary that a highly idealist version gained entry. Still, in mainstream studies what distinguishes a palatable ideas approach from 'soft' cultural or psychological models is that ideas are explicit programmatic ways of organizing institutions, and their distributions of benefits and costs. These ideas are 'shared beliefs', which exclude idiosyncratic and leader-specific notions. By definition they can be intersubjectively validated. So one may be attentive to cultural and/or psychological insights if they adhere to this shared character. The next section examines historical insights about the application of rationalist models as presented by social scientists, who, in a non-Marxian but dialectical vein, had come to conclusions very similar to those drawn by critical theorists. The 'silences' in rationalist social science extend well beyond treatment of Marxian scholarly critiques.

Psychology, Science and 'Silences'

Regarding B.F. Skinner's behaviorist fancies, a New Yorker cartoon long ago depicted two lab rats inside a cage chatting about a nearby scientist. One rodent brags: 'Have I ever got that guy trained. Whenever I press this lever, he gives me a pellet.' The point is that the subject, even in loaded-dice circumstances, 'elaborates and participates in that to which it responds'—that is, the stimulus intervenes according to what it signifies in the situational context for the subject.[28] In the field of psychology the notion of the isolated reflex or response long ago was exposed as 'a pathological dissociation of organismic activity prominent only within the luxurious confines of a laboratory—an anthropomorphic illusion.'[29] Human beings—if not ensconced in Dachau or held at gunpoint—are even more difficult to control or divine. 'A human being does not only have a hand and a heart,' Crozier observed. 'He also has a head, which means that he is free to decide his own game. This is what almost all proponents of human relations theories, as well as their early rational proponents, tend to forget.'[30]

In mainstream IR literature those beneath leadership level are regarded as 'natives' once were in the anthropological canon. These subalterns 'could be observed enacting their culture, fulfilling cultural obligations, and behaving in culturally appropriate ways, but they were not expected to be self-conscious or reflective, capable of subjectivity, choice or contestation,' a critic writes.[31] 'The cultural scripts that constructed them were written by "us"; these told them who they were and how they should behave. [Today, by contrast, through their own eyes] we see culture in the making as well as in the doing: how agency and structure interact, how culture shapes self, and how self shapes culture.' Constructivists, in their unduly restrictive social-psychological view of identity—a conceptualization of identity arising in reactive fashion from the 'reflective appraisals' of others—do not seem to fully grasp this otherwise congenial point. Even George Herbert Mead had a far more active, and arguably subversive, view of the perceiving subject than some disciples appreciate.[32] Still, constructivism improves upon rational choice theory in its view of the beings inhabiting its modeled universe.

Rational choice theory depicts its individuals as optimizing under a given set of constraints. But are constraints impervious to interpretative variations? For the sake of convenience interests are regarded as given and prior to the beliefs held by actors, so that ideas are relegated to the limbo of unexplained variance. Rational choice concedes that ideas can be important 'because unique predictions cannot be generated through an examination of interests and strategic interaction (utility functions and payoff matrices)' because almost all 'games with repeated play have multiple equilibria.'[33] The translation of 'interest into appropriate policy' (and preceding that, preference) is problematic.'[34] Because actors cannot guarantee the consequences of their actions, it is the 'expected effects of actions that explains them.' In short, what actors expect is elaborated 'in their heads' although the evidentiary basis for these expectations is not.

The mind lives 'on images, absorbing and re-creating them as a basis for all understanding and action': these shared images are 'the means of symbolically combining inner emotional experience with various prevailing ideological currents' in a given time and place.[35] When wielding this potent imagery, Erikson observed, 'no actor and no effective innovator is really independent, nor can he dare to be entirely original: his originality must consist in the courage and singular concentration with which he expresses an existing imagery—at the proper time.'[36] This imagery—'magic of the marketplace,' 'peace through strength,' 'Germany encircled,' 'evil empire'—cannot be spun out of nothing nor used any way one pleases, and when the context changes, so too will the credibility of the image, or the applicability of the model.

Rational choice itself is derived from a context-bound image of the way minds work. Fair enough when applied with caution, but formal frameworks generate irrational behavior when practitioners are insensitive to context-dependence. In Vietnam, local combatants on both sides of the 17th Parallel regarded the typical Western equation of what is real with what is countable (body counts, tonnage dropped, sorties flown) as a very violent form of mysticism indeed.[37] What was overlooked by authorities—apart from all discouraging data—was the overspilling of 'disintegrative tendencies into the realm of idea systems and images [causing] a breakdown not only of social institutions but of the shared symbols necessary to ordered existence—symbols defining rhythms of life and death, group loyalties, and the nature of reality.'[38] Rational reward–punish models employed by policy makers misunderstood the history, motives and strategies of their opponents.[39] What invariably gets lost is the connection between normative ends and instrumental means.

So a rationalist model, by deprecating 'soft' phenomena of culture or social psychology, frustrated the aims for which it was intended to be the most effective means.[40] One might have more confidence in hard-nosed realists if they were not inclined to such startling misjudgments as the claim that America lost the Vietnam War 'due to deficiencies of our ally' and declaring culture irrelevant because the NVA and Viet Cong, on the one hand, and the South Vietnamese army, on the other, 'were products of similar strategies and political cultures.'[41]

Culture is an extremely slippery and problematic term, but that is hardly a good reason for abandoning or deriding its use. 'One often is forced to resort to broad definitions,' as critical theory-oriented scholars note, such as 'any interpersonally shared system of meanings, perceptions and values.'[42] Still, even the way pain is experienced depends on 'genetic endowment, and on at least four functional factors other than the nature and intensity of the stimulus: namely, culture, anxiety, attention, and interpretation. All these are shaped by social determinants, ideology, economic structure and social character.'[43]

Even in diagnosing mental illness, culture defines certain symptoms as legitimate so that patients can latch onto approved ways of expressing their underlying anguish, whether this be invoking evil spirits, hysteria or genetic maladies.[44] For Williams culture consisted of 'known meanings and directions, what the members are trained to; [and] the new observations and meanings, which are offered and tested' and is 'always both traditional and creative.'[45] Culture requires its due, even if in the futile exercise of converting it into terms congenial to a positivist agenda.[46] I say 'futile' not because this cannot be done in principle but because no definition of culture which allows for adequate complexity and reflexivity (as Williams implies) ever pleased positivists, who cannot conceive that they themselves may form a 'culture' and not the last word in science, and to whom every 'soft' concept looks manipulable and untrustworthy.[47]

Yet ideas cannot be infinitely manipulable because an inhibiting cultural context—what Gramsci called 'common sense'—exists. Common sense, for Gramsci, 'define[s] the terms of public political discourse; it is embodied in social practices and therefore must be considered a material force' and 'civil society' is the sphere in which the struggle to define the categories of common sense takes place.'[48] I suggest below that context can function as a mainstream counterpart to Gramsci's 'common sense'— a sufficiently equivalent term that permits conceptual connections to occur across the intradisciplinary divide between mainstream scholars and constructivists, and between rival constructivist camps (Horkheimer and Adorno, of course, despised 'common sense' when construed as a keen folk wisdom). In non-mainstream studies the Gramscian definition of 'the constitutive character of common sense' has been put to provocative use.[49] Should and can mainstream scholars be lured by, or prodded into, the need to develop a counterpart theory of contexts?

Realists often allow that social beliefs influence how actors relate their interests to changing material circumstances (different contexts). For one domestic example, the reason why sterilization of 'mentally defective' people was spurned in Britain in the 1930s, and welcomed in 19 US states, Scandinavia and Germany, was rooted in 'the moral and ideological environment'; this eugenical measure 'infringed fundamental ideas about individual rights and social responsibility' in Britain. [50] (See Chap. 6 on this subject.) Citizens' judgments in both domestic and international realms not only seem to be shaped by calculations of material advantage and by propaganda but are mediated or balanced by collective notions of what is ethical in a given context too. A theory of contexts seems in order.

From a critical theory perspective, struggles about meaning are struggles about power—although, for critical theorists, reflexivity justifiably is intertwined with force only in order to mitigate violence, or its arbitrary use.[51] Scholars who promote policies purely on their scientific merits tend to get rudely awakened as to how ideas are adapted to suit the agendas of self-aggrandizing groups.[52] This is not to say that ideas mean exactly what their sponsors want them to mean; economic ideas, and the contexts in which they are presented, are contestable and never ultimately settled, at least not by argument. At the conclusion of the recent ideas debate, which saw a guarded welcome of 'conventional constructivists' into the mainstream, many scholars belatedly arrived at many of the same conclusions as critical theorists, if by a more roundabout and dubious path. The key liability of this latest disciplinary development is that ideas, whose power was beginning to be appreciated again, tended to become untethered from interests.

Reconnoitering the Ideas Debate

Peter Hall's influential volume on Keynesianism examined the ways in which ideas affect coalition-building and how 'administrative-political processes affected the selection of economic ideas.'[53] What matters is not the idea's intrinsic force in a given context but whether the idea reconciles the interests of elites within the institutional processes of a state so that a coalition emerges to enact the resulting agenda. The more powerful the sponsors, the more powerful the ideas. Goldstein went a step further in arguing that the 'power of the idea itself explains its acceptance,' but her trade policy study consistently retreated into a political sponsorship argument.[54]

The unabashedly idealist case advanced by some contributors—that ideas exert a force all their own—was never persuasive.[55] The inherent snarl is that the claim that the 'power of the idea itself explains its acceptance' first must demonstrate that interests are interpenetrated by ideas; then these same ideas must be shown to exert influence untainted by the very interests they have just been shown to interpenetrate.[56] This was an untenable move that anyone acquainted with critical theory would spot immediately. The hypothesis was afflicted by the tempting manoeuver where interests are shown to become embedded in an idea (e.g., Keynesianism) whose institutionalization supposedly proves that agents were mesmerized by the 'power of ideas' all along. One loses sight of the materialistic motives driving the success of an idea and so one ends by fetishizing ideas. Ideas and material circumstances, according to critical theory and Gramscian cultural studies, axiomatically are found together, mutually influence one another and are not reducible one to the other. The mainstream's challenge, as shown in the next section, was to arrive at a similar proposition without hauling tainted theoretical baggage along.

Mainstream scholars readily agree that ideas affect groups by influencing how they relate their interests to circumstances, and they agree that ideas trigger changes of the context—which itself is comprised of intellectual precepts and institutional arrangements fixing the limits of permissible action. At times the context itself can be at stake in contests among groups promoting rival projects. This context affects the kinds of issues that appear salient, by creating or altering expectations—that is, creating the 'background psychological operating system' within which new ideas and interpretative ploys come into play.

While ideas alone do not create interests, mainstream scholars concede that material constraints are subject to some significant degree to the ideas or to the perceptions that actors have about them. Ideas and interests are both concepts and therefore are ideas because 'interests are perceived through the lenses of the existing ideologies in various historical settings.'[57] But it does not follow from this tricky proposition that interests are 'only' ideas that change once we change our view of reality. It is impossible to describe an action without reference to the ideas and meanings that inform it.[58] The intrinsic interlacing of material interest by ideational influences appears to be an infernally difficult concept to grasp. Few positivists or even constructivists comprehend this point, and when they do, they slip quickly back to an interest vs. ideas dichotomy or else begin to fetishize the power of pure discourse.

Take a prominent scholar's survey of IR in which he equates the 'ideational approach' with a diarrhetically relativist rendition of constructivism emphasizing 'the capacity of discourse to shape how political actors define themselves and their interests, and thus modify their behaviour.'[59] Discourse is described as if divorced from interest or power. The author informs us that this approach 'largely replaced Marxism as the pre-eminent radical perspective in international affairs' when, in fact, important variants of constructivism stem precisely from this 'replaced' tradition.[60] In fact, the project of cultural studies aims to demonstrate that political economy is thoroughly 'cultural without ceasing to be material' and 'that what students of literature and art call "cultural" is economic, not as base to superstructure, but in its production, distribution and effects, including effects on reproducing class relations.'[61]

Another mainstream scholar employs the term 'nonmaterial explanations' to characterize ideas approaches, which supposedly 'attach key interest to how states purposes or goals are defined' because 'the ideas that policy makers carry around in their heads are very important in explaining their policy choices.'[62] This misleading formulation again detaches interest from ideas and restores readers to square one without any gain having been made from a decade-long ideas debate. Goldstein and Keohane, to be sure, 'recognise that ideas and interests are not phenomenologically separate,' but their prime question 'is the extent to which variations in beliefs, or the manner in which ideas are institutionalised in societies, affect political action' and it is in pursuit of this purpose where slips occur into dubious claims for the force of ideas. This tack also lures them into justifying ideas in terms of their fit to a formal model so that an 'idea as commodity' metaphor ultimately is deployed.[63]

Policy makers, they say, rely on causal models when making choices, and policy entrepreneurs 'depend on ideas about how to translate these forces into a political and economic program.'[64] However, these maps must meet interest-bound criteria so that even 'efficiency is valued only to the extent that the means to a goal adhere to existing ideas, values, and institutions.' Actors are usually very well aware that the rules established in the victory of an economic idea constrain future choices (via path-dependence), as exemplified by the recent protests against WTO policies.

The constructivist turn, as critical theorists behold it, is what is left after one removes the Marxian cores of critical theory and cultural studies.[65] Alex Wendt phrases his constructivist case as arguing for a 'cognitive, intersubjective conception of science in which identity and interests are endogenous to interaction' rather than 'exogenously given by structure.'[66] Interaction is again divorced from structure, or is left tenuously tied to it (through a 'rump materialism'). Wendt argued that anarchy acquires different meanings for different actors based on pre-existing 'communities of intersubjective understandings and practices'—a proposition that draws us close to the implication that some communities are privileged clubs whose privileges are bestowed by or wrung out of a material culture.[67] This claim approximates a critical theory position but simply is not teased out to any degree that threatens to link identity formation with material forces. The rupture point between conventional and critical constructivists is the formers' assertion that 'the structures of human association are determined primarily by shared ideas rather than material forces …'[68]

Critical theorists always view ideas and material forces in the realm of power politics as inseparably, if complexly, related. Wendt occasionally allows for the importance of ideas being 'mediated by power relations.'[69] But Checkel and Adler, among others, insist that constructivists are staking out a perfectly sensible middle ground between mainstream scholars and postmodernists.[70] Is this really the case?[71]

Going Conventional: A Critique

A key perk of mainstream scholars is ample freedom to misconstrue the theoretical character of challengers. Note how constructivism is conveyed for audiences of a major IR journal where the author imposes a neat but invidious distinction between 'critical' constructivism, based on critical theory, Gramsci and Foucault, and 'conventional' constructivism, which is cleansed of unsavory influences. Critical and conventional versions, Ted Hopf argues, share assumptions about the mutual constitution of actor and society, anarchy as a social construct, power as being both material and discursive and of interests as being variable with the context. So far, so good.

Critical constructivism 'rejects either the possibility of the desirability of a minimal or contingent foundationalism' and regards 'establishing causality as an illusory goal'—which would surprise the Frankfurt critical theorists who assiduously toiled to elaborate a profoundly subtle 'materialist conception of history.'[72] From the inaugural era of the Institute for Social Research through Habermas' endeavor to construct a 'universal pragmatics,' practitioners of critical theory exhibited little sympathy for the 'antifoundational' bent of postmodern theorists with whom they are conflated and confused here.[73] It says a great deal about the intellectual insularity of the discipline that no referee or editor had the knowledge or willingness to raise questions about this portrayal.

Critical constructivism aims at 'unmasking power,' which is true, while conventional constructivism is 'analytically neutral' as to its attitude to the distribution and nature of power in any society. No scholar evidently has any reason to unmask behind-the-scenes workings and purposes of powerful agents, which is just not a neutral to do. This is exactly the spurious sort of neutrality that critical theory arose to expose. Critical theory supposedly regards 'world politics as an array of fragments that can never add up to a whole' and so deems efforts to construct such a whole as the political imposition of 'some kind of rationalised, naturalised order on irrepressible differences,' which once again muddles up critical theory with a batch of postmodern theories, such as Saussure or Derrida, intent on conducting analysis exclusively within and between texts, as ungrounded systems of signs.[74]

Readers are informed that conventional constructivism aims at 'production of new knowledge and insights based on real understanding' while critical constructivists are interested in such unscientific notions as enlightenment and emancipation—and a presumption reigns here that the former task cannot legitimately be related to the latter.[75] What of *The Authoritarian Personality* series, the *Studies in Authority and the Family* project of which it was part, the *Studies in Prejudice* series and a host of other empirical studies conducted by the Frankfurt school and later followers like Habermas, especially at the Starnberg Institute? The overarching purpose of critical theorists, as Leo Lowenthal put it, was 'to accomplish scientifically meaningful work in a manner that would allow its application to political purposes.'[76] In Horkheimer's heyday, when the psychoanalytic slant was particularly strong, the school's objective was 'to research the psychic processing of economically induced behavioural imperatives and their transformation into specific cultural meanings.'[77] One hardly can come up with a more concisely stated 'constructivist' agenda, and many decades before anyone designated themselves, or were designated, as a constructivist.

Hopf avers that only conventional constructivists wish to 'discover identities and their associated reproductive social practices' and offer a responsible empirical account of 'how these identities imply certain actions.' As unveiled by conventional constructivism, the power of a social practice, Hopf explains, is to 'produce intersubjective meaning within a social structure'—which rather nicely also matches up with a Gramscian 'awareness of the material nature of ideology and of the fact that it constitutes a practice inscribed in apparatuses.'[78]

Critical constructivism 'aims at exploding myths associated with identity formation whereas conventional constructivists wish to treat these identities as possible causes of action.'[79] But what do these imputed identities, which are loosely defined as the 'basic character' of states, stem from? Did the American state under Jimmy Carter have the same 'basic character' as the American state under Nixon, or did the second

Reagan administration have the same 'identity' as his first administration?[80] Identity would be a very mercurial thing if the answers were all in the affirmative. Just what are the domestic and international components, and who are the agents involved, in creating (and recreating) this 'basic character'? You don't have to be a critical theorist to tell that identity 'cannot be constituted without reference to place, to conditions of existence' that help to define 'who we are' and 'what we are doing here.'[81] Conventional constructivism relies on Mead's and follower Harry Stack Sullivan's view that the 'self is made up of reflected appraisals'—a zealously passive notion that is extended to the way states supposedly acquire identities. Yet utilizing Sullivan's own term 'parataxic distortion,' one easily poses the scenario that, given such passivity, one's identity is likely to be composed of nothing but parataxic distortions, that is, the sum of distorted identifications in which all the deluded participants—who internalize one another's misapprehensions—consensually validate a Lewis Carroll reality.[82]

Hopf observes that conventional constructivists really offer no causal theory of identity construction and that critical theory is 'more advanced in this regard but it comes at a price that one may or may not be willing to pay,' which is an admirably candid appraisal.[83] Hopf and the conventional constructivists speak of many possible identities available for each state (a proposition that keeps scrutiny fixed at state unit level), but not of many identities—bearing diverse interests and projects—competing within each state for power.[84] So much for 'second image reversed' studies and for linking domestic and international realms of politics.[85] Curiously, one finds a ready recognition in this literature that factions compete for dominance within substate organizations, such as the military, though not in the overall apparatus of the state itself[86] (this oversight stems, in part, from the interchangeable use of 'state' and 'government'—and not only or universally by conventional constructivists).[87]

Identities rarely are 'reconstituted.' What usually is at stake in such constructivist studies are political projects of domestic groups striving to demonstrate to dominant elites (where they do not already comprise part of these elites) that a preferred course of conduct is in their interest too. Does it really make sense to say that industrialists and bankers were 'reconstituted' in their grudging acceptance of Keynesianism and welfare state policies in the early post-war era? This was no small change, but how embedded does this liberalism appear today? In the USA and UK, are corporations and banks—not to mention, the state—reverting to their 'pre-reconstituted' (pre-Keynesian) identities? The surface clearly is all that is being scratched by such a question. Still, what even the conventional constructivist literature usefully, if not uniquely, emphasizes is that there usually are several paths—with different immediate consequences for the distributions of costs and benefits by which to accomplish a particular goal.

In assigning meaning, however, Hopf finds that conventional constructivism's amazingly hazy notion of identities and identity-formation does the analytical service of reducing uncertainty.[88] The implicit interest that a critical constructivist detects here is the managerial mission to control uncertainty even when, by different criteria, uncertainty can be a 'good thing'—indicating, for example, that the range of participants and of policy choice is widening or that the governing coalition is reformulating its views to meet changed conditions. Ultimately, Hopf praises conventional constructivism's 'nonpareil richness of the elaboration of causal/constitutive mechanisms in any given social context'—nonpareil except for a critical constructivism rooted in critical theory.

On Theories of Contexts

For non-mainstream scholars a latent theory of contexts already is found in Gramscian studies where, as Weldes, Rupert and others have sketched, interpellation and articulation comprise the stuff of common sense, and porous lines are drawn between this 'common sense' and allegedly sophisticated theories. What are required then are mainstream counterparts with which to critically engage. Minimally, any such theory will be forced by this competition to give an account of how ideas arise from and alter social structure (and if not, why not), provide a defensible concept of causal relations regarding links between the cognitive-cultural and the socio-economic spheres, and demonstrate why the analyst is or is not implicated in the analysis and what the consequences and/or remedies are.

Laffey and Weldes are on right track in saying that competing conceptions of causal relations ultimately were at stake in the ideas debate.[89] They argue, as did the critical theorists, that ideas are 'inextricably embedded in material practices and other social relations' because power relations are entailed in all representational practices.'[90] Further, the ideological effects of representations 'are closely bound up with the contexts in which they are deployed.'[91] Examining core values (which presumably form part of Weldes' 'security imaginary') Herman adds that the use of force against an ally might be unthinkable whereas against an enemy it would be easy due to 'the image of the other actor and the norms this image defines as relevant.'[92] Where the image (say, Iraq in 1989 and Iraq in 1991) springs from and why it takes the form it does are questions that no ideational school of thought has sorted out convincingly.

The critical theory/Gramscian approach scrutinizes the play of organized interests always striving to gain the interpretative upper hand, propagating their views in elite circles and public forums and seeking sympathetic decision-making sites (congressional committees, the executive branch, the courts, regulatory agencies, etc.) in which most favorably to wage their fights. Conventional constructivism can aid us here although there remains a strong tendency, despite its avowed concern to sort out the murky process of 'mutual constitution,' to weight structure over agency and, indeed, to eschew agency altogether.[93] This happens because many constructivists—even some who wield critical theory or Gramscian sympathies—search for, and are captivated by, speech (linguistic) structures through which, as the notorious postmodernist phrase goes, people are 'spoken.'

Germain and Kenny clearly regard it as a failing that, for Gramsci, consciousness 'could not be understood independently of the exigencies of the economic substructure.'[94] Apparently, no theoretical advance is possible until released from such exigencies. Why this is necessary is not explained by authors who apparently regard the inclusion of any role for economics at all as vulgar economic determinism. Weldes in a Cuban missile crisis study succumbs to this postmodernist bent. After making much of variable meanings that can be attached, apparently at the pleasure of the authorities, to 'visceral feelings' about the discovery of the missiles, the 'security imaginary'—a pool of working concepts, disparate rules of thumb and half-baked beliefs—gathers irresistible cultural momentum and supposedly determines the outcome. In the wobbly span of a single sentence the USA is endowed with a 'well-established cold war identity' but still suffers from an 'always precarious self.'[95] The American state—a unitary actor, or embodied momentarily as such by Excomm—is an insecure and highly sensitive entity which nonetheless ignores Europe—also a unitary actor—which does not share the same common sense as the USA about Cuban missiles, or later, Vietnam, the 'evil empire' and much else. States, funnily enough, seem able to turn identity-formation 'receptors' on or off depending on whether it seems advantageous to those in charge, or is forced upon them. Conventional constructivism's influence crowds out Gramsci here. Yet actors clearly can rise above (or sneak around) the 'security imaginary' too, as JFK clearly and fortunately did.

Actors devised self-interested but plausible interpretations of changing circumstances and promote programmatic messages to the citizenry (or those potential allies within it) to reinforce dominance or to displace that of others. People can 'reconfigure what is happening to attain their own advantage or meet their needs.'[96] Indeed, as Goffman shows, even patients in total institutions elude self-identification with the roles imposed upon them by 'working the system' for forbidden advantages.[97] Of course, one should be wary of cheery portrayals of citizens as 'rascally independent decoders of texts, forever spinning off his or her own individualized forms of resistant readings.'[98] As evidenced in the success of the 'political correctness' bogeyman concocted in the 1990s, 'well-targeted money can create debates out of thin air.'[99] While ideas are interpreted within the context into which they are inserted, the context itself is not an inert background although dominant groups are all too happy to portray a favourable one as 'the way the world works.'

Yet all political actors 'work' their environments in light of changing circumstances and play upon the ideational elements available in their cultural contexts to protect or to advance their concerns and are well aware that rivals do too.[100] To be implemented, the 1995 *Framework on Climate Control*, for example, had to have different social meanings, each of which is context-dependent, but each of which may be 'essentially contested' by other parties. '[R]eports on the International Negotiating Committee meetings directed to prepare for the first Conference of the Parties in March 1995, and that meeting itself, suggest that numerous different social meanings still stalk the meeting halls. If this is so, then which meaning(s) are accepted as legitimate, and how their legitimacy is established, become central to the exercise.'[101]

Similarly, the fraught peace process in Northern Ireland can be consolidated only if rival leaders succeed in presenting the same documents to their respective followers, clothed in persuasive interpretations about the terms of institution-building. The Ulster Unionist Party leader explains why the agreement fastens the six counties forever in the bosom of Britain while his republican confreres must argue that it is instead a stepping stone to a united Ireland. Neither group is deceptive in any way that a polygraph can detect: the different contexts in which the Unionists and republicans are situated generate different interpretative possibilities and plausibility.

It isn't that Unionists see in the gestalt card image two faces (as is their habit) while Sinn Fein perceives a chalice, they both comply with their audiences' views of the minimum concessions they can live with.

'Given the same measure of racial or cultural pluralism,' as Price observes in South Africa, 'different contexts (especially with respect to political institutions and the distribution of resources) equal different outcomes.'[102] Likewise, 'the mere existence of ethnic difference does not produce the politicisation of those differences.'[103] Politicizing ethnicity and race can take a variety of forms 'with substantially different consequences for the quality of a society's political life—particularly in regard to levels of political conflict and stability. The introduction of a socially constructionist view of cultural and quasi-cultural (race) identity has sensitized us to the role of context in the derivation of seemingly given and fixed identity.'

Facets of critical theory, through the vehicle of what mainstream scholars might call an interactionist approach, can provide a conceptual bridge to investigate relations between cognitive and socioeconomic processes which retains elements of both while avoiding the excesses of either.[104] As evidenced by the acceptance of conventional constructivism, mainstream studies still resist the historical materialist notion that culture 'must be finally interpreted in relation to its underlying system of production.'[105] Still, there are signs that the need to examine context entails an attendant recognition that norms are 'not divorced from the material world and impervious to the activities of agents such as nation-states'— and substate actors.[106] The concept of articulation can guide formulation of theories of contexts outside its original Marxian realm.[107] The field is tantalizingly open since 'we have no theory for contexts, no rules for it, and no clear idea of what limits it may have.'[108]

Articulation, a familiar term in these pages, links 'elements which have no necessary relation to each other' (e.g., what advertising executives do for a living) and 'involves delinking or disarticulating connections in order to link or rearticulate others [and] is a continuous struggle to reposition practices within a shifting field of forces, to redefine the possibilities of life by redefining the field of relations—the context—within which a practice is located.'[109] Contexts generate puzzles, which often are puzzles only so long as we take a particular context as given rather than to see it as both variable and interest-laden. Where one goes from there will vary depending on the degree of awareness one comfortably has that these analytical procedures, and the results they yield, are value-bound too.

Because you put something in context does not mean you are being critical, but if you are critical, you will put something in context. This is a difference of some importance because the sociology of knowledge, as rendered by Karl Mannheim, also puts everything in context but is mainstream-oriented. The issue here is one of reflexivity, or critique of the intersubjective context in which the subject is operating: What marks critical theory, after all, is less simply a concern with the context than its normative contestation of the context.[110]

Habermas' early work *Knowledge and Human Interests* with its emphasis on the ideal speech situation (rather than his later dalliance with a 'universal pragmatics') projected an 'emancipatory interest' without which a contestation of the structural context becomes impossible. Only its inclusion in the equation, so to speak, makes the contextual argument critical rather than purely analytic. This, however, raises the question whether there is a place for critical theory in a mainstream unconcerned with radical political aims and norms. Palen is correct that constructivism, as rendered by Wendt, 'arrived at a definition of the task of social science that precludes any form of social criticism.'[111] This hardly is surprising. Nonetheless, a theory of context derived from, or in dialogue with, Gramsci can enable mainstream scholars to conduct deep explorations of relations between agent and structure when sifting out the sources of policy choice. Such a dialogue would keep Gramscians and critical theorists on their toes too.[112]

The Gramscian/critical theory approach makes one, or should make one, exquisitely aware of the material basis of ideology, sensitive to contests to control the political context, and attunes one to the social construction of reality without capitulating to relativist drivel or a fetishism of ideas.[113] One does not construct a context 'by bringing the pieces together, and showing how the pieces fit together [which is] not the same as defining the mode of that articulation, the nature of that fit.'[114]

Who or what else but agents, finally, can articulate this fit and these links? The links do not articulate themselves. The mainstream ideas literature tried to avoid any suggestion that ideas are manipulable entities, although at the same time it quite properly demanded stress on the role of agency. Any hint that agents employ ideas for gain was chalked up as mere or theoretically uninteresting manipulation. Yet it is always agents who put any issue 'into context' just as, in turn, it is analysts such as ourselves who put what those actors do into context too. The issue of elite manipulation, and how it is treated in scholarship, is very tricky yet promising terrain for applying and appraising competing theories of contexts. A Vietnam War veteran, for example, recounts being asked by a classroom of secondary school students decades later if the American antiwar movement had demoralized him in combat[115]:

> What had damaged my morale, I told them, was the discovery that the people we had been sent to defend did not want us there—and indeed, more often than not and with good reason—hated us; that we had been ordered by our government to win the hearts and minds of the people of Vietnam with nothing but rifles and bombs and bullets and American arrogance; that what we were involved in had nothing to do with the cause of liberty and democracy and freedom for which I had enlisted in 1966 at the age of 17; that we were redcoats, not patriots, and that our national leaders had put us up to it; that we were killing and dying for something worse than nothing.

The pupils had been taught that America lost the Vietnam War because wicked protesters undermined troop morale. One may hypothesize that the more citizens accept such unchallenged beliefs, the easier life will be for national leaders and for mainstream analysts. The omitted variables are behaving themselves; the 'data' are conforming. But 'counter-elites,' like this veteran, inhabit the public realm too and convey their own sober experiences. So cumulative public judgments about past foreign policy affect the 'identity' of the American State—in the form, in this case, of a Vietnam syndrome constraining military adventures for which there formerly was carte blanche. Can scholars in or out of the mainstream realistically omit this level of analysis, this continuous and crucial conflict over situating facts in their proper contexts?[116]

Conclusion

In mainstream IR ideational factors remained a residual factor within the dominant frameworks of analysis or else were imported in the form of a 'conventional constructivism' which is, if anything, less empirically inclined than critical theory ever was. At the height of the 1990s debate ideational approaches promised to open an analytical avenue between elites, institutions and the public realm as well as to alert scholars to the subtle political dynamics at play when elites devise public policy. Critical theory's point is that political and economic institutions are permeated with 'significations and norms' and that 'even the most discursive cultural practices have a constitutive, irreducible political-economic dimension; they are underpinned by material supports.'[117]

Secondly, rationality is itself a concept and so is the notion of interest although they are not only concepts once they acquire material support and institutional expression (indeed, as Adorno pointed out, positivists are reluctant to acknowledge their own emergence from and relation to a particular context, which may account for their reluctance to examine contexts at all).[118] This formulation, if by no means novel, may be the key contribution that the ideas debate brought to the mainstream. Constructivists of all stripes seem to agree that it is vital to theorize links between subjective experience and social/institutional structures, although constructivists differ radically over the nature of issues such as reifying the state, the proper unit level of analysis and the adequacy of a social psychological approach for understanding formation of identities.[119]

Rational choice theory, a proponent asserts, 'does not presume that actors possess perfect and complete knowledge about future events. It merely assumes that, given the information they have, they try to pursue the best available means to achieve their ends.'[120] Yet psychotherapists long have strived to detect reasons behind the behavior of psychotic patients, and therapeutic successes occurred based on this belief that patients' actions are meaningful if one tries to understand their viewpoint. If so, have psychotics evidenced forms of rationality all along? The question arises as to what, according to this elastic criterion, is not rational? What evidence do we need to decide case by case that rational choice is applicable, partially useful or useless.[121]

Rational theories typically treat contexts as inert backgrounds, independent of activities under study. But the practice of analyzing articulation 'does not separate the focus from the background; instead, it is the background that actually articulates the focus [and] the task is made even more difficult when the analyst is located in the context' in which he or she is working. And this is probably the hardest nut to crack. Why weren't mainstream scholars, steeped in realism, drawn more to historical materialism than idealism during the debate? It is at first glance puzzling why scholars, who usually consign ideas to the status of supplements to interest-based paradigms, opened a space for conventional constructivists who skirt so perilously along the edge of philosophical idealism. One explanation is that what unites unlikely allies is that they both are fond of the fiction of the neutral scientific observer who supposedly plays no role in influencing or being influenced by the wider social system. Everything looks exquisitely 'scientific' in a positivist mode when critical theorists and their ilk are not around to chip away at that conceit. Conventional constructivists nonetheless have widened a small breach in IR, perhaps even permitting entry of insights from other social sciences and other frameworks.

Just how 'small [a] part of what constitutes interests is actually material' is a question which conventional and critical constructivists can engage in useful dialogues.[122] For mainstream IR, entering dialogues not with Marxism per se but with psychology, anthropology and historical sociology would be a considerable step in the direction of 'interdisciplinary materialism.' A serious dialogue by both mainstream scholars and conventional constructivists with critical constructivists would be valuable for all, although each scholar will have to decide for himself or herself whether this game is worth the candle. Still, the competing constructivisms are surely in agreement when Wendt warns that the 'dependence of theory on method' becomes 'problematic if one method comes to dominate a field' inasmuch as in 'such a context, certain questions never get raised, certain possibilities never considered.'[123]

Notes

1. Jurgen Habermas, 'On Systematically Distorted Communication', in Hans Peter Dreitzel (ed.) *Recent Sociology* (New York: Vintage, 1972).
2. Peter Berger and Thomas Luckmann label one variant 'nihilation' in *The Social Construction of Reality* (New York: Doubleday, 1967), pp. 106, 107. One example is the argument that Realists, correctly understood, are not 'really' Realist at all. See Jeffrey Legro and Andrew Moravscik, 'Is Anybody Still a Realist?' *International Security* 24, 2 (Fall 1999), pp. 5–55.
3. Terry Eagleton, *The Idea of Culture* (Oxford: Blackwell, 2000), p. 48.
4. Ash Amin and Ronan Palen, 'Editorial: The Need to Historicise IPE', *Review of International Political Economy* 3, 2 (Summer 1996), p. 209.
5. See Knud Erik Jorgenson, 'Continental IR Theory: The Best Kept Secret', *European Journal of International Relations* 6, 1 (March 2000), 1–33, and, almost aberrantly, Ole Waever, 'The Sociology of a Not So International Discipline: European and American Developments in

International Relations', *International Organization* 52, 4 (Autumn 1998).
6. Jeff Checkel, 'The Constructivist Turn in International Relations Theory', *World Politics*, 50, 2 (January 1998) and Emanuel Adler, 'Seizing The Middle Ground: Constructivism in World Politics,' *European Journal of International Relations*, 3, 3 (1997).
7. On the derivative relation of Theda Skocpol's neo-Weberian stance to neo-Marxist scholarship see Paul Cammack, 'Bringing the State Back In?', *British Journal of Political Science*, 19, 2 (April 1989).
8. Friedrich Kratochwil, 'Constructing A New Orthodoxy?: Wendt's 'Social Theory of International Politics' and The Constructivist Challenge', *Millennium*, 29, 1 (2000). p. 89.
9. Beate Jahn, 'One Step Forward, Two Steps back: Critical Theory As The Latest Edition of Liberal Idealism', *Millennium* 27, 3 (1998).
10. Ted Hopf, 'The Promise of Constructivism in International Relations Theory', *International Security*, 23, 1 (Summer 1998), pp. 183–184.
11. The Frankfurt theorists were divided: at one extreme Adorno 'saw an internal reform of the social sciences as futile.' Horkheimer thought prospects were a bit better. Seyla Benhabib, Wolfgang Bonss and John McCole, *On Max Horkheimer: New Perspectives* (Cambridge: MIT Press, 1993), p. 11.
12. Amin and Palen, 'Editorial: The Need to Historicise IPE,' p. 212.
13. Robert Keohane, 'International Institutions: Two Approaches', *International Studies Quarterly* 32, 4 (December 1988), pp. 390–391.
14. Max Horkheimer, 'The State of Contemporary Social Philosophy and The Tasks of An Institute for Social Research', in Stephen Eric Bronner and Douglas Kellner (eds.) *Critical Theory and Society: A Reader* (London: Routledge, 1989), p. 32.
15. They aimed 'to show how repressive interests were hidden by the supposedly neutral formulations of science no less than ontology and, in this way, the movement always retained a commitment to the sociology of knowledge and the critique of ideology (ideologiekritik). This internal or immanent encounter with the existing order, however, retained a transcendent or utopian component. The objective was to foster reflexivity, a capacity for fantasy, and a new basis for praxis in an increasingly alienated world. Critical theory, in this way, stood diametrically opposed to economic determinism and any stage theory of history. It sought to examine the various 'mediations' between base and superstructure.' Stephen Eric Bronner, *Of Critical Theory and Its Critics* (Oxford,: Blackwell, 1994), p. 3. Also Martin Jay, *The Dialectical Imagination* (Boston: Little, Brown, 1973). pp. 103, 105.

16. Horkheimer, 'Traditional and Critical Theory,' in *Critical Theory: Selected Essays* (New York: Herder & Herder, 1972), p. 240.
17. Thomas Nemeth, *Gramsci's Philosophy: A Critical Study* (Atlantic Highlands, New Jersey: Humanities Press, 1986), p. 15. Also Georg Lukacs, *History and Class Consciousness: Studies in Marxist Dialectics* (Cambridge, Mass: MIT Press, 1971), pp. 6–7.
18. Jurgen Habermas, 'Remarks on the Development of Horkheimer's Work,' in Benhabib, *On Max Horkheimer*, p. 50.
19. I preface cultural studies with 'Gramscian' to indicate that there are other currents within that variegated field. The version I believe most compatible—indeed, almost interchangeable—with Frankfurt critical theory stems from Stuart Hall's trail-blazing work.
20. On American and British IR practices see J. K. Jacobsen, 'Are All Politics Domestic?: Perspectives on the Integration of Comparative and International Relations Theories,' *Comparative Politics* 22, 4 (October 1996).
21. See Ellen Schrecker, *Many Are the Crimes: McCarthyism* in America (New York: Beacon Press, 1999).
22. For a Realist response see John Mearsheimer, 'The False Promise of Institutionalism,' *International Security* 19, 3 (Winter 1994–95).
23. Ben-Ami Scharfstein, *The Dilemma of Context* (New York: New York University Press, 1989), p. 1.
24. This is assumed even when scholars distinguish between a 'proximate context' (in which a specific policy operates) and 'macro context' (including ramifications in larger political and economic spheres) Martin Rein and Donald Schon, 'Reframing Policy Discourse,' in Frank Fischer and John Forester (eds.) *The Politics of Problem Definition: Shaping The Policy Agenda* (Durham: Duke University Press, 1993), pp. 154–155.
25. Herman J. Loether and Donald G. McTavish, *Descriptive Statistics for Sociologists: An Introduction* (Boston: Allyn & Bacon, 1974), pp. 285–290.
26. See James Tully (ed.) *Meaning and Context: Quentin Skinner and His Critics* (Cambridge: Polity Press, 1988).
27. William Greider, *One World, Ready or Not* (New York: Simon & Schuster, 1997), p. 34.
28. Maurice Merleau-Ponty, *The Structure of Behavior* (Boston: Beacon Press, 1963), p. 45.
29. Merleau-Ponty, *The Phenomenology of Perception* (New York: 1962), pp. 67–174.
30. Michel Crozier, *The Bureaucratic Phenomenon* (Chicago: University of Chicago, 1967), pp. 158, 162.

31. Lloyd I. Rudolph, 'The Self Constructing Culture: The Ethnography of the Amar Singh Diary' *Economic and Political Weekly* 30 September 2000, pp. 3557, 3558.
32. George Herbert Mead, *Mind, Self and Society* (Chicago: University of Chicago Press, 1934), p. 114. See the discussion of Mead in Floyd W. Matson, *The Broken Image: Man, Science and Society* (New York; Anchor Books, 1964). pp. 170–175. Mead may be closer in spirit to Stuart Hall than to Harry Stack Sullivan's theory of 'reflected appraisals,' which is the usual touchstone of the conventional constructivists.
33. Judith Goldstein and Robert Keohane (eds.) *Ideas and Foreign Policy* (Ithaca: Cornell University Press, 1993), p. 17; Kowert and Legro, 'Norms, Identities and Their Limits', pp. 456, 461.
34. Goldstein and Keohane, *Ideas and Foreign Policy*, pp. 13, 240.
35. Robert J. Lifton, *History and Human Survival* (New York: Random House, 1970), p. 23
36. Erik Erikson, *Childhood and Society* (New York, Norton, 1955). Put bluntly: 'creativity is the last thing wanted in any culture because of its potentialities for disruptive thinking' Jules Henry, *Culture Against Man* (New York: Vintage, 1963), p. 288.
37. Michael Novak, *The Experience of Nothingness* (New York: Harper & Row, 1970), p. 35.
38. Lifton, *History and Human Survival*, pp. 216–217.
39. In contrast to a 'conventional warrior mentality,' a former central committee member contends that in the NLF, '[e]very military clash, every demonstration, every propaganda appeal was seen as a part of an intelligible whole: each had consequences far beyond its immediate apparent result. It was a framework that allowed us to view battle as a psychological event and to undertake negotiations in order to strengthen the military posture. The Americans seemed never to appreciate fully this strategic perspective ... It was after all a traditional Vietnamese approach to warfare, a technique refined over centuries of confrontation with invaders more powerful than ourselves.' Truong Nhu Tang, *A Viet Cong Memoir* (New York: Harcourt, Brace, Jovanovich, 1985), pp. 86–87, 212.
40. Why policy makers cling to such models despite persistent adverse 'feedback' has not to my knowledge been the subject of the application of rational methods.
41. Michael C. Desch, 'Culture Clash: Assessing the Impact of Ideas in Security Studies' *International Security* 23, 1 (Summer 1998), p. 147. 'The functions, actions, and values of officers and soldiers are the inevitable consequence of the kinds of societies they are seeking to create or defend. This social context defines the character of the officer corps and

the soldiers, their relationship to each other, and their human, social and economic impact on the population. Strategy mirrors this reality and in turn weighs strongly on the balance of forces. This framework exerts an overriding influence on soldiers' motivations in battle and an army's ability to endure protracted war. In this vital regard the Vietnam War was from its inception a very unequal battle between radically different kinds of armies.' See Chap. 20, 'The Character and Consequences of the Two Vietnamese Armies' in Gabriel Kolko, *Vietnam: Anatomy of War* (London: Allen & Unwin, 1986), pp. 252.

42. *Millennium* 'Special Issue on Culture in International Relations' 22, 3 (Winter 1994), p. 376.
43. Ivan Illich, *Medical Nemesis* (New York: Bantam, 1976), p. 132.
44. Joel Pfister, 'Cultural History of Emotions in Psychological Life', in Joel Pfister and Nancy Schnog (eds.) *Inventing The Psychological: Toward a Cultural History of Emotional Life in America* (New Haven: Yale University Press, 1997), pp. 18, 19.
45. Raymond Williams, 'Culture is Ordinary,' in his *Resources of Hope: Culture, Democracy, Socialism* (London: Verso, 1989), p. 4.
46. Katzenstein, *The Culture of National Security*, p. xiv.
47. See, e.g., Ido Oren, 'Is Culture Independent of National Security? How America's National Security Concerns Shaped 'Political Culture' Research,' *European Journal of International Relations* 6, 4 (2000) pp. 543–571.
48. Antonio Gramsci, *The Modern Prince* (New York: International Publishers, 1971), 112.
49. Jutta Weldes, *Constructing National Interests: The United States and The Cuban Missile Crisis* (Minneapolis: University of Minnesota Press, 1999), p. 241.
50. Matthew Thomson, *The Problem of Mental Deficiency: Eugenics, Democracy, and Social Policy, 1870–1959* (Oxford: Clarendon Press, 1998), p. 299.
51. Eagleton, *The Idea of Culture*, p. 107.
52. See Robert Reich, *Locked in The Cabinet* (New York: Knopf, 1997). On domestic welfare reform, see the profile of Professor David T. Ellwood in The *New York Times Magazine* 8 December 1996; and, on defence policy, see the JASON group case related in Christopher P. Twomey, 'The Vietnam War and The End to Civilian-Scientist Advisors in Defense Policy' *Breakthroughs* IX, 3 (Spring 2000).
53. Peter Hall (ed.) *The Political Power of Economic Ideas: Keynesianism Across Nations* (Princeton: Princeton University Press, 1989). Essentially the same argument is advanced in a Gramscian guise by Steve Bernstein who looks at the 'social fitness of new norms with extant social

structure' in his 'Ideas, Social Structure and The Compromise of Liberal Environmentalism,' *European Journal Of International Relations* 6, 1 (March 2000), p. 465.
54. Judith Goldstein, *Ideas, Interests and American Trade Policy* (Ithaca: Cornell University Press, 1993), p. 2, fn. 1.
55. J. K. Jacobsen, 'Much Ado About Ideas: The Cognitive Factor in Economic Policy,' *World Politics* 47, 2 (January 1995).
56. Goldstein, *Ideas Interests and American Trade Policy*, p. 2, fn. 1.
57. Robert H. Jackson, 'The Weight of Ideas in Decolonization: Normative Change in International Relations', in Goldstein and Keohane, *Ideas and Foreign Policy*, p. 37.
58. Rodney Barker, 'Hooks and Heads, Interests and Enemies: Political Thinking As Political Action,' *Political Studies* 48, 2 (2000), p. 224.
59. Stephen M. Walt, 'International Relations: One World, Many Theories,' *Foreign Policy* 110 (Spring 1998), p. 34.
60. Ibid., pp. 40, 41.
61. Iris Marion Young, 'Unruly Categories: A Critique of Nancy Fraser's Dual Systems Theory', *New Left Review* 222 March/April 1997 (Summer 1992), p. 120.
62. Helen Milner, 'International Political Economy: Beyond Hegemonic Stability,' *Foreign Policy*, 110 (Spring 1998), pp. 116, 117.
63. Mark Laffey and Jutta Weldes, 'Beyond Belief: Ideas and Symbolic Technologies in the Study of International Relations,' *European Journal of International Relations* 3, (1997) pp. 194–195.
64. Charles Maier, *In Search of Stability* (Cambridge: Harvard University Press, 1986), p. 45.
65. See George Steinmetz, *State/Culture*, pp. 13–76. 'Any attempt to distinguish the abstract or ideal appearance of the state from its material reality ... will fail to understand it' (p. 76).
66. Alexander Wendt, 'Anarchy is What States Make of It: The Social Construction of Power Politics', *International Organization*, 46, 2 (Spring 1992), p. 393.
67. See Kratochwil, 'Constructing a New Orthodoxy?', p. 95. 'Scientific inquiry is based on certain ethical principles that govern arguments and the allocation of burden of proof' in debates among fallible authorities.
68. Alexander Wendt, *Social Theory of International Politics* (Cambridge: Cambridge University Press, 1999), p. 1.
69. Ibid., pp. 132, 330.
70. Checkel, 'The Constructivist Turn', p. 326. Their approach, incidentally, stems from a frequently justified suspicion that ideas get used as rhetorical camouflage for self-interest—a gambit which, where proven, vindicates realists. Rarely noted is the opposite tack that actors motivated

by ethics cast their motives in terms of self-interest in order to buttress their case before a wider and less ethically fussy audience. Yet this formulation too misses the point that high-minded ideas inevitably are interwoven with interest too.

71. On the dubious practice of arriving at wise choices by 'splitting the difference' see Alexander Cockburn, *Corruptions of Empire* (New York: Verso, 1987), pp. 199–211. Perhaps ideas are 'distinguished from interests in that ideas-based proposals are driven by principles or values that are informed by a wider perspective on causes and effects, costs and benefits.' M. Stephen Weatherford and Thomas B. Mayhew, 'Tax Policy and Presidential Leadership: Ideas, Interests and the Quality of Advice,' *Studies in American Political Development* 9 (Fall 1995), p. 289. But who suffers from supporting 'tax fairness' if it means that they fork out less tax or reap more services? Who suffers from opposing militarism if the result is oneself or one's children kept out of body bags? Saints are still saints but high-minded behavior exerts an impact on material fortunes which cannot be ignored.

72. Hopf, 'The Promise of Constructivism', pp. 183, 198. It is the case though that from Korsch to Adorno and even up to Habermas there is a rejection of the metaphysical foundations of 'traditional theory.' All these critics, however, retain a concern with thematizing the whole whether in terms of a 'totality' (Hegel/Lukacs) or a 'constellation' (Adorno/Benjamin) of fragments. There was never a need for metaphysical foundations in order to thematize the whole: these are very different things.

73. See Rudiger Bubner, 'Habermas' Concept of Critical Theory,' in John Thompson and David Held, *Habermas* (Cambridge, MA: MIT Press, 1980), pp. 50–51.

74. Hopf, 'The Promise of Constructivism,' p. 199. On the critical theory-compatible contributions of Bakhtin, see Andrew Chadwick, 'Studying Political Ideas: A Public Political Discourse Approach,' *Political Studies* 48 (2000).

75. Hopf, 'The Promise of Constructivism', p. 185.

76. Leo Lowenthal, *Critical Theory and Frankfurt Theorists: Lectures-Correspondence-Conversations* (New Brunswick: Transaction Publishers. 1989), p. 238. Indeed, a 1930 survey revealing the underlying authoritarian attitudes of German working class and lower middle class supporters of the SDP stirred the School to begin plans to relocate—a rare instance where research probably saved the researchers' own lives (pp. 245–246).

77. Wolfgang Bonss, 'The Program of Interdisciplinary Research,' in Benhabib, *On Max Horkheimer*, p. 120.

78. Chantal Mouffe, 'Hegemony and Ideology in Gramsci,' in Tony Bennett, Graham Martin, Colin Mercer, Janet Woolacott (eds.) *Culture, Ideology and Social Process* (London: Open University, 1987), p. 223.
79. Hopf, ' The Promise of Constructivism,' pp. 183–184.
80. See, for e.g. Frances Fitzgerald, *Way Out there in The Wild Blue Yonder: Reagan and Star Wars and The End of The Cold War* (New York: Simon & Schuster, 2000).
81. Ronald Lipschutz, *Global Civil Society and Global Environmental Governance* (Albany, NY: State University of New York Press, 1998), p. 220.
82. 'These psychotic elaborations of imaginary people and imaginary personal performances are spectacular and seem very strange. But the fact is that in a great many relationships of the most commonplace kind—with neighbors, enemies, acquaintances, and even statistically determined people as the collector and the mailman—variants of such distortions exist. The characteristics of a person that would be agreed to by a large number of competent observers may not appear to you to be the characteristics of the person toward whom you are making adjustive or maladjustive movements. The real characteristics of the other fellow at that time may be of negligible importance to the interpersonal situation. This we call parataxic distortion.' Harry Stack Sullivan, The *Psychiatric Interview* (New York: W. W. Norton, 1956), pp. 24–25. On Sullivan's relation to the 1920s 'Chicago School' of Mead, Dewey and Cooley see Helen Swick Perry, Psychiatrist *of America: The Life of Harry Stack Sullivan* (Cambridge, Mass: Belknap Press of Harvard University Press, 1982), pp. 251–260.
83. Hopf, 'Promise of Constructivism', p. 193.
84. Lipschulz, *Global Civil Society*, p. 197.
85. Wendt, to be fair, observes that his target is Waltzian system level theory, which he criticizes at the system level, and he does not want to give short shrift to domestic factors. Wendt, 'On the Via Media: A Response to Critics,' *Review of International Studies* 26, 1 (2000).
86. See Jeffrey Legro, *Cooperation Under Fire* (Ithaca: Cornell University Press, 1995), p. 20 and Elizabeth Kier, 'Culture and French Military Doctrine Before World War II,' in Katzenstein, *The Culture of National Security*, pp. 186–215. Compare this approach to the use of currents in analysis of grand strategy in Franz Schurmann, *The Logic of World Power* (New York: Random House, 1974), Paul Joseph, *Cracks In The Empire* (Boston: South End Press, 1981), and Michael Brenner, *Nuclear Power and Non-Proliferation* (Cambridge: Cambridge University Press, 1981).
87. Jepperson, Wendt, and Katzenstein, 'Norms, Identity and Culture in National Security,' in Katzenstein, *The Culture of National Security*,

p. 37 fn. 13. Wendt does make such a distinction in *Social Theory of International Politics*.
88. Hopf, 'Promise of Constructivism', p. 188.
89. Laffey and Weldes, 'Beyond Belief,' p. 209.
90. Ibid., pp. 210.
91. Ibid., p. 211.
92. Richard K. Hermann, James F. Voss, Tonya E. Schooler And Joseph Ciarrochi, 'Images in International Relations: An Experimental Test of Cognitive Schemata,' *International Studies Quarterly* 41, 1 (January 1997), p. 423.
93. Checkel, 'The Constructivist Turn in International Relations,' p. 325.
94. Randall D. Germain and Michael Kenny, 'Engaging Gramsci: International Relations Theory and The New Gramscians,' *Review of International Studies* 28, 2 (January 1998), p. 12. See responses by Craig Murphy and Mark Rupert two issues afterward.
95. Weldes, *Constructing National Interests*, p. 219.
96. Alaine Touraine, *The Return of the Actor* (Minneapolis: University of Minnesota, 1988), 1–14; Kurt Jacobsen, *Chasing Progress In The Irish Republic: Ideology, Democracy and Dependent Development* (Cambridge: Cambridge University Press, 1994), pp. 1–31.
97. Erving Goffman, *Asylums: Essays on the Social Situations of Mental Patients and Other Inmates* (New York: Anchor Books, 1961), pp. 130, 305.
98. Andrew Martin, *Receptions of War: Vietnam in American Culture* (Norman, OK: University of Oklahoma Press, 1993), p. 25.
99. Susan George, 'How to Win The War of Ideas: Lessons From The Gramscian Right,' *Dissent* (Summer 1997), p. 50.
100. Margaret Archer, *Culture and Agency: The Place of Culture in Social Theory* (Cambridge: Cambridge University Press, 1988), p. xxiv.
101. Lipschutz, *Global Civil Society*, p. 246.
102. Robert Price, 'Race and Reconciliation in South Africa,' *Politics and Society* 25, 2 (June 1997), p. 151.
103. Ibid.
104. Stuart Hall, 'Cultural Studies: Two Paradigms,' in Bennett et al., (eds.) *Culture, Ideology and Social Process*, p. 12.
105. Williams, *Resources of Hope*, p. 7.
106. Leonard J. Schoppa, 'The Social Context in Coercive International Bargaining,' *International Organization* 53, 2 (Spring 1999), p. 309.
107. Lawrence Grossberg, *We Gotta Get Out of This Place: Popular Conservatism and Modern Culture* (London: Routledge, 1992), p. 54.
108. Scharfstein, *The Dilemma of Context*, p. 3.
109. Grossberg. *We Got Get Out of This Place*, p. 397.

110. My thanks to Steve Bronner regarding this point.
111. Ronen Palan, 'A World of Their Making: An Evaluation of The Constructivist Critique in International Relations,' *Review of International Studies* 26, 3 (October 2000), p. 592.
112. Germain and Kenny, 'Engaging Gramsci,' p. 21.
113. The Gramscian notion of ideology 'as a collective structure suggests that it is a product of social action.' Michael Freeden, 'Practising Ideology and Ideological Practices,' *Political Studies* 48, 2 (2000), p. 317.
114. Laura Kipnis, 'Refunctioning Reconsidered: Towards a Popular Left Culture,' in Colin McCabe (ed.) *High Theory/Low Culture: Analysing Popular Television and Film* (Manchester: Manchester University Press, 1986), pp. 56, 61.
115. W. D. Ehrhart, *In the Shadow of Vietnam* (London: McFarland & Co., 1991), p. 17.
116. 'The very concept of a fact,' Horkheimer argues, 'is a social process.' *The Eclipse of Reason* (New York: Oxford University Press, 1947), p. 82.
117. Nancy Fraser, 'From Redistribution to Recognition: Dilemmas of Justice in a Post-Socialist Age,' New *Left Review*, 212 (1996), p. 72.
118. Theodor W. Adorno, 'Introduction,' in Adorno (ed.) *The Positivist Debate in German Sociology* (London: Heinemann, 1976), p. 5.
119. Roxanne Lynn Doty, 'Desire All The Way Down, *Review of International Studies* 26, 1 (January 2000).
120. HeeMin Kim, 'Rational Choice Theory and The Third World,' Comparative *Politics* 30, 1 (October 1997), p. 98.
121. Stephen Walt, 'A Model Disagreement,' International *Security* 24, 2 (Autumn 1999). pp. 178–179.
122. Wendt, *Social Theory of International Politics*, pp. 114–115.
123. Ibid., p. 35.

Why Do States (Bother to) Deceive? Managing Trust at Home and Abroad

'Every government is run by liars,' I. F Stone found, 'and nothing they say should be believed.'[1] Why do states deceive their own populations as to certain foreign policies they practice, the purposes behind them and their consequences? The reasons seem as self-evident as the reasons why states deceive one another. They do so when they need to soften noxious aspects of their actions for a public audience; to sell or conceal policies at variance or in contradiction to national or party values; to allay fears of domestic groups who thereby stand to lose quality of life, or even their lives; to portray disputable decisions as inevitable or optimal ones; to cloak ulterior purposes in fine moral raiment, and, as Hannah Arendt added, because of an expeditious urge to turn 'pleasing hypotheses' into 'facts.'[2]

Citizens (other than the 5% customarily deemed well informed) are largely regarded by foreign policy elites as easy marks, if not security risks, which only makes the temptation to deceive them all the greater. For realists it is self-evident that the general citizenry is ignorant, fickle and impressionable. So in international politics the public is neither expected nor welcome to inquire too closely into security or economic arrangements arranged by seasoned and dispassionate diplomats on their behalf. 'Foreign affairs,' Metternich enjoined, 'is not for the plebs.'[3]

Statesmen strive to keep it that way by painstakingly hiding inconvenient realities from foes, colleagues and the public, especially when partisan, ideological or ego issues come into play. The 'nature of power,' Hans Morgenthau readily noted, 'is concealed by ideological justifications and rationalizations.'⁴ Alexis de Tocqueville doubted that democracies would permit a stratum of sly experts to perform adroitly in the intricate game of international balancing acts, given that it is the public's 'nature to have, for the most part, the most confused or erroneous ideas on external affairs, and to decide questions of foreign policy on purely domestic considerations.'⁵ One can compile many pages of similar sentiments. Democracy is duly regarded as an added onerous burden, and policy makers situated in such polities must make the best of it, often by resorting to deception or concealment, like counterparts in authoritarian regimes.⁶

Contrary to these corrosive views, Charles Merriam, for one, saw it as 'a great argument for democracy and the soundness of the judgment of the mass of the people that the so-called 'better sort'—the wealthy and well born who, as John Adams said, are the 'natural rulers of mankind' are so often wrong, as in the case of FDR, TR [Theodore Roosevelt], Wilson, Lincoln, Jackson, Jefferson, Washington—defending the Stamp Act, against the income tax, defending slavery, opposing regulation of monopoly, against social security, against all forms of planning, willing to trade the League of Nations for Harding's election.'⁷

Merriam's robust democratic stance placed him in a distinct minority of those who see themselves as members of elites, especially IR experts who, when they regard the public at all, see lack of knowledge or understanding as its critical characteristic. It is doubtless tempting to express derision when the public fails to know within a factor of 10 how many nuclear weapons the USA wields, or how comparatively small the foreign aid bill is, or that Iraq had no link to 9/11.⁸ Realists go so far as to claim that the public *prefers* to be ignorant and, deep down, wants authorities to help to keep them that way.⁹ In any case, few parties, realist or otherwise, seem very interested in wising up the feckless rabble.

Responding to a 1954 Covert Action Report, President Eisenhower, for example, rejected its blunt exhortation that 'the American People be made acquainted with, understand and support [the] fundamentally repugnant philosophy of ruthless imitation of the enemy.'¹⁰ Apparently, if only the public were as cynical as policy makers, there would be less need to deceive it. However, there may be good reasons why one might not want the public to be as cold-blooded as its leadership. Notions of justice, liberty and truth, as George Orwell appreciated, 'may be illusions but they are powerful illusions. The belief in them influences conduct [so that] hypocrisy is a powerful safeguard.'¹¹

States deceive their citizens because they are, potentially, constrained by them. Leaders craft 'likely stories' to disguise seamy or disputable activities because they believe they *must* do so inasmuch as they are vulnerable to a punitive or obstructive public. Otherwise, why bother? Theories derived from realpolitik make scant allowance for such domestic 'interference'—apart from deploring it—and therefore do not do a good job of explaining it and its effects. Yet there is mounting evidence that in democracies the role of mass publics in curbing or modifying the conduct of foreign policy is a force to reckon with.[12] I examine this domestic level phenomenon and its troublesome implications for the realist tradition. What the essay argues, at minimum, is that particular realist tenets today need to be treated as contingent propositions, not axioms.[13] Here realpolitik refers to the core propositions (anarchy, states as key units of analysis, self-help, power-seeking, etc.) that realists of all prefixes share.[14]

Defining Deceit

Given the risk of exposure or electoral comeuppance, why bother to deceive? One reason is that risks are deemed low compared to prospective gains. The government may enjoy media control or, close enough, mainstream media collaboration. Another reason is that revelations of legerdemain often occur after the period that matters for decision-makers. If leaders are caught, they can blame blundering intelligence agencies or an intervening layer of expendable underlings. Deception therefore is enticing as (1) a diversionary tactic, (2) 'public relations,' to put a favorable gloss on events, (3) a desperate ploy in a tight spot or (4) Platonic 'noble lies' fooling the public for the sake of an imputed higher good.[15] While the truth indeed may be so precious that it 'must be accompanied by a bodyguard of lies,' a gloriously glib Churchill phrase cannot settle the question of their necessity. Our concern here is deliberate misleading statements—outright lies as well as untruths formed from mixes of cagey omissions and selective use of facts to serve the purposes of a policy elite, a party, a coalition, a social class, a status group or any blend of the above.

Hans Blix justly cautions us that diplomacy 'devises language that understates the divergence of positions so as to minimize the gaps that have to be bridged and make reconciliation less difficult [and so] lying is not part of diplomacy, at least not of good diplomacy.'[16] Distinguishing lies from errors can be tricky. The most effective propaganda, after all, is based on technically true but re-contextualized statements.[17] So the critical ingredients of deception in, or about, international politics are that policy makers are aware of essential information unknown to the public or particular interest groups, must choose to act in a certain way in response to the information and must explain (or keep hidden) that action in a way which misrepresents or ignores the information relevant to the action taken. Further, deceit is likelier when the stakes are high, the chances of exposure are low and the costs are zero-sum or nearly so.

Because deceit is intentional any neutral party obviously must regard it as the researcher's responsibility to document instances. In foreign policy each decision-making apparatus is labyrinthinely interwoven with secret agencies, backdoor dealing and off-the-books operations. So, ironically, the eminently reasonable demand for documented proof can become yet another incentive to deceive. Protective state mechanisms make it all the more difficult to prove deceit beyond a shadow of a doubt. Anyone disclosing information that state leaders prefer to conceal is sure to face reprisals too.[18]

The Utility of Deceit

A prominent realist recently assessed the role of deceit in international politics, wondering why the question is so rarely addressed (one reason, I suggest, is because a thorough examination of motives for deceit might well produce an acute challenge to the realist tradition). In Mearsheimer's view, however, justified distinctions may be made between 'spinning' and 'concealment', on the one hand, and outright lying, which is presented as a 'positive' act in the sense of actually doing something.[19] The flaw in this subcategorizing is that liars always are pleased to portray their lies as mere 'spinning' or 'concealment' which, according to Mearsheimer's generous criteria, they are free to do. Spinning facts in one's favor, and the concealing of contrary data to craft a specific distortion of reality, is the very essence of lying. Who wants to be on the other end of it?

Mearsheimer's intriguing distinctions ultimately are misconceived because these lesser kinds of deception are the stuff out of which grandiose lies are composed. They are *all* deceits and they all invite unwitting penalties. US Intelligence agencies 'can spin their reports to get along with the White House,' Loch K. Johnson instructively notes about such choices. 'Or the White House can ignore the intelligence estimates. Either way, the danger is that the country can delude itself. When you start bending the facts, you can make very bad decisions.'[20] Exactly.

But aren't there extenuating circumstances for resorting to lies? 'Few statesman,' E. H. Carr wrote, 'fail in an emergency to recognize a duty to lie for their country.'[21] State leaders, Mearsheimer accordingly explains, may try to hoodwink citizens 'because they believe that their public (or their political system) is incapable of dealing effectively with threats to national security, and therefore the people must be lied to so that they do the right thing.'[22] Mearsheimer offers a few concrete examples; however, the archetypal IR cases, pre-World War II British appeasement (in which Carr was implicated) and American 'unpreparedness,' are reexamined below.

Sensitive security data need to be guarded, although how material comes to be so labeled is often almost comically arbitrary.[23] Still, citizens do not require full access to blueprints of invasion plans or missile defense schemes in order to assess whether they approve of them or believe they will work. The standard rationale for citizen deference is that elites alone are able to devise sagacious solutions for complex foreign policy problems. Yet, in retrospect, to invoke Robert McNamara's repentant phrase, few foreign policy problems ever have one best solution where the 'common good' or 'national interest' is concerned.[24] This tacit latitude enables a host of factors—institutional missions, class and 'club' biases, bureaucratic rigidities, interest group lobbying, ideology, careerism, foibles, blinkered behavior, misunderstandings and accidents—to inflect policy outcomes and practices.

Insofar as policy makers in democracies encounter more attentive publics, the touchy issue of legitimacy arises. Trust is a crucial political asset and is not easily restored once lost. Because trust engenders low-cost cooperation, it diminishes the resources needed to attain desired objectives. The 'Vietnam syndrome,' prematurely pronounced dead by President George H. W. Bush in 1991, is one durable legacy of such a loss, such that only a third of the American public twelve years later trusted his son to make a unilateral decision to go to war against Iraq.[25] Four years of conflict lowered public support for the Iraq war to that gung-ho third (which Joseph finds are the percentage of Americans who tend to support militarism unreservedly).[26] The post-Vietnam 'Powell doctrine' earlier affirmed a domestically driven necessity to assemble overwhelming force, define the national interest credibly at stake, set clear military goals and work out an exit strategy for any large-scale intervention abroad. A determined administration certainly could violate this doctrine, but not with impunity, as the mid-term 2006 US election would seem to show.

Instead of invoking the imputed iron necessities of realpolitik, democratic leaders appeal to high moral purposes for the sake of citizens whose qualms must be assuaged if they are to consent to questionable actions abroad.[27] As a result of this 'extra step' states often incur added costs and, as a result, may modify policy to conform more closely to stated values, though at first they usually modify only their presentation of policies. This factor works not only to curb policy but, on occasion, to drive it. A survey of public opinion about intervention in Bosnia in the 1990s found that cautious British, French and Russian governments slowly came around to match that of a public more eager than they were to deploy troops[28] (President Clinton, attentive to public opinion, was compelled to 'frame' his reluctant deployment of US troops to Bosnia purely as a peacekeeping operation, not a commitment to a far more controversial combat role).[29] Any state's responsiveness in this regard will depend on its domestic structure, the strength of 'actually existing' civil rights, divisions within elites, the degree of media freedom and concentration of ownership (the more concentration, the less that legal freedom assures diversity of opinion), personal beliefs of leaders and the public memory that grew out of experiences of earlier interventions or non-interventions ('lessons of Munich') .

States may not be moral entities but the people residing within their borders are. So an inherent clash of amoral collective and moral individual 'identities' creates tensions that pose an interesting challenge to realism. If it is 'utopian to ignore the element of power,' Carr chided, 'it is an unreal kind of realism which ignores the element of morality in any world order'.[30] Still, leaders chafe at inhibiting forces and usually try to co-opt domestic values to justify policy preferences, override ethical concerns by contriving 'emergencies' or make tactical concessions.[31]

The focus of this essay is US and, to some degree, UK foreign policy, a shortcoming that needs to be remedied in future comparative studies. Nonetheless, this critical approach ranges over the gamut of domestic–international interaction, and the dilemmas involved in leaders relating to different audiences, releasing or withholding information, building coalitions of support and mobilizing resources. In so doing, it cites several means—education, polls, mobilization, etc.—by which the political sociology (of public influence upon elites) underpinning realist accounts has shifted. Accordingly, the theme of deceit throws light on an embedded weakness in realism as well as upon particular specimens of political hypocrisy.

Realpolitik, and How it Plays in Peoria[32]

Ever since Thrasymachus, the dictum 'might makes right' cut to the core of insecurity and power seeking of the sort that sows more dragons' teeth than it slays dragons.[33] Thucydides narrated a seemingly fatalistic chronicle of tragic overreaching, but some readers argue that he composed a cautionary tale—one intended to stir learning—and not just a grieving shrug of the shoulders at hardwired human folly.[34] In this perspective, people are beheld as being as 'good' or 'reasonable' as the structures in which they move allow, and it is open to them to recognize structural constraints and, under propitious conditions, to alter structures to accord with their reconsidered goals. So there is a ray of hope for agency in Thucydides' work, in the very fact of (not only the facts in) the narrative's existence.

Does the primal fault lie in structure, in human nature, in organizational codes or in their interplay? While Waltz divides theories of international conflict into 'first image' (base human nature), 'second image' (the state) and 'third image' (structure) explanations, in practice these 'images' typically intersect in international conflicts.[35] Realist propositions, of course, are ignored at one's peril. The precept that one cannot acquire too much power is hard to ignore, even if unchecked acquisitiveness damages the security one seeks, which is a plight spawning the ironies, perplexities and tragedies of which realists ably write. Few such scholars, though, are willing to be corralled by a handful of axioms about anarchy, insecurity and self-help, so realism has expanded into a highly diversified tradition.[36]

All models, theories and frameworks, of course, are limited, selective and liable to extensive ad hoc amending.[37] As Waltz attests, the 'third image describes the framework of world politics, but without the first and second images there can be no knowledge of the forces that determine policy, the first and second images describe the forces in world politics, but without the third image it is impossible to assess their importance or predict their results.'[38] While there are acknowledged instances where realists agree that ideology and other non-material factors play an important role, these moments nonetheless are regarded as unusual ones and anyway the structure sooner or later reasserts its primacy.[39]

This stringent approach displays the virtue of parsimony, but interests in achieving parsimony and in illuminating reality can and do threaten to part company. One reason why states deceive citizens is that the public—unorganized actors who may lack an immediately perceived stake in an outcome—seems easily fooled or intimidated, especially during wartime.[40] Further, Mearsheimer describes a public 'hungering' for 'nationalist myth making,' as if citizens were congenitally gullible and as if intensive indoctrination, or coercive agencies, had nothing to do with acquiescence.[41] 'To maintain and transmit a values system,' Barrington Moore reminds us, 'people are punched, bullied, sent to jail, thrown into concentration camps, cajoled, bribed, made into heroes, encouraged to read newspapers, stood up against a wall and shot, and sometimes taught sociology.'[42] The home populace, moreover, is usually kept in the dark much more so than are the people of a targeted state. Examples range from Operation Mongoose saboteur operations against Castro's Cuba through the 1960s Phoenix assassination program in Vietnam to selective sanctioning of drug trafficking for covert Cold War purposes. Can this high-level penchant for secrecy be imputed to reasons other than a fear that ordinary citizens, if fully aware of such activities, would impede the will of policy makers?

After all, a primal anxiety for a domestic audience is that realpolitik ends at no known shore. 'People with power have the right to do to us anything we can't stop them from doing,' as Joseph Heller Thucydideanly summed up his classic novel *Catch-22*.[43] One way of reading *Catch-22* is as a tale of realism carried to its logical conclusion in personal as well as in international conduct. Behavior in one realm infects the other. Citizens—even many who cheer high-handed acts abroad—will grow nervous when they start to spill over at home.[44] The US Patriot Act, instantly enacted after 9/11, is 'Exhibit A' of such a disturbing tendency.[45] In the twenty-first century blowback no longer is a bit of jargon known only inside intelligence agency corridors. The term is 'another way of saying that a nation reaps what it sows,' Johnson notes.[46] 'Although people usually know what they have sown, our national experience of blowback is seldom imagined in such terms because so much of what the managers of the American empire have sown has been kept secret.'

The relevant analysis then is not one of separate domestic and international dimensions but rather one asking which dimension has primacy at a given time and under what conditions. The opposite of realpolitik is not idealism (which is invariably caricatured anyway)[47] but domestic primacy arguments that contest the notion that systemic international forces impose one-way changes upon domestic realms. Far from devaluing international influences, domestic primacy arguments claim that internal politicking is a significant explanatory factor in comprising the international dimension 'out there.' Some realists seem to agree inasmuch as one way of reading the 'two-level games' literature is as the insertion of domestic influences in an albeit subordinate way into realism.[48]

If states plainly must maneuver in a self-help and anarchic world then why would leaders need to resort to deceit? Why can't citizens understand that force and fraud are indispensable facts of life in power politics? Mearsheimer suggests that the shortfall between what he characterizes as the elite's hard-nosed acuity and the public's soft-headed ignorance is good grounds for lying if it is done 'in service of the national interest.' This is a big 'if,' and Mearsheimer concedes how problematic it is to identify the national interest with whatever elites in charge say it is.[49] Arch-realist George Kennan, by contrast, fretted that 'generic' average Americans 'in our sentimentality, in our bumbling good will' cannot help but be 'flattered and misled by the obsequiousness' of talented liars abroad.[50] One doubts this upper-crust diplomat had much contact with 'generic' Americans, but it is worth recalling that over his long distinguished career Kennan decried the China Lobby, disdained McCarthyism, regarded General MacArthur in Korea as 'out of control,' opposed aid to the French in Indochina, rued 'our military-industrial addiction,' detested nuclear posturing and regretted 'our misunderstanding of Soviet expansionist policies and intentions.' Kennan lost a lot of policy battles for someone who maintained knee-jerk faith in the wisdom of the upper ranks. Neither does the interwar period offer as much comfort as elitists imagine it does.

Appeasement and Unpreparedness Reconsidered

During the 1930s appeasement debate, Churchill, he of the 'bodyguard of lies,' urged Prime Minister Stanley Baldwin to tell the truth to 'a tough people and a robust people [who] may be a bit offended at the moment, but if you have told them exactly what is going on you have insured yourself against complaints and reprisals, which are very unpleasant when they come home in the manner of some disillusionment.'[51] Rowse's classic analysis, lest we forget, lacerated Tory elites for 'not letting the real issues penetrate through to the people' and for succumbing to 'a fatal confusion in their minds between the interests of their social order and the interests of their country'—a 'fatal confusion' that might confuse realists for whom such a malign possibility does not even arise.[52] The many clarion calls to rearm at the time were spoken in vain not because they were unheeded but because rearmament indeed was well under way within a year of Hitler's rise to power, especially in aircraft and naval production.

The appeasement literature focuses on anemic land forces as if these were the best gauge of grand strategy and were the sole indicator of overall military spending; hence, naval and air rearmament were systematically underestimated. UK air defense spending alone rose from 9 billion pounds in 1935 to 19 billion in 1936, 30 billion in 1937 and 56 billion in 1938.[53] Contrary to standard accounts, which have evolved over time into the near-invincible status of a moral tale, rearmament was really quite vigorous inasmuch as the technologically 'militant' UK Treasury 'wanted air power and mechanization as a substitute for manpower.'

At the outbreak of war the RAF and the Luftwaffe were 'about equal,' and a year later the UK was producing half again as many warplanes.[54] Keith Robbins allows that public opinion was 'volatile' throughout this period but other scholars put the public well ahead of the government in terms of correct threat assessment.[55] The 'appeasement' controversy deals less with the willingness by an imperial offshore island to adopt a rational defense strategy (for it arguably did just that) than with whether it made sense for imperial Britain to intervene on the European continent with a huge land army. More seriously, the debate failed to differentiate between disarmament and appeasement (Britain appeased and rearmed) and to recognize that often it was the proto-realists such as Carr who were for appeasement and the 'deluded idealists' who wanted to prepare for war.[56]

Regarding FDR's America one historian instructively alleges that 'democracy failed the test' despite his own cited data attesting otherwise.[57] The USA, another offshore 'island' with imperial priorities (the Pacific and Caribbean), rearmed rapidly, likewise focusing on naval and air power. In hard times of the 1930s the American public, though wary of international adventurism, saw the advantages of military preparedness and of job-creating expenditures to achieve it. Isolationist sentiments, in practice, applied only to Europe; isolationists often thirsted for war with Japan, given the imperial rewards in the offing.[58] Scholars chided FDR for failing to push for war for fear not of the public but of the well-funded and vocal right, which, as a matter of definition, is a minority that wields more resources than all other shades of political opinion put together.[59]

After an FDR address on September 21, 1939 on the need to revise the Neutrality Acts public opinion 'jumped sharply' in Roosevelt's favor, but he failed to exploit the opening.[60] The 1940 Act extending conscription passed by one Congressional vote but, less advertised in the literature, with 71% public approval.[61] Upon the Fall of France in May 1940, 85% of the public favored aid to Britain and two of three did so at the risk of entering the war. In May 1941 FDR proclaimed an 'unlimited national emergency' linking ship protection against U-boats to national security.[62] Telegrams were 'ninety-five percent favourable' for what Admiral Leahy saw as a virtual declaration of war. It most definitely was not the case that after that point (and indeed long before) the 'American public did not appreciate the danger that Nazi Germany presented to the United States.' These moral fables of British appeasement and of American unpreparedness continue to blame the mass public for actions/inactions for which smaller potent groups in both countries are far more culpable.

CREDIBILITY AND DISSENT

State leaders deceive in order to acquire room for action and consequently, as word leaks out or consequences become apparent, credibility gaps occur. So is deceit worth the trouble once one assesses all the costs and benefits? Historical deceptions are plentiful, ranging from artfully planted tales of German troops crucifying Belgian babies in 1914 to Adolf Hitler in 1939 'retaliating' for an impudent Polish incursion on German soil.[63] In the latter half of the twentieth century, one beholds the 1964 Tonkin Gulf incidents, the 'secret' bombing of Cambodia and Laos, the 1990 Kuwait incubator babies story hatched by PR firm Hill & Knowlton, the abetting of a six-figure massacre in Indonesia in 1965 (via CIA hit lists), fabrication in the 1980s of phony documents on communist infiltration into Central America and stories describing Osama Bin Laden as a theocratic fascist (which he is) but omitting the 'blowback' aspect of his history.[64] No government permits hot pursuit of terrorists to lead back to its own doorstep if it can help it.

Gabriel Almond, like Harold Lasswell and Walter Lippman earlier, contended that the public 'lack intellectual structure and factual content. Such superficial psychic states are bound to be unstable.'[65] Benjamin Ginsberg argues that mass polling, rather than hampering elites, enables wily authorities to shape and anticipate public opinion.[66] Citizens notoriously do succumb to 'rally-round-the-flag' government propaganda, but this rallying effect also happens to be a rapidly wasting asset. A burgeoning literature indicates that citizens are, as Merriam argued, capable of 'shrewd enough' appraisals.[67]

Bruce Jentleson, in a study of post-Cold War military interventions, finds that 'Americans do appear to have a much more pragmatic sense of strategy than they are given credit for'—prudently relating supportable costs to principle policy objectives.[68] Sam Popkin cites a 'low-level gut rationality' that usually yields reasonable appraisals.[69] Ronald Inglehart argues that better education and an increase in the volume of low-cost news (and the internet) improved the sophistication and depth of public knowledge.[70] Perhaps a 'populist realism'—to coin another prefix—someday explicitly will incorporate this factor but, if so, it is unlikely to fit comfortably into a realist tradition which has no use for non-elites, except as suckers and cannon fodder.

Yet 'reasons of state' can wither under sensible scrutiny, as Mearsheimer concedes, rather than simply be too esoteric for the public to grasp.[71] Authorities always have an interest in portraying public distrust as street-level cynicism, rather than as an outgrowth of valid understanding. Are average citizens ineligible as serious critics because they are so full of 'bumbling good will'? Schumpeterian formal democracy and Burkean representation propagate such dismissive views. Rousseau too thought the people must be 'taught to know what they require.'[72] During the 2004 US elections few mass media commentators turned a hair at polls showing that a majority of Americans believed Saddam Hussein abetted the 9/11 plot—a carefully cultivated assumption that aided Bush's return to office. Highly placed members of government agencies and media organizations perpetuated it. What, exactly, was their excuse?

Is the public too squeamish to behave with necessary steeliness in international affairs? Kull and Ramsay argue that it is a myth that the American public automatically shrinks from overseas operations that incur casualties.[73] The public's inclination is to 'respond assertively,' at least in the short term. The authors questionably assert that what matters in sustaining an intervention or peacekeeping exercise is whether it is seen as successful, regardless of the stakes or the nature of the conflict. Yet their own findings indicate that majorities are concerned not with assertiveness for its own sake but with humanitarian objectives ('stop famine') and resisting aggression ('stop ethnic cleansing'), which likewise carry moral freight.[74] Purposes, and their credibility, matter.

Is realism dependent on one-way top-down dominance by policy elites? If so, and this condition is relaxed, then realist tenets bear reexamining. What if states aren't impervious, and voices from below actually serve to improve rational scrutiny? Indeed, can a dissident public prove to be more 'realist' in respect to allocating limited resources in service of sound policy aims?[75] The reigning conceit is that any public interference with foreign policy comes at the cost of rationality. Participation endangers rationality even though some realists (not to mention, Aristotle) have warned that elites, unchecked, tend to commit grave hubristic errors. Hans Morgenthau, who usually urged leaders to ignore ignorant citizens, shed this stance with some chagrin during the tortuous course of the Vietnam War.[76] (Jervis aptly observed that Morgenthau need not lecture citizens on the necessity of heeding the 'national interest,' if his premises had been correct).[77] Still, the need to deceive citizens implies that citizens, weighing the authorities' case, may well find it wanting or will arrive at incompatible conclusions. When elites conflict over an issue, as they often do, the issue no longer is purely a matter for experts. If the image of omnicompetent elites becomes questionable, then what authority do they really retain? If partisan factors clearly operate regarding the foreign policy realm then why should citizens defer to partisan depictions of reality?

Realism—in the form of *primat der aussenpolitik*—was articulated in the nineteenth century within an authoritarian agenda and accordingly reaffirmed an asymmetrical distribution of domestic as well as international resources. An ingrained disdain for the 'masses' was reinforced. Yet citizens do 'deepen their judgment and [calibrate] their understanding on the basis of relevant experience, even if their grasp of specific events remains hollow.'[78] The intrusion of formerly powerless players also alters the nature of the game (E. E. Schattschneider's 'scope of conflict') unless, as realists insist, domestic configurations must respond over time in much the same way to international exigencies. This *contingent* quality of realist propositions cannot be addressed unless one takes seriously the study of the interplay of domestic interests with malleable international influences.

Why does realism seem to its critics to be at least occasionally unrealistic? This question differs from asserting that, or asking why, realism is unpopular.[79] This essay next turns to key examples—the Vietnam War, the Iran-Contra affair, the 2003 Iraq invasion—to highlight situations under which it is incumbent on elites to make their preferred but disputable policies make sense to a wide domestic audience. These cases attest that the citizenry is quite sensible in its judgments, despite low levels of information, and that, thus far, realism doesn't remotely appreciate, let alone adequately factor in, the role of the public.

As impressive in its ghastly way as was the Nazis' industrialized mass murder machine, for example, almost as extraordinary were the 'nacht und nebel' (night and fog) lengths to which Hitler's regime went to hide it (despite the 'willing executioners' hypothesis predicting otherwise.)[80]

Nazi officials were dab hands at euphemisms: occupation costs were 'rebuilding' costs, hostages were expiators, deportation was 'resettlement,' and 'special treatment' entailed limitless horrors.[81] Yet there were implicit internal limits that the Nazis sought to avoid violating. Hitler's regime definitively was aberrant, but the Nazis tried anyway to uphold a prim self-image as 'guarantor of legality.'[82] Nazi tact, such as it was, remains a telling datum.[83] The instruments of 'spin' and 'concealment' sufficed nicely to cloak activities inside the concentration camps. No 'lies,' as defined by Mearsheimer, needed to be told.

Allied forces, for their part, concealed the inaccuracy of their vaunted bombsights as 'dehousing' became their main objective. There is ample evidence that the public was not squeamish about inflicting civilian casualties on enemies during a time of total war. Still, authorities emphasized precision for the sake of imputed civilian sensibilities. Indeed, the first military force to employ poison gas in Iraq were not other Iraqis but the RAF in the 1920s, which 'doctored its reports to conceal its policy of 'control without occupation' via gas and phosphorous bombing and strafing of the Arab population.'[84] The realist case is that foreign policy elites, by means of such spin and concealment, achieve a necessary degree of leeway to act 'in service of the national interest.' Does the realist belief hold up that the more autonomy policy elites enjoy, the better the quality of their policies?

Vietnam and the 'Bounds of Reasonable Dishonesty'

The Bay of Pigs fiasco in 1961 was a moment when John F Kennedy wondered if a more feisty press wouldn't have been a blessing and stayed his hand.[85] Yet soon Kennedy and then successor Lyndon Johnson were badgering editors to rein in reporters who revealed more about Vietnam than US authorities wished. 'The newsmen, no less than the Viet Cong, were the enemy,' a White House press aide affirmed.[86] President Johnson in early 1964 hastened contingency planning because of deteriorating friendly governments in Laos and South Vietnam, a fact 'concealed from Congress and the public as much as possible to provide the Administration with maximum flexibility to determine its moves as it chose from behind the scenes.'[87] Deceptions multiplied but the flexibility thereby acquired hardly produced anything one would call rationality. In May 1962 Robert McNamara expressed confidence in the outcome in Vietnam because every 'quantitative measurement we have shows that we're winning this war.'[88] A genial cycle of deception developed: 'Ah, les statistiques!' A South Vietnamese general told [Roger] Hilsman, 'Your Secretary of Defense loves statistics. We Vietnamese can give him all he wants. If you want them to go up, they will go up. If you want them to go down, they will go down.'[89]

The Tonkin Gulf resolution almost literally was in Johnson's pocket awaiting a pretext for action (as apparently was the 2000 *Project for A New American Century* treatise on George W. Bush's shelf awaiting a 'Pearl Harbor-style attack' which al-Qaeda obligingly provided).[90] In the first Tonkin incident North Vietnam tried to drive off a US destroyer aiding ARVN attacks; in the second melee American sailors fired wildly at figments of their sonar.[91] Although Johnson later resisted eager advisors who urged bombing Hanoi and Haiphong, his 'peace feelers' were aimed to placate a US audience and were never meant to be offers that the Southern resistance or North Vietnam could take seriously.[92] A US general admitted the primary objective was to 'keep the American public in the dark.'[93] Deliberately self-sabotaging peace offers are familiar gambits from Vietnam to Rambouillet (where the Serbs were presented with impossibly intrusive demands) but only so long as citizens can imagine that their government, like themselves mostly, prefer to avoid bar room brawls. This charitable attribution is perhaps an offshoot of the 'bumbling sentimentality' Kennan lamented. Realist policy makers, far from dispensing with public 'soft-headedness,' as they deem it, could hardly do without it.

Bombing pauses in Vietnam were 'packaged' so as to persuade domestic audiences that the 'enemy has left us no choice' except escalation.[94] Shortly before the 1969 moratorium, President Nixon wrote Henry Kissinger that 'it would be very helpful if a propaganda offensive could be [mounted], consistently reporting what we have done in offering peace in Vietnam in preparation for what we may have to do.'[95] Nixon leaked plans to mine Haiphong harbor and to invade the North ('Operation Duck Hook'), but by November, for a variety of reasons—not least of which was adverse public opinion—he scrubbed it.[96] In September 1970 Nixon denounced against 'those who protest that if the verdict of democracy goes against them democracy itself is at fault, who say if they don't get their own way the course is to burn a bus or building'[97] The day before, he ordered the CIA to help to overthrow elected Chilean President Salvador Allende.[98]

Despite official disdain, the peace movement stirred Gene McCarthy's and, fatally, Robert Kennedy's presidential bids, which affirmed perception in high places that the public had turned against the war, and induced Johnson to give up a reelection bid (Bombing intensified after Johnson stepped aside, and an offer to meet Communist factions soon was withdrawn).[99] Still, the peace movement applied pressure on Nixon to negotiate a settlement.[100] Spurred by an antiwar surge after the 1970 Cambodia 'incursion,' Congress passed the Cooper-Church amendment denying ground troops entry to Laos and Cambodia. Kissinger blamed the breakdown of the Paris Peace Accords, and the fall of the South Vietnam regime, on 'our domestic situation,' which prevented a revival of bombing that Nixon intended as a prop-up measure.[101] After US withdrawal in 1973, and once the Saigon regime was teetering, the public and Congress prevented reintroduction of ground troops or a resumption of bombing.[102]

In 1971 Daniel Ellsberg and Anthony Russo disclosed a Defense Department study chronicling three decades of systematic deception of Congress and the public. Nixon ironically began unraveling his own administration once he dispatched 'plumbers' to plug leaks of government misdeeds.[103] Flaws permeated the patchwork antiwar movement, but the case usually mustered against it is incoherent, e.g., if only the movement had not taken to the streets, it would have grown more quickly, even though it had no effect at all.[104] Contrary to widespread belief, it was less-educated groups who most opposed the war and who were less liable to be swayed by abstract anti-communist invocations (though there are conflicting data as to how people with multiple degrees responded).[105] The accusation that the public was discouraged by televised carnage or defeatist reporting cannot stand up to scrutiny.[106] Declining faith in America's leadership was a direct consequence of the uncovering of cumulative lies. The mid-1970s Congressional investigative reports would flush out state crimes whose extent surprised even antiwar activists.

Wed the reasonable dishonesty of 'spinning' and 'concealment' to a team player mentality and you get lies of ever-greater magnitude, with tragic consequences. In 1967 CIA analyst Sam Adams found that Viet Cong forces were more than double what the US military stated. Under political pressure CIA Director Richard Helms signed off on a National Intelligence Estimate endorsing the Army's disputed undercount of some 200 thousand. 'Had Helms told the truth, the war could have ended much sooner. Rather, it dragged on for seven more years,' recalls CIA veteran Ray McGovern. 'I have a vivid memory of Sam Adams telling me at the time about a comment made to him by one of the most senior CIA officials: 'Have we gone beyond the bounds of reasonable dishonesty?''[107]

The White House diligently pretended that the peace movement exerted no influence upon it.[108] The antiwar movement interwove with broader forces: enemy resilience, a faltering economy, Saigon's corruption and a renewed concern about superpower relations. The more the domestic resource base was squeezed—given LBJ's reluctance to test the war's popularity by raising taxes or mobilizing reserves—the more domestic politics mattered. Policy makers, far from being fearlessly foresightful, usually succumbed to intense institutional pressures to conform. Mavericks do not get perks or promoted or even niches as media pundits. So the transformative sequence was that of a grass roots outcry emboldening critics in the administration and the media, not vice versa, although a mutually reinforcing dynamism kicked in.[109]

Iran-Contra

In the Iran-Contra scandal US policy makers contrived a convoluted means to sell weapons through an Israeli link to Iran to gain help to free hostages in Lebanon and then divert the heavily marked-up proceeds to illegally arming Nicaraguan rightwing paramilitary forces.[110] Many summoned personages, after the story broke in November 1986, lied to Congress, which is a felony. Official inquiries included the 1986 Tower Report, the 1987 Senate-House hearings and an Independent Counsel's lengthy investigation, leading to several high-profile trials.

The Israelis approached the US with the arms-for-hostages deal in July 1985.[111] In December Reagan signed a presidential 'finding' approving the deal despite a congressional embargo on arms to Iran and despite the Boland amendment, strengthened in 1984, forbidding aid 'for the purpose of overthrowing the Nicaraguan government.' The Reagan administration eluded these barriers by using the National Security Council, which was not directly answerable to Congress, to run its pet covert projects. A 'compartmentalized' operation was created, responsible only to the National Security Advisor, as a private procurement agency to serve Reagan administration whims.

One reason why governments resort to back channels evidently is so that lieutenant colonels may tote birthday cakes and bibles to bemused Middle Eastern clerics, with no questions asked. The benighted public clearly would not understand the subtleties involved. Reagan officials themselves were confused by these extensive intricacies. 'Contracting out' dirty work conjured up a Rube Goldberg transnational apparatus that intermingled South Korea, Saudi Arabia, Brunei, Argentina, Israel, South

Africa, Panama, Cuban exiles, the Unification Church, Vietnam era soldiers of fortune, American tycoons, an Iranian arms dealer and clandestine Swiss bank accounts. The policy reverberations were far-flung. South African aircraft, for example, pitched into supply the contras, which helps to explain US 'opposition to economic sanctions and CIA director William Casey's efforts to line up Saudi oil for the apartheid regime.'[112]

The term 'conspiracy' was deemed wholly appropriate by Independent Counsel Lawrence Walsh. This 'government within a government' scandal was not 'an aberration,' Theodore Draper, following the investigation, finds, but was 'brought on by a long process of presidential aggrandizement, congressional fecklessness and judicial connivance,' which 'threatened the constitutional foundation of this country.'[113] Reagan first denied there was such a deal but reversed himself a week later, pleading he acted with the best intentions. The Reagan-appointed Tower Committee criticized Reagan's 'passive' presidential style but the 1987 congressional committees reported that Reagan certainly bore 'ultimate responsibility.' Independent Counsel Walsh afterward summarized: 'the Iran/contra affair was not an aberrant scheme carried out by a 'cabal of zealots' on the National Security Council staff, as the congressional Select Committees concluded in their majority report. Instead, it was the product of two foreign policy directives by President Reagan which deliberately skirted the law and which was executed by the NSC staff with the knowledge and support of high officials.[114] In relaying Walsh's findings many newspapers, including the New York Times, 'incorrectly asserted in the subhead that [Reagan] did not break the law. In fact, the report makes it clear that Reagan displayed a 'disregard for civil laws.' When told by Weinberger that the sales were unquestionably illegal, Reagan is quoted as saying: '[They] can impeach me if they want; visiting days are Wednesday.'[115]

For a personally popular president whose actual policies at home and abroad encountered strong opposition, the temptation to evade the law—given ample means—to enact his will was irresistible.[116] 'The strong executive essential to the pursuit of hegemony is fundamentally at odds with the constitutional system of checks and balances and the restraints afforded by public opinion,' argue Marshall, Scott and Hunter. 'Thus the Iran-contra affair is an urgent challenge for all those who see hegemony, and not our open society, as the curse to be mitigated.'[117]

Many Iran-Contra figures reappeared in George W. Bush's government.[118] The short-lived appointment as director of the Pentagon's

Information Awareness Office of John Poindexter, convicted of lying to Congress, demonstrates that spin and concealment—and lies that meet Mearsheimer's stringent criteria—are rewarded, if performed on behalf of the right authorities. Poindexter asserted unapologetically that he deceived Congress in service of unspecified higher goals. Elliot Abrams, one of six presidential pardoned felons, is another case. As Congressman Henry Hyde (R-Ill) put it with, for him, untypical charity, 'All of us at some time confront conflicts between choices that are evil and less evil, and one hardly exhausts moral imagination by labeling every untruth and every deception an outrage.'[119]

Perhaps realists are correct to aver that some citizens are glad to be kept 'out of the loop' regarding vile activities their leaders perform, inasmuch as these acts improve their sense of security and personal prosperity. This assumption certainly fits conformist segments of any populace but, nonetheless, majorities in the seventy percent range consistently say that authorities should not lie to them, no matter what.[120] So it is not permissible to be, as British Tory wit Alan Clarke once put it, 'economical with the actualite.'

Post-9/11

Did Realpolitik ordain US arming of religious zealots in Southwest Asia, and the abetting of the drug trade to finance covert wars, which policy spokespersons considered, like dying Iraqi children under the 1991–2003 sanctions regime, a worthwhile price to pay? The American public was likely to differ had it known (or bothered to find out).[121] The George W. Bush White House proposed an Office of Public Diplomacy to persuade taxpayers to hail his policies, which was quashed after a public uproar but quickly reconfigured in the Defense Department. Here one may hazard a realist-style tragic proposition for the domestic sphere, where governing groups wind up sacrificing legitimacy in the course of deceiving to achieve it.

One can argue that 'lies' are outcomes of these cumulative inflections as information travels from the interiors of intelligence agencies through various 'desks' to the lips of unwitting policy makers. A recent case is Colin Powell, who later complained that he was a victim of false information when he made his February 5, 2003, pro-intervention speech in the UN Security Council. But this hardy agnostic view begs the questions of why these particular pieces, and patterns, of misinformation, this particular diagnosis, and this particular prescription were promoted at that time by the Bush administration.[122]

After observing, in light of evidence, that 'it would take some nerve to claim that this was an intelligence-drive war [and that] policy makers wanted to hear confirmation of their preconceived views,' Blix concludes:[123] 'I am not suggesting Bush and Blair spoke in bad faith, but I am suggesting that it would not have taken much critical thinking on their own part or the part of their advisers to prevent statements that misled the public. Under national laws individuals are often held responsible if they 'had understood or should have understood' something they did was potentially damaging. It is at least the latter kind of responsibility that large bodies of public opinion now ascribe to the political leaders who unleashed the war.'

Since 9/11 the USA experienced a resurgence of the 'imperial presidency.' The trouble with it is that 'enormous responsibility and power plus enormous capability to avert or conceal failures is likely to 'corrupt the most resolute human being.'[124] Many, if not all, of Nixon's illegal deeds are now perfectly and disgracefully legal in Patriot Act era America. For all that, the initial post-9/11 Afghanistan intervention affirms the power of the Vietnam syndrome. Whether the Afghan civilian death toll was 5000 or half that during the late 2001 overthrow of the Taliban regime, carpet-bombing did not cause it. Was this restraint strategic, or a nod to the home folks? The 'CNN Effect,' such as it exists, is employed and treated as a 'strategic asset' for the military.[125] One military analyst concedes that 'the media and the military share a commitment to American freedoms, and neither wants a news story to be the cause of a single soldier's death.' Perhaps this proviso will apply to stories that can avert unwise or immoral military action, though one has good reason to doubt it.

A dwindling minority of the US public accepts that the Bush Administration believed that Iraqi Weapons of Mass Destruction existed, or that WMD were the real reason for invasion. If so, one must ask why insiders attest Bush wanted to invade Iraq upon assuming office, why phony reports such as that of Niger Yellowcake uranium acquisition were circulated assiduously, why high administration officials continually linked 9/11 to Iraq, why intelligence reports which undermined WMD claims were ignored, why Iraqi exiles hitherto regarded as unreliable were suddenly rehabilitated into sources of gospel truths and why the self-described 'coalition of the willing' prematurely ended the

UNMOVIC search team mission even as it was proving its value.[126] As a New York Times columnist in late October 2002 deduced[127]:

'... in the last few days, The Wall Street Journal reported that senior officials have referred repeatedly to intelligence [which] remains largely unverified. The CIA 's former head of counterterrorism was blunter: "Basically, cooked information is working its way into high-level pronouncements." USA Today reports that "Pressure has been building on the intelligence agencies to deliberately slant estimates to fit a political agenda." Reading all these euphemisms, I was reminded of Monty Python's parrot: he's pushing up daisies, his metabolic processes are history, he's joined the choir invisible. That is, He's dead. And the Bush administration lies a lot.'

One columnist, even at America's 'paper of record,' does not clinch a case. In May 2005, however, the 'Downing Street memo' implicated British and American policy makers for fabricating grounds for invasion.[128] Minutes taken by aide Matthew Rycroft at a Prime Ministerial meeting July 23, 2002, attest that in the USA 'intelligence and facts were being fixed around the policy [and it] seemed clear that Bush had made up his mind to take military action, even if the timing was not yet decided.' Earlier, on March 13, 2002, a memo by advisor David Manning assured Americans that Blair supported regime change. Blair denied he said any such thing. The memo, however, says: '[to Condoleezza Rice] that you [Tony Blair] would not budge in your support for regime change but you had to manage a press, a Parliament, and a public opinion that was very different [from] anything in the states.'

In short, the British public, like Americans, could be manipulated, but required a different style of deceit. Lying—the deliberate misrepresentation of what is thought to be true—clearly characterizes US and UK activities in the run-up to war.[129] Even Mearsheimer seems to agree unreservedly.

Contrary to most strains of realism, actors (including foreign policy elites) commonly angle to interpret external events so as to buttress their own interests and policy predilections.[130] Some acts by nations, or impersonal global trends, may support particular domestic forces over others, but many are ambiguous and therefore open to interpretations. The international realm we see actually is a politicized interpretation of aspects of it—a politicization constructed with targeted domestic audiences in mind. Neorealism accommodates this process inasmuch as it conceives structure as 'akin to a field of forces in physics: Interactions within a field have properties different from those they would have if they occurred outside of it, and as the field affects the objects, so the objects affect the field… A influences B. B, made different by A's influence, influences A' so that 'A's own activity enters into the stimulus which is causing his activity.'[131] If A is the international realm and C is the domestic audience whose reactions to A likewise affect B, the state, we begin to come up with a parallel, if uninvited, approach.[132]

Neoclassical realism aims to mingle realist tenets with attention to the internal dynamics of states.[133] Rose places international variables first since 'foreign policy cannot transcend the limits and opportunities thrown up by the international environment.' The key word is 'opportunities,' for his formulation implies that the state is a passive receptor. Yet states always work diligently to shape their external environment, as do citizens and interest groups. British IR scholars, and neo-Gramscians such as Robert Cox, long have commended interactionist models to account for this fact of political life.[134] International forces acquire social meaning and political muscle only as they are factored into national politics in ways that accommodate the interests, strategies and ideologies of dominant local players. Domestic actors may not make foreign policy as they please, but they are adept at adapting external constraints to suit the exigencies of local contests over the distribution of power, status and wealth.

Conclusion

If 'hypocrisy is the tribute that vice pays to virtue,' then hypocrisy—symbolic concessions, policy modifications or concealment—imposes a significant constraint. A democratic state can opt for repression but 'tough guy' measures are not always effective or costless. States play a delicate game of persuasion and coercion with their citizens. States also strike moral poses that they occasionally are compelled to honor. How far one can generalize about deceit, and how much difference political systems make to behavior and outcomes, is a matter for further research. Nothing is more foolish than, as former Secretary of State George Schulz put it, 'ignore the power element in the equation'—except to ignore everything but the power element. Governments are composed of individuals with histories—class backgrounds, personal and partisan ambitions, private allegiances, ideologies, and mixed motives.

Most citizens expect some indefinable minimum level of observance of law and of the 'soft power' of morality. These expectations, as some realists concede, are a force to reckon with. Indeed, one anticipates that some sort of 'populist realism' soon will emerge from the ranks to account for wider public influences, at least to the satisfaction of realists. Still, it appears that realists fret about the consequences of lying only when it prevents a state elite from lying successfully when these same experts imagine the state elite needs to gull the citizenry.[135]

Meanwhile, a persistent gap between actual and 'perceived' public opinion ironically works to fortify realpolitik stances.[136] Americans consistently overestimate the percentage of fellow citizens who are hard liners (quite possibly an effect of the mass media slants they encounter daily), which in turn affects the activities of everyone else because 'people are willing to accept outcomes and policies that do not favor them to the extent that they perceive these outcomes and policies as legitimate.'[137] US 'hawks' as a proportion of their nation (22%) outnumber European hawks three to one. while UK hawks (13%) outpaced continental European hawks by 2 to 1, which interestingly matches the magnitude of their defense establishments.[138] How a minority consistently came to leverage foreign policy in its favor by fostering an impression of majority support is a topic well worth exploring.

Especially after the 2003 attack on Iraq, the perception of the US abroad differed drastically from self-perceptions of the Bush administration. Inveterate deceit generates an identity crisis, if not for the liars, then for beholders, which in turn has consequences for the liars. Yet by the following year most of the US public seems to have understood how alienated, even hostile, the rest of the world became toward unbridled American policy.[139] The more a state resorts to deception, the more costly it is to 'signal' other states and its own public as to its intentions. This lugubrious plight includes a temporal dimension (how long the lie works), a historical dimension (how many lies has a government told before) and a reputational dimension (is this individual or group liable to lie in a tight spot or just because it can?). Is it possible for political elites to practice something that is recognizably realism in the absence of successful deception or de facto disenfranchisement of the public? It may be realism, to paraphrase a Star Trek character, but probably not as we have known it.

Citizens treated to torrents of doctored information are liable to be a much more wary audience. Cynicism may be 'cheap wisdom' but it is a form of critical wisdom to reckon with, especially when it is a result of experiences, not prejudgments, of the behavior of authorities. Discontented domestic audiences can and sometimes do wring foreign policy concessions from their governments. These moments require investigation by IR theorists as to the pathways by which dissent is transmuted into effective pressure.[140] Under what conditions do the manifold forms of dissent tip the balance? Mass dissent acts as a sobering corrective force wherever a governing elite pursues dubious policies. '[For in national as in personal affairs,' as Kennan cautioned, 'the acceptance of one's limitations is surely one of the first marks of a true morality.'[141] Western publics today no longer are inclined automatically to assume that political leaders and economic elites have their best interests at heart.[142] Some will call that a shame; some of us will call that progress.

NOTES

1. I. F. Stone cited in John Pilger, *Heroes* (New York: Vintage, 2001), p. 571, and in Philip Knightley, *The First Casualty* (New York: Harcourt, Brace Jovanovich, 1975), p. 373.
2. Hannah Arendt, *Crises of The Republic* (New York: Harcourt, Brace, Jovanovich, 1972), p. 42.
3. Cited in Bruce Russett, *Controlling The Sword: The Democratic Governance of National Security* (Cambridge: Harvard University Press, 1990), p. 146. More recently 29% were 'very interested' in events in other countries. Meg Bostrum, 'Public Attitudes about Foreign Affairs: An Overview of the Current State of Public Opinion' (Washington DC: Framework Institute, 2001).
4. 'Politicians have a 'tendency to deceive themselves about what they are doing'. Hans Morgenthau, *Politics Among Nations* (New York: Knopf, 1967, 4th ed), pp. 83–84. See Michael William's essay on Morgenthau's unappreciated subtleties: 'Why Ideas Matter in International Relations: Hans Morgenthau, Classical Realism, and the Moral Construction of Power Politics,' *International Organization*, 58 (Fall 2004).
5. Quoted in George Kennan, *At A Century's End* (New York: Norton, 1996), p. 135. Also see Eric Alterman, *Who Speaks for the People?* (Cornell University Press, 1998), Chap. "Introduction: Politics All the Way Down".
6. 'The modern propagandist, like the modern psychologist, recognizes that men are often poor judges of their own interests, flitting from one alternative to the next one without solid reason or clinging timorously to the fragments of some mossy rock of ages.' Dwaine Marvik (ed) *Harold Lasswell on Political Sociology* (Chicago: University of Chicago, 1977), p. 236.
7. Quoted in Barry D. Karl, *Charles Merriam and the Study of Politics* (Chicago: University of Chicago Press, 1974), pp. 301–302.

8. The 2004 Pew Study, finding 4 of 5 citizens underestimated US nuclear weapons, is at http://peoplepress.org/reports/display.php3?PageID=1016.
9. A realist referee at another journal stated exactly this objection to the essay's argument. The author will be happy to relay the entire document to inquirers. This stance is also taken in John J. Mearsheimer, 'Lying in International Politics,' Paper presented at the Annual Meeting of the American Political Science Association, 2–5 September 2004), p. 8. Available at http://www.learnedhand.com/mearsheimer-lying.html.
10. Eisenhower balked at publicizing such activities—not at performing them, to be sure—because he believed the propaganda costs of abandoning the high ground were too high. Stephen Ambrose, *Ike's Spies: Eisenhower and the Espionage Establishment* (Jackson, Miss: University Press of Mississippi, 1999), p. 188. The U-2 shootdown in 1960, and its initial denial via a 'cover story,' was a diplomatic setback. See Philip Taubman, *Secret Empire: Eisenhower, The CIA, and the Hidden Story of America's Space Espionage* (New York: Simon & Schuster, 2003), pp. 26, 308.
11. George Orwell, *Inside the Whale and other Essays* (London, Penguin, 1957), pp. 75, 76.
12. See Paul Joseph, *Are Americans Becoming More Peaceful?: A Counterintuitive Examination of the US Public's Attitude Toward War* (Chicago: Paradigm Publishers, 2007).
13. See Jeffrey Legro and Andrew Moravscik, 'Is Anybody Still a Realist?' *International Security* 24, 2 (Fall 1999).
14. 'There is no debate among realists, however, that, at a minimum, states are worried about their security and that they act vigilantly to enhance their security in an environment which offers them no choice but to do so.' Benjamin Frankel, 'Introduction,' in Frankel (ed.) *Roots of Realism* (London: Frank Cass, 1996), p. ix.
15. For contrasting assessments of the costs see Sissela Bok, *Lying: Moral Choice in Public and Private Life* (New York: Pantheon, 1978) and Jeremy Campbell, *The Liar's Tale: A History of Falsehood* (New York: Norton, 2002). On 'noble lies' see Shadia Drury, *Leo Strauss and The American Right* (New York: St. Martins Press, 1997).
16. Hans Blix, Disarming Iraq: *The Search for Weapons of Mass Destruction* (London: Bloomsbury, 2nd ed. 2005), p. 9.
17. Propaganda is desensitizing such that a 'cry wolf' reaction arises, most terribly with stories of the death camps, which many were inclined to ascribe to what the Nazis termed 'horror propaganda.' The opposite also occurs. When the public finds it was mistaken in attributing a 'cry wolf' motive to a genuine mass crime, it is likely to credit future accusations.
18. For a contemporary case, see James Dao, 'Physicist Says Pentagon Is Trying to Silence Him,' *New York Times*, 27 July 2001. 'A leading critic of the military's missile defense testing program has accused the Pentagon

of trying to silence him and intimidate his employer, the Massachusetts Institute of Technology, by investigating him for disseminating classified documents.' For a follow-up related report, see William J Broad, 'Accounting Office Finds Itself Accused,' *New York Times* 2 April 2006.

19. '[S]pinning is all about assembling known facts in a way that presents a favorable picture to the person telling the story. No false statements are involved and no attempt is made to present an untrue bottom line. Concealment simply involves withholding information from others... A lie is a positive action; an individual must actually do something to lie.' Mearsheimer, 'Lying in International Relations,' pp. 2, 4. See his expanded argument why 'their are good strategic reasons for leaders to lie to their publics' in *Why Leaders Lie: The Truth about Lying in Interntional Politics* (New York: Oxford University Press, 2010), p. 12. Is it credible that a political figure is not 'doing something,' or something 'positive' (for themselves, at least), when they spin or conceal?

20. Scott Shane, 'Some worry U.S. may bend facts for policy Intelligence: Analysts pressured to spin reports to support White House position,' *Baltimore Sun*, 4 April 2003.

21. Cited in Charles Jones, *E.H. Carr and International Relations: A Duty to Lie* (Cambridge: Cambridge University Press, 1998), p. iii. By the same token, few unfaithful spouses fail in an emergency (threat of exposure) to recognize a duty to lie for the sake of their marriages. Motives matter.

22. He calls this 'fear-mongering,' which has positive and negative variants. Mearsheimer, 'Lying,' p. 9. The question, who is to judge which is which, is an interesting one that goes unasked.

23. Witness Ronald Reagan's order in the 1980s to re-classify declassified materials, and George W. Bush's administration order that the US National Archive reclassify formerly public records. 'Secrecy-Obsessed White House a Nightmare for Historians.' *Chicago Sun-Times*, 24 April 2006. p. 35.

24. Robert McNamara, *In Retrospect: The Tragedy and Lessons of Vietnam* (New York: Times Books, 1995). Apart from the 'national interest' being usurped by subnational, other-national or supranational forces, one ought to distinguish the 'necessary and variable elements' of the national interest such that consequent acts can survive 'rational scrutiny.' Hans J. Morgenthau, 'The National Interest,' in Michael Smith, Richard Little, Michael Shackleton (eds.) *Perspectives in World Politics* (London: Open University, 1981), p. 52.

25. Public support for war without a new U.N. vote authorizing it was 30%, according to a poll conducted 17–18 February 2003. David W. Moore and Frank Newport, 'Gallup News Service Poll Analyses "Powell 'Bounce" Fades But Majority of Americans still open to War with Iraq.'

Gallup News Service February 21, 2003. The phrasing of the headline is itself an interesting exhibit of media slant.
26. Versus 55–60% whose support for war is highly conditional and 15% who are pacifist, according to Joseph in Are Americans becoming More Peaceful?, pp. 3, 5–6. A similar breakdown of categories is found in Peter Feaver and Christopher Gelpi, *Choosing Your Battles: American Civil-Mlitary Relations and the Use of Force* (Princeton: Princeton University Press, 2004). By February 2007 polls were reporting 72% disapproval of Bush's handling of Iraq, and 53% wanted withdrawal of troops 'as soon as possible.' *The Guardian* February 2007.
27. Victor Kiernan, *The Lords of Human Kind: European Attitudes to Other Cultures in The Imperial Age* (London: Serif, 1995, 2nd ed), p. 240. The post-war lesson widely drawn from defeating fascism was a fear of public mobilization. See William Kornhauser, *The Politics of Mass Society* (Chicago: Free Press, 1959).
28. Richard Sobel and Eric Shiraev eds. *International Public Opinion and the Bosnian Crisis* (Lanham Md: Lexington, 2003), pp. 66–67, 107, 303.
29. Douglas C. Foyle, *Counting the Public In: Presidents, Public Opinion and Public Poicy* (New York: Columbia University Press, 1999), p. 249. Foyle's analysis, though, boils down to saying some leaders are inclined to heed public opinion and some just aren't.
30. E. H. Carr, *The Twenty Years Crisis, 1919–1939* (New York: St. Martins Press, 1961), p. 235.
31. Realists confer enormous latitude on leaders. So if a leader presumably believes her own untruths then she is truthful, if not telling the truth. True believers therefore cannot lie—which is preposterous. Absent a foolproof polygraph, the best test is to investigate whether the actions a leader advocates accord with their demonstrable interests or ideological convictions. If they do, one has strong grounds to suspect lying at work.
32. Richard Nixon's advisers used the phrase 'How will it play in Peoria?'—a solidly Republican Party community in rural Illinois—when anticipating the relevant impact of proposed policies.
33. Plato, *The Republic* (London: Penguin, 1963), pp. 62–83.
34. See Richard Ned Lebow and Robert Kelly, 'Thucydides and Hegemony: Athens and The US', *Review of International Studies* 27, 4 (October 2001) and Nancy Kokaz, 'Moderating Power: A Thucydidean Perspective,' *Review of International Studies* 27, 1 (January 2001).
35. Kenneth Waltz, *Man, The State and War* (NY: Columbia University Press, 1959), p. 28.
36. Jack Snyder describes neorealists as 'truncated realists' as opposed to the broader approaches of Morgenthau, Machiavelli and Thucydides. 'Aggressive Realism' is exemplified by John Mearsheimer, and 'defensive

Realism' by Stephen Walt. See Snyder, *Myths of Empire: International Ambitions and Domestic Politics* (Ithaca: Cornell University Press, 1992), pp. 12, 19. Stephen G. Brooks distinguishes between 'worst-case possibilistic neorealism' and 'probability-oriented postclassical realism' in 'Dueling Realisms,' *International Organization* 51 (Summer 1997), p. 446.
37. Legro and Moravscik, 'Is Anyone Still a Realist?' pp. 8, 23, 53–54. On the delicate question as to what point is it that an accumulation of ad hoc statements should scuttle a theory, see Paul Feyerabend, *Against Method* (London: Verso, 1975).
38. Waltz, Man, States and War, p. 238. For a detailed account of neorealism see his *Theory of International Relations* (Reading, MA: Addison-Wesley, 1979).
39. John J. Mearsheimer, *The Tragedy of Great Power Politics* (New York: W. W. Norton, 2001), pp. 10, 11.
40. See Oliver Thomas, *Easily led: A History of Propaganda* (London: Sutton, 1999); Jacques Ellul, *Propaganda: The Formations of Men's Attitudes* (New York: Vintage, 1971); Walter Lippmann, *Public Opinion* (New York: Free Press, 1922); and J. A. C Brown, *Techniques of Persuasion* (London: Pelican, 1963); (New York 1992).
41. Mearsheimer, 'Lying,' p. 9 and Mearsheimer, *Why Leaders Lie*, p. 104.
42. Barrington Moore, jr, *The Social Origins of Dictatorship and Democracy* (Boston: Beacon Press, 1966), p. 486. 'To speak of cultural inertia [or complicity], is to overlook the concrete interests and privileges that are served by indoctrination, education and the entire process of transmitting culture from one generation to the next.'
43. BBC television documentary 'Great Books: *Catch-22*', 27 December 2003.
44. 'Every argument used to justify Athenian imperialism abroad could be applied with equal force to the justification of tyranny at home... and the sort of treatment that the Athenians had once meted out to the Melians they ended up, during and after the Sicilian expedition, meting out to one another.' Paul Rahe 'Thucydides Critique of Realpolitik,' in Frankel, *Roots of Realism*, 134–135.
45. See Robert C. Byrd, *Losing America* (New York: Norton, 2004). The mistreatment of prisoners in Guantanamo Bay in Cuba and in Abu Ghraib prison, among others, in Iraq became an election issue. See Ronald Dworkin, 'The Supreme Court & Guantanamo,' *New York Review of Books* LI, 13 (12 August 2004).
46. Chalmers Johnson, *Blowback: The Costs and Consequences of American Empire* (New York: Henry Holt, 2001), p. 40.
47. On systematic misconstruing of liberal internationalists in the interwar period as pacifists see David H. Edgerton, *Warfare State: Britain 1920–1970* (Cambridge: Cambridge University Press, 2006).

48. Andrew Moravscik, 'Integrating Domestic and International Theories of International Bargaining,' in Peter Evans, Harold K. Jacobson and Robert D Putnam (eds.) *Double-Edged Diplomacy: International Bargaining and Domestic Politics* (Berkeley: University of California, 1993), p. 12. Also see Gideon Rose, 'Neoclassical Realism and Theories of Foreign Policy.' *World Politics* 51, October 1998.
49. Mearsheimer, 'Lying,' p. 18.
50. George Kennan, *Memories 1950–1963* (New York: Pantheon, 1972), p. 56.
51. Quoted in A. L. Rowse, *Appeasement: A Study in Political Decline 1933–1939* (New York: Norton, 1963), p. 12.
52. Ibid, pp. 14, 117. Rowse said that only a 'ruinous foreign policy' separated him from Conservatives since he had 'no illusions about people's average intelligence' and the 'humbug of the welfare state.' The Labour Party 'for all the lunatic fringe it had to carry of pacifists and illusionists—did stand for collective security' (pp. 111, 112).
53. See David H. Edgerton, *England and The Aeroplane* (London Macmillan, 1991) p. 71; Clive Ponting: *1940: Myth and Reality* (London: Hamish Hamilton, 1990), p. 30; and Keith Robbins, *Appeasement* (London: Basil Blackwell, 1988), p. 44. Martin Gilbert and Richard Gott in *The Appeasers* (London: Weidenfeld & Nicolson, 1963, p. 59) mistakenly state that in 1935 the three major British parties refused to endorse a White Paper recommendation for rearmament and suggest that by 1939 British air power lagged behind Germany. During a flap over aviation hero Lindberg's overestimate of German airpower in 1938, British intelligence knew very well that they were not outnumbered but were not going to say so. See Rowse, *Appeasement*, p. 80.
54. Edgerton, *England and the Aeroplane*, pp. 37, 43.
55. Robbins, *Appeasement*, p. 44. On the British public showing more perspicuity than their goverment, see Richard Rosecrance and Zara Steiner, 'British Grand Strategy and the Origins of World War II,' in Rosecrance and Art Stein (eds.) *The Domestic Bases of Grand Strategy* (Ithaca: Cornell University Press, 1993), 136, 139, 147–148.
56. See Lucian M. Ashworth, 'Where are the Idealists in Interwar International Relations?' *Review of International Studies* 32, 2, (April 2006).
57. William O'Neill, *A Democracy at War* (New York: New Press, 1993), p. 59. By his own account an arms buildup began in 1934–1935, with a massive naval construction program under way in 1936. Actually, FDR ordained naval rearmament during his first year in office. See William McBride, The Unstable Dynamics of a Strategic Technology:

Disarmament, Unemployment, and the Interwar Battleship,' *Technology and Culture* (April 1997), pp. 386, 389.
58. O'Neill, *A Democracy at War*, pp. 107–108. On the interest-laden idiosyncracies of isolationism see Franz Schurmann, *The Logic of World Power* (New York: Pantheon, 1974) Like Mearsheimer, John Schuessler argues that without deception FDR would have failed to gain public consent for entry to WWII. See his 'The Deception Dividend: FDR's Undeclared War' *International Security* 34, 4 (Spring 2010), p. 165.
59. Robert Shogan, *Hard Bargain* (New York: Scribners, 1994). p. 267; Kenneth Davis, *FDR: Into The Storm 1937–1940* (New York Random House, 1993), p. 565.
60. Shogan, *Hard Bargain*, pp. 267–268.
61. O'Neill, *A Democracy at War*, p. 86.
62. By September 1941 Rooseveltian deception about the USS Greer incident, which Mearsheimer cites approvingly, was secondary and even superfluous. Mearsheimer, *Why Leaders Lie*, pp. 67–71, 128. Joseph E. Persico, *Roosevelt's Secret War: FDR and World War II* Espionage (New York: Random House, 2001), pp. 86, 87.
63. *Wehrmacht* troops were punishing Polish 'aggression.' Initially soldiers also were kept in the dark about *einsatzgruppen* activities but *Wehrmacht*-SS cooperation was so high as ultimately to make little difference in their respective conduct. Alexander B. Rossino, *Hitler Strikes Poland: Blitzkrieg, Ideology and Atrocity* (Lawrence: University of Kansas Press, 2003), pp. 10, 27, 58–59, 87. See also Peter Stargardt, *The German War: A Nation Under Arms, 1939–1945* (New York : Basic Books, 2015).
64. Blowback is a cost that elites inflict on their own populations, partly because it often (though not always, as the 2004 Spanish election attests) redounds to the elites' advantage.
65. Almond, *The American People and Foreign Policy* (New York: Praeger, 1950, p. 69. The people make 'a dangerous master' in foreign policy according to Walter Lippman in *his Essays on the Public Philosophy* (Boston: Little, Brown, 1955), p. 558. In response, see Ole Holsti, 'Public Opinion and Foreign Policy: Challenges to the Almond-Lippman Thesis,' *International Studies Quarterly* 36 (1992).
66. Benjamin Ginsberg, *The Captive Public: How Mass Opinion Promotes State Power* (New York: Basic Books), p. 21.
67. Kaase and Newton, *Belief in Government*, p. 107. Also see Benjamin Page and Robert Shapiro, *The Rational Public* (Chicago: University of Chicago, 1992).
68. Bruce Jentleson, 'The Pretty Prudent Public: Post-Vietnam American Opinion and the Use of Military Force,' *International Studies Quarterly*

36 (March 1992), p. 71. Also see Bruce Jentleson and Rebecca Britton, 'Still Pretty Prudent: Post-Cold War American Public Opinion on the Use of Military Force,' *Journal of Conflict Resolution* 42, 4 (August 1998).
69. Samuel Popkin, *The Reasoning Voter* (Chicago: University of Chicago, 1991).
70. Ronald Inglehart, *Culture Shift in Advanced Industrial Societies* (Princeton: Princeton University Press 1990). Also see Robert Shapiro and Lawrence Jacobs, 'Who Leads? Who Follows?: US Presidents, Public Opinion and Foreign Policy,' in Brigitte L. Nacos, Robert Shapiro, and Pierangelo Isneria (eds.) *Decision-making in a Glass House: Mass Media, Public Opinion, and American and European Foreign Policy in the 21st Century* (Lanham, Md: Rowman & Littlefield, 2000).
71. Mearsheimer, 'Lying,' p. 19.
72. Jean Jacques Rousseau, *The Social Contract* (Hetrtfordshire: Hammondsworth, 1998), p. 39.
73. Steven Kull and Clay Ramsay, 'The Myth of the Reactive Public: American Public Attitudes on Military Fatalities in the Post-Cold war Period,' in Philip Everts and Pierangelo Isernia (eds.) *Public Opinion and the International Use of Force* (London: Routledge, 2001), p. 6.
74. ibid. p. 12. 'In Korea and Vietnam it is more likely that support diminished as the public came to *question the purposes of the wars* and their likelihood of success.' (emphasis mine) p. 20. Also see Joseph, *Are Americans Becoming More Peaceful?*, pp. 3–10.
75. Captain Marc Hedahl, who teaches ethics at the Air Force Academy, notes: 'Most military members have used the Washington Post test at some point in their careers. If you are facing an ethical dilemma, then you simply ask yourself what you would do if you knew that your actions would make the front page of tomorrow's *Washington Post*. The test is easier to remember and employ than Kant's Categorical Imperative.' 2 February 2003 http://www.msnbc.com/news/752664.
76. Hans J. Morgenthau, 'Vietnam and the National Interest,' in Marvin Gettleman (ed.) *Vietnam: History, Opinions and Documents of a Major World Crisis* (New York: Fawcett, 1965), pp. 365–375. Kurt Vonnegut told Morgenthau in the early 1970s that 'we've learned over the past eight years that the government will not respond to what we think and what we say. It simply is not interested.' Morgenthau ruefully agreed. See Vonnegut, *Wampeters, Foma, and Granfallloons* (New York: Delacorte Press, 1974), p. 271.
77. Robert Jervis, 'Realism in the Study of World Politics,' *International Organization* 52, 4 Autumn 1998, p. 976.

78. Miroslav Nincic, *Democracy and Foreign Policy* (New York: Columbia University Press, pp. 38, 39–42, 54–55.
79. Mearsheimer, *The Tragedy of Great Power Politics*, p. 23.
80. Daniel Goldhagen, *Hitler's Willing Executioners* (New York: Knopf, 1996).
81. Ian Ousby, *Occupation: The Ordeal of France 1940–1944* (London: Pimlico, 1999), p. 178.
82. Mark Mazower, *Inside Hitler's Greece* (New Haven: Yale University Press, 1993), p. 191.
83. Paul Rahe similarly notes that Thucydides 'invites his readers to ponder why human beings caught up in circumstances in which religious restraints are largely ineffectual nonetheless persist in making religious appeals.' Why bother? Rahe, Thucydidies Critique of Realpolitik,' in Frankel, *Roots of Realism*, pp. 108–109.
84. Charles Townshend, 'Civilization and "Frightfulness": Air Control in the Middle East Between the War,' in Chris Wagler (ed.) *Warfare, Diplomacy and Politics: Essays in Honour of A.J.P. Taylor* (London: Henry Hamilton, 1986), p. 151.
85. Roger Hilsman, 'Difficulties of Covering Vietnam,' in Harrison Salisbury, *Vietnam Reconsidered* (New York: Harper & Row, 1984), p. 126. 'American reporters should go out and seek the truth,' deduced Morley Safer, 'but only within the context of serving American foreign policy.' p. 159.
86. William Prochnau, *Once Upon a Distant War* (New York: Vintage, 1996), pp. 59, 109, 130.
87. Neil Sheehan, *The Pentagon Papers* (New York: Bantam Books, 1971), p. 241.
88. Neil Sheehan, *A Bright Shining Lie* (New York: Random House, 1988), p. 290.
89. Prochnau, *Once Upon a Distant War*, p. 69.
90. See www.projectforaNewAmericanCentuy.org/rebuildingamericasdefenses.pdf.
91. Mike Gravel, *Pentagon Papers* vol. III (Boston: Beacon Press, 1974), p. 108. Mearsheimer readily agrees that the Tonkin Gulf incident(s) involved two major official lies. Mearsheimer, *Why Leaders Lie*, pp. 72–74.
92. 'I have one more problem for your computer,' Johnson told advisers, 'will you feed into it how long it will take five hundred thousand angry Americans to climb that White House wall out there and lynch their President if he does something like that.' David Halberstam, *The Best and The Brightest* (New York: Random House, 1974), p. 641.

93. Bruce Franklin, *Vietnam and other American Fantasies* (Amherst: University of Massachusetts Press, 2000), p. 43.
94. James William Gibson, *The Perfect War* (New York: Atlantic Monthly Press, 1986), pp. 64, 332. Also see the Sheehan, *Pentagon Papers*, pp. 316, 321, 470, 515.
95. Stephen Ambrose, *Nixon: The Triumph of a Politician* v. II, (New York: Simon & Schuster, 1989), pp. 377–378.
96. Larry Berman, *No Peace, No Honor: Nixon, Kissinger and Betrayal in Vietnam* (New York: Free Press, 2001), p. 57.
97. Ambrose, *Nixon*, p. 301.
98. Ambrose, *Nixon*, p. 291.
99. Gabriel Kolko, *Vietnam: Anatomy of a War* (London: Allen & Unwin, 1986), p. 321.
100. Tom Wells, *The War Within* (Berkeley: University of California Press, 1994), p. 5–6. Also the Clifford Group report in Sheehan, *The Pentagon Papers*, p. 601–602; Terry Anderson, *The Movement and The Sixties* (New York: Oxford University Press, 1995), pp. 237–238; and Seymour Hersh, *The Price of Power* (New York: Simon & Schuster, 1983), pp. 129–131, 195. On LBJ's decision not to run again, see Ginsberg, *The Captive Public*, p. 67.
101. Berman, *No Peace, No Honor*, pp. 6, 7.
102. Ibid., p. 262. A Gallup poll found 71% said no to bombing North Vietnam if it 'does try to take over South Vietnam' and 79% opposed sending in ground troops.
103. Interview with Daniel Ellsberg, 2002.
104. Adam Garfinkel, *Tell Tale Hearts: The Origin and Impact of the Vietnam Antiwar Movement* (New York, 1995), pp. 17–19, 264.
105. A Gallup poll in 1971 showed 60% with college education favoring withdrawal, 75% with a high school diploma and 80% of those with only a grade school education. Bruce Franklin, *Vietnam and Other American Fantasies*, p. 57. Other studies indicate the relationship is curvilinear to educational levels.
106. See Lawrence Lichty,' Comments on the Influence of Television on Public Opinion, in Peter Braestrup (ed.) *Vietnam as History* (Washington DC: Woodrow Wilson Center, 1989), p. 158.
107. Ray McGovern, 'CIA Director Caves in,' *Counterpunch* 13 February 2003. Also see C. Michael Hiam, *Who the Hell are We Fighting? The Story of Sam Adams and the Vietnam Intelligence War* (South Royaton, VT: Steerforth Press, 2006).
108. Rhodri Jeffrey-Jones, *Peace Now!: American Society and the Ending of the Vietnam War* (New Haven: Yale, 1999), p. 83.

109. See Daniel Hallin, *The 'Uncensored War': The Media in Vietnam* (Berkeley: University of California Press, 1986) and Sheehan, *A Bright Shining Lie*, pp. 342–348.
110. See Theodore Draper, *A Very Thin Line: The Iran-Contra Affair* (New York: Hill & Wang, 1991), Bob Woodward, *Veil: The Secret Wars of the CIA 1981–1987* (New York: Simon & Schuster, 1991) and, a Reagan administration viewpoint, Michael Ledeen, *Perilous Statecraft* (New York: Scribner, 1992).
111. See Samuel Segev, *The Iranian Triangle: The Untold Story of Israel's Role in the Iran-Contra Affair* (New York: Free Press, 1988).
112. Jonathan Marshall, Peter Dale Scott, Jane Hunter, *The Iran-Contra Connection: Secret Teams and Covert Operations in the Reagan Era* (South End Press, 1987), p. 29.
113. Draper. *A Very Thin Line*, p. 21.
114. *Final Report of the Independent Counsel for Iran/Contra Matters, Volume I: Investigations and Prosecutions*, Lawrence E. Walsh Independent Counsel August 4, 1993 Washington, p. 21. http://www.fas.org/irp/offdocs/walsh/. Also see Lawrence Walsh, *Firewall: The Iran Conspiracy and Cover-up* (New York: WW Norton, 1998).
115. Malcolm Byrne and Peter Kornbluh, 'The Press Indicts the Prosecutor,' *Columbia Journalism Review* (March–April 1994), p. 23. 'An April 11, 1993, Washington Post Magazine profile of Walsh by Marjorie Williams dismissed Walsh's 'sense of duty' as 'anachronistic,' and cited as an example his insistence 'that it was a serious matter—a serious crime—for members of the executive branch to lie to Congress' (p. 24). Also see Byrne and Kornbluh, *The Iran-Contra Scandal: The Declassified History* (New York: The New Press, 1993).
116. On the unpopularity of Reagan's policies versus the popularity of the man, see Thomas Ferguson and Joel Rogers, *Right Turn* (New York: Hill & Wang, 1989).
117. Marshall, et al., *The Iran-Contra Connection*, p. 27.
118. Duncan Campbell, 'Bush Appointments tainted by Reagan Era Scandal,' *The Guardian* 20 August 2001.
119. Quoted in David Brock, *Blinded by The Right* (New York: Crown, 2002), p. 44.
120. Alterman, *Who Speaks for the People?*, p. 132.
121. The information was available in non-mainstream sources, which only a small minority seek out. See Alfred McCoy, *The Politics of Heroin: CIA Complicity in the Drug Trade* (Chicago: Lawrence Hill, 1991) Peter Dale Scott and Jonathan Marshall, *Cocaine Politics* (Berkeley: University of California Press, 1991) and Alexander Cockburn, *Whiteout* (London: Verso, 1998).

122. See James Bamford, *A Pretext for War* (New York: Doubkleday, 2004).
123. Blix, *Disarming Iraq*, pp. 260, 272. 'While the Iraqis had become frantic, though not very successful, about finding evidence of their innocence, the U.S. had become frantic—but also not very successful—about finding convincing evidence of Iraqi guilt' (p. 11).
124. Daniel Ellsberg, *Secrets: A Memoir of Vietnam and The Pentagon Papers* (New York: Little, Brown, 2002), p. 23.
125. Margaret H. Belknap, 'The CNN Effect: Strategic Enabler or Operational Risk?' *Parameters* (Autumn 2002).
126. On American insiders see Richard A. Clarke, *Against All Enemies: Inside America's War on Terrorism* (New York: Free Press, 2004) and Ron Suskind, *The Price of Loyalty: George W. Bush, The White House and the Education of Paul O'Neill* (New York, 2004). Also see Bob Woodward, *Plan of Attack* (New York: Simon & Schuster, 2004); Michael Sheuer, *Imperial Hubris: Why the West is Losing the War on Terror* (New York: Potomac Books 2004), and Blix, Disarming Iraq.
127. Paul Krugman, *The Great Unraveling* (New York: Norton, 2004), p. 260.
128. Reported in London's *Sunday Times* 1 May 2005. The Downing Street memo likewise is cited as incriminating in Mearsheimer, *Why Leaders Lie*, p. 81.
129. Mearsheimer identifies four major lies that the Bush administration told about Iraq. Mearsheimer, *Why Leaders Lie*, pp. 14–17. On systematic shortfalls in British governmental veracity, see David Miller, Big and Little Lies in David Miller (ed.) *Tell Me Lies: Propaganda and Media Distortion in the Attack on Iraq* (London: Pluto 2004).
130. Kurt Jacobsen, *Chasing Progress in the Irish Republic* (Cambridge: Cambridge University Press, 1994), pp. 1–22.
131. Kenneth N. Waltz, 'Laws and Theories,' in Robert O. Keohane, ed., *Neorealism and its Critics* (Columbia University Press, 1986), pp. 62–63.
132. For constructivists, norms shape identities and preferences in ways that transcend material or instrumental aims. Talk about norms can alter the content and efficacy of international norms. A problem arises regarding 'identities' when they are cultivated as deceptions. Receding mirror images appear. The concept of 'identity' of states looks less compelling when one confronts the problems of prevarication, or dual/triple messaging, with respect to different audiences. When a peddled illusion becomes the basis for policy, it becomes a dangerous 'social fact.' Myths generate an entrancing reality of their own, which does not make them any less myths. So is 'lies all the way down' the bedrock for identities inasmuch as every state deceives? Yet this proposition suggests that there

is a recognizable basis—perhaps itself composed of a mélange of misconceptions and prejudices—from which the liar departs. If identity can be a veneer—different things to different audiences—then what, one is entitled to ask, is it a veneer over? See Chap. 3.
133. Rose, 'Neoclassical Realism and Theories of Foreign Policy,' pp. 144–154.
134. For a reconsideration of Carr's 'historical realism,' see David Goldfisher, 'E.H. Carr: An Historical Realist' approach for the Globalization era,' *Review of International Studies* 28 (2002), pp. 697–717.
135. Mearsheimer, 'Lying,' p. 12. One can concede that the closest case to a 'noble lie' in Mearsheimer's terms is the Kennedy Cuban Missile crisis deal, which in our view was more a matter of appeasing the American right than the public as a whole. Mearshiemer, *Why Leaders Lie*, pp. 25, 97.
136. Alexander Todorov and Anesu N Mandisodza, 'Public Opinion on Foreign Policy: The Multilateral Public that perceives itself as Unilateral,' *Policy Brief*, Woodrow Wilson School of International and Public Affairs, September 2003, p. 1.
137. Todorov and Mandisodza, 'Public Opinion.' The 16% who are unilateralists thought 54% shared their views while the 71% who believed the 'US should do its fair share' assumed only 49% shared their views.
138. The four categories are hawks, pragmatists, doves and isolationists. Ronald Asmus, Philip Everts and Pierangelo Isernia, 'Power, War, and Public Opinion: Thoughts on the Nature and Structure of the Trans-Atlantic Divide,' *Policy Review* 123 (February/March 2004), pp. 73–88.
139. See the Pew Research Centre for People and the Press Study at http://peoplepress.org/reports/display.php3?PageID=1016.
140. The UN Security Council appeared, prior to the invasion of Iraq, as a last resort in order for Americans to restrain their own government. One sees similar motives in the case of European Union, where citizens sometimes use the EU institutions as a means to establish fair rules and practices they cannot count on their own governments to provide.
141. Kennan, *At A Century's End*, p. 279.
142. The University of Michigan Center for Political Studies polls find that whereas in 1958 over three quarters (76.3%) of respondents said they believed their government was run for the 'benefit of all the people'; by 1972 only 37.7% did, and by 1994 the figure had fallen under a fifth (19%). Two-thirds said that the country was governed for the sake of a 'few big interests.' Cited in H. Bruce Franklin, *Vietnam and Other Fantasies* (Amherst: University of Massachusetts, 2000), pp. 43, 46.

COIN Flips: Counterinsurgency Theory and American IR

Why intervene? Counterinsurgency, according to the 2006 *Manual* guided foremost by former General and now CIA Director David Petraeus, is 'the process by which the government asserts its influence and control in an area beset by insurgents,' which includes 'local security efforts, programs to distribute food and medical supplies, and lasting reforms (like land redistribution).'[1] The stated objectives are—familiar ones—too familiar, according to friendly critics who argue a radically different context obtains today.[2] Yet counterinsurgency in the crucial case of Vietnam was responsible for enormous non-combatant casualties and ended in withdrawal.[3] There is no reason, scanning twentieth century history, to be surprised at this glum outcome in what the Lyndon Johnson administration dubbed, as a genus, 'the other war.' The more 'we won, the more we lost,' observed Jonathan Schell.[4] Why? Because 'our policies were destroying whatever support that [the South Vietnam] government might ever have had.'[5] Can a foreign military force ('third-party counterinsurgency') ever do anything else?

Schell's summation is one that few, if any, experts today accept is a necessary fate for counterinsurgent enterprises. Studies of counterinsurgency, especially in American IR journals, are framed so that there is a salvageable formula to win any given conflict at acceptable costs, even if it means trading off one or two of three major counterinsurgency goals (force protection, discriminating between combatant and non-combatant, and physical elimination of insurgents).[6] To notice this management-oriented bias is regarded by many IR specialists as itself a sign of egregious bias.[7] COIN experts, in any case, rarely are in position to advise governments to forego contemplated operations, though they do quibble about aspects of implementation.[8]

This paper attempts a deeper scouring of the theory and practice of COIN. No American IR journal has yet published an article on counterinsurgency that does not ultimately aim to 'improve' it, rather than fundamentally questioning its utility. This latter tack, however ample the warrant for it, is way beyond the pale.[9] Accordingly, the essay examines a recent ascendant reinterpretation of counterinsurgency which reinforces this stance, and is concerned foremost with the doctrinal justifications guiding US counterinsurgent interventions. The Vietnam War remains the pivotal case for parties in and out of academe who have refashioned the history of counterinsurgency operations as one of eminently worthy and effective endeavors, as they were originally imagined to be. One therefore is tempted to call them revivalists, not revisionists, but will stay with the latter term.

Insurgencies elsewhere are drawn into this critical essay but the new revisionists' case hinges on Vietnam, so it occupies center stage. The ensuing sections consider the research parameters that COIN studies operate within and the exaggerated demise of COIN after Vietnam, scrutinize the influential 'triumph forsaken' argument that the USA won the counterinsurgency aspect of the Vietnam War, flush out faulty presuppositions of recent COIN theory, challenge skewed accounts of COIN successes, ferret out rules of counterinsurgency based on behavior rather than aspirations and argue for inclusion of interveners' motives in analyses of COIN experiences.

RESEARCH PARAMETERS

The Counterinsurgency *Manual* tends to overlook evidence attesting to intrinsic operational flaws. So Civil Operations and Revolutionary Development Support (CORDS), a coordinating committee of US agencies formed in 1967, is credited by the Manual authors, according to metrics of their own devising, with 'considerable success' at pacification.[10] Counterinsurgency incorporates 'civic action *and* pacification programs' *and* is broadly defined as 'the employment of military resources for purposes other than conventional warfare.' French Algerian war veteran David Galula refers to '[p]acification, rather than military operations,' which are 'both aspects of counter-insurgency warfare.'[11]

While some analysts stress a neat distinction between pacification (pure repression) and counterinsurgency (developmental consent-seeking devices mixed with repression), this distinction, by virtually all accounts we have, dissolves out in the field.

The 'developmental' and the 'repressive' aspects customarily come under different agencies which in practice find themselves coming quickly at odds.[12] Regardless of the degree of centralization of command, the 'population-centric' (in COIN jargon) element yields to the 'enemy-centric' emphasis to the point of eclipse or until the costliness of the endeavor becomes apparent. This realization of unacceptable costs evidently takes as long to be felt in policy circles in democracies as in non-democracies.[13] In response to the Phase IV fizzling of the 2003 Iraq invasion counterinsurgency doctrine was hastily refurbished. Counterinsurgent capability did not stir recent interventions abroad; rather, the summoning of COIN did enable prolonging of military engagements in Iraq (until 2011), Afghanistan and elsewhere.

One cannot fault the US military for alleged neglect of counterinsurgent expertise if scholars such as Laqueur concluded that, given the end of decolonization, insurgencies, insofar as they existentially threatened states, were a thing of the past.[14] If the USA slighted counterinsurgency prowess it was because of a prudent desire to avoid plunging into another Vietnam inferno that also wreaked havoc inside the military services and across the domestic scene.[15] If a counterinsurgent capability were believed to exist, military chiefs could be vulnerable to the pressure of civilian militarists in government to apply it in unwise expeditions. The decline of counterinsurgency lore nonetheless was highly exaggerated, as the Manual itself attests.

Fishel highlights the robust lineage from the 1981 *Military Operations in Low Intensity Conflict Army Manual* (FM 100–20) through the Small Wars Research Operations Directorate (SWORD) model to the joint doctrine for Military Operations Other Than War (JP-3-07) in the 1990s.[16] An Army/Air Force Center for Low Intensity Conflict was sited at Langley Air Force base in 1986 at the same time as the Reagan administration created a post for Assistant Secretary of Defense for Special Operations and Low Intensity Conflict. Indeed, El Salvador in the 1980s was viewed by counterinsurgency proponents as an 'ideal testing ground,' although that conflict did not resolve quite as the Reagan and Bush I administrations wished.[17] Ongoing 'drug wars,' preceding 9/11, incorporated key ingredients from COIN programs although arguably in Columbia, Peru and Afghanistan these often roughshod measures 'served primarily to increase the guerrilla's legitimacy among the population involved.'[18]

Counterinsurgency has been reinterpreted over the last few decades as an unacknowledged triumph so that this upbeat recasting has acquired the status of standard history.[19] Even a scholar who is very critical of the *Manual* concedes that reputed counterinsurgency skills were applied 'too late in the Vietnam debacle.'[20] The conventional account today is that US/GVN forces, after a grisly trial-and-error process, vanquished the South Vietnam's insurgency. Only after the USA withdrew did regular North Vietnamese forces overrun South Vietnam: ergo, counterinsurgency prevailed. The books treated below are regarded in American IR studies as a reliable body of work attesting to this 'ironic' experience. So supporters contend that counterinsurgency, given enough 'learning and adopting' to local milieus, can suppress all armed opposition, if properly applied. 'With the right mindset and with a broader, deeper knowledge of lessons from previous successes,' a military scholar concludes, 'the war against the flea can be won.'[21] This lesson, boosted in credibility by this series of related revisionist works, and resurrected by the *Manual* during a post-invasion crisis over Iraq strategy, requires much more scrutiny than it is getting.

The *Manual* is a stirring brief for deploying a dynamic 'learning organization' that curiously is forbidden to learn or even to entertain certain lessons. Does a tactical concern, for example, about the 'information starvation' that mechanized outfits suffer in the field ever extend to reassessing the geopolitical purposes those forces are dispatched to serve in the first place?[22] The drawbacks of using mechanized forces against guerrillas, in any case, have been on record since the French defeat in Indochina.[23] The credo of the *Manual*, regardless of the dismaying record, is its invocation of Galula's adage that 'if the individual member of the organization were of the same mind, if every organization worked to a standard pattern, the problem would be solved.'[24]

The predominant characteristic of the *Manual*'s narrative is its 'mission fixation,' which entails axiomatic beliefs—rooted in French doctrine and echoed in British works[25]—that the insurgents lack merit, a passive population is unconnected to insurgents except by intimidation and that the extant power structure must be preserved.[26] A particular leader may be ditched for the sake of expedience but replacements naturally must align with the interests of the intervening power. Managerial fixation entails utmost identification by analysts with the goals set by state managers, which cannot help but impose analytical blind spots. A 'mafia rivalry' model of insurgency—greed, not grievance—arises as the default depiction of conflict because it recasts complex relationships into a stripped-down framework of asymmetrically armed and equally extortionate gangs. Even more so than Galula, Roger Trinquier's blunt Algerian lessons align with this reductive mindset.[27] In this restricted conceptual light, an intervening power is never a counter-revolutionary or invading force; rather, it is a neutral arbiter quelling unjustified civil conflict.[28]

So it is no social scientific revelation that 'groups whose attacks on civilians targets outnumber military targets' are less likely to achieve their goals, since they alienate potential mass support through which success otherwise might be achieved.[29] The trouble is that not all or even most designated terrorists behave in so self-sabotaging a manner. Bernard Fall observed that a 'guerrilla force must eventually build up a working administrative structure, maintain or provide schooling, and a modicum of economic life (i.e. 'construct' rather than simply destroy) within its area of operations if it wants to survive and succeed in the long run'— and cited China, Algeria and Vietnam as stellar examples.[30] Questions of justice and equity are dispensable issues for analysts who prefer to treat actors as utility maximizers (with those same analysts assigning and measuring pertinent utilities).[31] In this cramped analytical zone, greed is good because it renders opponents open to *divisa et impera* deals and makes them rational by dint of being acquisitive.[32] Material goods are all that are at stake.

COIN accordingly offers a civic action dimension that requires 'nation-building,' even if in a bottom-up 'localized' form.[33] A concomitant COIN presupposition is that the intervening counterinsurgent possesses sufficient power and will to reform local rulers so as to shore up legitimacy.[34] The reason routinely given for the misfires in Southeast Asia is that the Marines (and/or the CIA or Army Special Forces) earlier had amassed an impressive stock of fine-grained wisdom but that this vital information was inexplicably mislaid or ignored.[35] A contemporary admirer quotes the 1940 Marine Corps *Small Wars Manual* admonition that 'in small wars, tolerance, sympathy, and kindness should be the keynote to our relationship with the mass of the population.'[36] Surely worth recalling, of course, but the Marine Corps, despite the use of 'combined action platoons' in village settings, has never been renowned for promulgating these traits.[37]

The core assumption of COIN is that violent methods, when unslung, must succeed regardless of local conditions, regardless of overarching superpower interests and regardless of meddlesome domestic elites with goals of their own. A host government pursuing selfish ends need not negate the interests of the intervening counterinsurgent though it does complicate and undermine an ongoing counterinsurgency enterprise.[38] Evaluation depends on what the intervening counterinsurgent power really seeks to accomplish. The third-party counterinsurgent is usually averse to a two-front war, that is, unwilling to reform a recalcitrant host government, though pressures occasionally may be exerted at the margins.[39] For all the Manual's advocated attentiveness to local sensitivities, it is concerned above all with the application of power with the most, if not the best, intelligence available.

The Manual's authors believe that the populace won't be incensed about erroneous local fatalities if the populace is handled with a firm and friendly hand. The Manual states that the task of the insurgents 'is to break the ties between the people and the government,' as if such ruptures can occur only as a result of terrorist coercion.[40] The insurgents are depicted as attracting, and themselves becoming, criminal elements, even if there often are obvious social limits to the extent they can do so.[41] Grievance and greed nonetheless can mix with and spur one other. Yet it takes only one greedy party to make war on aggrieved others, and greed, when present, does not supersede deeper issues driving a conflict.[42] An insurgency as a whole can be greater than the sum of its faulty parts. In Indonesia over 1945–1946, as British forces aided restoration of Dutch rule[43] many of the more organized and politicized pemuda militias made common cause with the underworld of large cities such as Jakarta to draw on the expertise of men experienced in violence. The bersiap amounted to social revolution in some areas—in north and east Sumatra the old aristocracies came under bloody attack—but in Java much of the republican leadership fought shy of its implications; here the social revolution remained a feral population, without program or direction. In many places it simply meant a struggle for scarce resources or settling of old scores. 'The Indonesia revolution,' admitted the Islamicist leader Abe Hanifah, 'was not totally pure.'

Encountering fierce nationalist resistance, the British in November 1945 bombarded and devastated Surabaya city.[44] The history of governments hiring criminals to do their dirty work, where they do not already engage in widespread criminality themselves, is quite extensive.[45] Earlier, surveying El Salvador, a military analyst finds that the US resource boost to 'counterinsurgency capacity during the 1960s created a robust system of repression controlled by oligarchs and conservative military officers who thwarted the political reforms that might have prevented the insurgency in the first place.'[46] The *Manual* excludes ruthless expedience, incompetence and willful negligence on the part of local authorities as factors in the genesis, and/or fanning, of an insurgency, which is a rather unscientific set of omissions. In this vein, a recent RAND study is determined to view cases such as El Salvador—'regimes incapable of governing'—as welcome opportunities for 'state capacity building,' rather than as a spur to examine whether to support such regimes at all.[47]

Vietnam as 'Ironic Victory'

The revisionists' case hinges on an exquisitely 'ironic' notion that counterinsurgency triumphed at the very moment American withdrawal began. The upshot is that military strategy made good sense. The bedrock assumption is that there was a way to win the Vietnam War without decimating the local populace, rending US society or expanding the conflict into China. Moyar's upbeat saga of the Phoenix program, devised to destroy the NLF infrastructure, is representative and instructive.[48] Moyar suggests that mass murder can be 'an effective counter-insurgency tool' and that Diem's Strategic Hamlet program was a sound scheme, though he admits that the villages 'were almost all on the Viet Cong's side' in what started out as an 80% rural population.[49] The populace readily forgives authorities for killing the wrong people if authorities demonstrably meant well.[50] Moyar's argument uncannily reincarnates in all its particulars Leon Goure's 1965 RAND works on Vietnam, a jumble of optimistic wishful thinking, gratefully hailed at the time by McNamara, Walt Rostow, McGeorge Bundy and other seekers of a swift military solution.[51]

Torture was used but 'almost always against hard-core Communist cadres and soldiers rather than civilians of uncertain loyalties.'[52] The insurgents mingled with the population, which Moyar regards as a violation of the Geneva Convention.[53] The Phoenix program merely aimed to attain a 'crossover point' where NLF casualties exceed ability to replenish their ranks. During Nixon's first two and a half years the State Department reports that Phoenix eliminated or abducted 35,708 Vietnamese. The GVN claimed 41,000 were killed. Former Phoenix agents and associates later testified that orders were given to kill South Vietnamese Army and even US personnel who were deemed security risks.[54] Phoenix deployed CIA-trained assassination squads and counter-terror teams called provincial reconnaissance units (PRU). 'In practice,' Sheehan notes, 'the PRUs anticipated resistance in disputed areas and shot first.'[55] If you weren't an NLF sympathizer beforehand you became one afterward, providing you survived the initial encounter with authorities.

If brute force is prescribed, as Trinquier openly did in the lost cause of Algeria, there are indeed seemingly successful cases such as Hitler's vastly punitive policies in Western Europe—though they were markedly less successful in the Balkans and Russia.[56] Even some members of Hitler's staff viewed these harsh and expensive policies—anti-guerrilla operations require force ratios of 15–20 to one—as counterproductive.[57] Nonetheless, unchecked repression exerts an irresistible appeal inside any military organization under fire. Lyell, among many others, accordingly argues in line with the Manual that democracies are far better served by 'relative restraint' insofar as they avoid creating more insurgents and lower-key supporters than they eliminate.[58]

The 'crime of Phoenix,' Blaufarb concludes, was 'ineffectiveness, indiscriminateness, and, in some areas at least, the violation of the local norms to the extent that it appeared to the villagers to be a threat to them in the peaceful performance of their daily business.'[59] This verdict suggests that Americans 'erred in not appreciating the extent to which the pathology of Vietnamese society would distort an apparently sound concept.' The GVN was reckless in carrying out the program. Moyar assures readers that in the 'overwhelming majority of cases the people whom allied forces picked off were found with deadly weapons or incriminating documents in their possession.'[60] So the 385 thousand dead targets must have been mostly armed. Yet the 9th Infantry Division in the Mekong Delta during pacification sweeps over the first half of 1969 reported an 'official body count of 11,000 with only 748 captured weapons.'[61] Still, the COIN system revisionists claim worked in Vietnam was a panoply of primarily coercive techniques; it was not COIN in the refined form that the *Manual* endorses.

Military and Intellectual Pacifiers

In 1967 the NLF shifted strategy, avoiding US or GVN patrols instead of ambushing them at every chance. Government intelligence reported that the NLF decided not to fight 'pacification efforts. Rather, the guerrillas gathered intelligence and acted as guides and reinforcements for the main forces.'[62] By 1969, after Tet and the Mini-Tets, the CIA concluded that the North shunned major engagements in order instead to glut the GVN government with spies so that Thieu's regime would crumble from within.[63] Post-war accounts are rife with Americans discovering trusted South Vietnamese aides were NLF agents. 'There is probably not one government army unit, camp, public agency, or even ministry without its share of Viet-Cong informants,' a Swedish correspondent judged.[64] Not even Moyar imagines that friendly Iraqi or Afghan zones were less riddled with informers and double agents, not to mention 'green on blue' attacks.[65] In 2004 the first US-trained Iraqi battalion declined to fight in Fallujah, and reports do not indicate anything changed before the USA pulled (mostly) out.[66]

Moyar avers that villagers moved to whichever side suited their immediate safety.[67] Villagers, who would have to be suicidal to openly contest the government narrative, told officials that they deplored the VC for bringing ruin upon them through indiscriminate shelling. Moyar points to Vietnamese who enlisted to fight the NLF, though most youths were conscripted.[68] In a South Vietnam of 18 million people, 1.1 million were drafted into the military and 4 million more posted in local security units often riddled with NLF sympathizers.[69]

Zalin Grant based his kindred revisionist argument on the reckonings of a South Vietnamese master spy whose plan to defeat the communists 'was perverted by the CIA.' Grant argues that certain players he endorses had a good handle on how to neutralize the enemy through a deft blend of political action and aid programs. Just as big strides were being made, however, they were thwarted by 'corruption in Saigon and by big bang, big-bucks conventional-warfare mongers like [General] William Westmoreland.'[70] So then, if only 'we' disposed of the unpopular regime 'we' were defending and the incompetent US military high command who were defending it, 'we' would have won.

Lewis Sorley argues that 'accelerated pacification' conducted from November 1968 onward triumphed.[71] Sorley estimates 465,000 South Vietnamese civilians were killed with most being 'assassinated by Viet

Cong terrorists or felled by the enemy's indiscriminate shelling and rocketing of cities'—a level of firepower improbably equal to American/GVN levels.[72] Sorley complains that Westmoreland's strategy emphasized attrition of the North Vietnamese Army in a 'war of the big battalions.' Westmoreland's successor General Creighton Abrams, on the other hand, 'wisely emphasized not the destruction of enemy forces *per se* but protection of the South Vietnamese population by controlling key areas—a unified "one war" strategy,' which would have saved the day, at least until the next.[73] Yet Abrams, according to declassified documents, judged in December 1968 even 'after modernization of GVN forces [that] Saigon would not be able to contain indigenous VCI forces.'[74] As it evolved, Abrams' 'clear and hold' strategy differed little from Westmoreland, Elliot observes, and 'pacification was achieved mainly through depopulation through firepower.'[75]

Sorley undercuts his own argument severely by drawing attention to the potent April 1968 Mini-Tet, the August/September 'Third offensive,' and subsequent NLF-spurred actions, who appear unusually aggressive for an almost extinct organization. This startling energy accords with a CIA analyst who, after Tet, 'noted that although the enemy suffered heavy losses, their forces appeared to be regrouping and could mount further large-scale action in a matter of weeks.'[76] RAND interviews with captured NLF members after Tet also disclosed an unshaken belief in the insurgency and in ultimate victory.[77]

Moyar asserts that Americans, via Land-to-the-Tiller reforms, won over Vietnamese villagers who bore no hard feelings toward American and GVN forces for previous rough treatment. The 'impressionable villagers' were 'attracted by military presence and strength,' Moyar writes, echoing Galula's denigrative perception of Algerian villagers. Hence, the 'use of highly destructive weaponry in the villages' resulted in a 'weakening of communists and an increase of support for Americans.'[78] The Vietnamese peasant was depicted as an apolitical and childish being, but one who luckily was just rational enough to be amenable to the analyst's tools of persuasion. In El Salvador later, a more realistic analyst lamented that 'civic actions emphasising pep talks and charity assumes that the local population is either ignorant of political issues or that its loyalty can somehow be purchased.'[79]

In Malaya British officials presumed that ethnic Chinese 'support which [the communists] get is almost wholly through intimidation and cannot by any stretch of the imagination be described as "popular,"' and furthermore opined that the 'Chinese are accustomed to acquiesce under pressure.'[80] These opinions seem especially obtuse given that Chinese Malayan Communists comprised the strongest element in the anti-Japanese WWII campaign and that British officers conducting counterinsurgency learned much of what they knew serving alongside some of those same guerrillas.[81] Lord Mountbatten personally decorated a future Malayan communist guerrilla leader.[82] One can find reports with identical misestimates filed wherever insurgencies occur.[83] Malayan pacification eventually absorbed half the public budget, police state measures, mass relocations, 'seven British infantry battalions, eight Gurkha battalions, three "colonial" battalions and the Malayan Scouts, two Royal Armoured Corps regiments, ten RAF squadrons, two Royal Australian Air Force squadrons, and a small naval contingent'—some unacknowledged luck and, finally, a promise to withdraw.[84] The notion 'that "winning hearts and minds" was a carefully prepared strategy is a myth,' Bayly and Harper note.[85]

The classic manual was written by Sir Robert Thompson—an ex-Chindit, Chinese affair officer and later secretary of defense in Malaya—only after the Emergency was ended. At the time the strategy was 'an agglomeration of trifles,' and it proceeded mainly by trial and error. Many of the aftercare measures, as they were termed, arrived in fits and starts sometime after the worst effects of resettlement—the uprootings, banishments, loss of income, exposure to corruption and exploitation—had already been experienced by the rural Chinese.

Moyar quotes Sir Robert Thompson issuing his verdict about Vietnam in 1972 that 'the VC side of it is over. The people have rejected the VC.'[86] Other creditable sources, however, found that the VC 'remained strong in the villages despite accelerated pacification,' that the Hamlet Evaluation System number crunchers 'conflate control and loyalty' and rued an institutionalized 'inability to see the VC as a vital, organic part of rural society.'[87] In Malaya—widely regarded as the ideal counterinsurgent success story—General Gerald Templer publicly counseled winning 'hearts and minds' even as he inflicted harsh collective punishments.[88] Contradictions of this kind are plentiful, given the nature of the enterprise, because acquiescence, not consent, is what really is sought. John Paul Vann is quoted by Moyar as declaring from inside a ferocious police state that 95% of South Vietnamese prefer Thieu. In 1969 Vann's close friend Daniel Ellsberg put pro-GVN support as closer to 20%.[89] That same year a dissident group of RAND researchers published a remarkable letter in the *New York Times* urging the USA to withdraw from Vietnam.[90]

Summers' Discontent, Colby's Complaint

Harry Summers is a noted revisionist whose *On Strategy* argued that US leaders were misled gravely by a 'new model of Communist revolutionary war.' The mischievous work of wrongheaded experts such as the aforementioned Sir Robert Thompson 'channeled our attentions toward the internal affairs of the South Vietnamese government rather than toward the external threat.' Americans concentrated on guerrillas, a wasteful diversion. Summers, who concedes the First Indochina War (not the Second) 'was a revolutionary war,' regrets that 'expending military resources on inconclusive military and social operations' exhausted the 'patience of the American people.' The American military could have continued fighting, presumably to the present day, if only objectives had been clear. Yet the supreme US objective clearly was to sustain Thieu's regime. Revolutionary war theory never asserted that guerrillas 'achieve decisive results on their own,' although Summers fails to mention American reckoning that the NLF would have overthrown the Southern regime if the USA stayed out.[91] Yet the more the USA took control of the war the greater was the ability of Hanoi to portray the USA as neocolonialists and the GVN as a puppet regime. The dilemma was inescapable.

The 'ultimate irony,' former CIA Director William Colby echoes, 'was that the people's war launched in 1959 had been defeated, but the soldiers' war, which the United States had insisted on fighting during the 1960s with massive military forces, was finally won by the enemy.'[92] The accelerated pacification campaign was a 'great success' and 'the basic objective of increasing the population living in security from the enemy was indeed achieved.' Since 1968 the Phoenix program 'captured 29,978 communist 'leaders' in the Viet Cong infrastructure, 17,717 more had taken advantage of the amnesty program, and 20,587 had been reported killed, 'mostly in combat situations.' If there were thirty thousand leaders, then how many followers existed?, is a very ticklish question that went adamantly unasked. Precisely '87.6% of those killed were killed by regular or paramilitary forces, and only 1.4% by police or irregular forces.'[93] Another unasked question is how can a counterinsurgency apparatus kill so many people under the sober auspices of civil/police authority? The PRU and local militia fought 'superbly,' Colby asserts, although he conceded that they also were guilty of numerous atrocities.[94]

Thieu set up a 'Central Pacification and Development Council,' but 'Americans had no apologies for putting huge pressure on officials to see and do things our way.'[95] Colby oversaw special centers across South Vietnam where serious abuses were rampant.[96] CORDS reported that from January 1968 to May 1971, 20,857 insurgents were killed. The GVN notched 40,994 assassinations from August 1968 to July 1971. According to CORDS, Phoenix accounted for 12% of enemy losses. Phoenix set a 1969 target of eliminating 1800 VC per month, which invited a lot of room for error. The USA also funded a national identity registration project for Vietnamese age 15 and above.[97] A state-of-the-art computer tabulated some 15 million suspects. Neither Vietnam nor Northern Ireland accord with the notion that democracies such as the USA or UK are especially constrained when gathering information.[98] US/GVN intelligence services pooled fallible data with misbegotten data from informers and prisoners to guide official activity in extinguishing threats.[99] Rural folk 'showed little or no inclination to join the insurgents.'[100] One might wonder then why authorities wasted resources on extravagant ID tracking systems. Colby, like Sorley, strays revealingly from the official narrative when acknowledging in 1968 'the Communists mounted another surge of attacks during the coming months to try to pick up the momentum the initial Tet attack had lost.'[101]

Vietnam was a defeat of 'the entire learning process we went through there,' Colby regrets. 'After years of trial and much error, we had finally learned how to meld our military, political and economic efforts in support of a single strategy and of a unified mechanism for its execution.'[102] This 'learning process' is what the *Counterinsurgency Manual* champions. For a clinching anecdote Colby recalls his stunt in 1969 driving columnist Stewart Alsop down a former VC-controlled road in complete safety. General Douglas Kinnard offers a revealingly different angle on this stage-managed trip.[103] A former Army colonel, weighing up the propaganda dimension, makes all due allowance for the Phoenix Program in improving observable civilian behavior. Nonetheless, 'the corruption, the heavy-handed treatment of the civilians, the torture and imprisoning of innocent persons, and the use of the [Phoenix] program to disguise political repression of non-communists outside of the Thieu government doubtlessly destroyed much of the good will created by the pacification effort.'[104] As the pacification machine threshed ahead its achievements rolled up right behind it, like a mower bag catching blades of cut grass.

'Peasants were attached to private property'—which the Saigon regime did not provide much of, except under duress—and so these rustic materialists had no truck with 'abstract ideas like nationalism and communism.' Colby's refrain that villagers side with whomever had the upper hand is *de rigueur* for purveyors of McNamara era systems analysis. Rational choice, derived from a context-bound image of the way minds work, is reasonable enough when applied with requisite humility, but formal frameworks inevitably generate irrationality of their own when practitioners are insensitive to, or plain ignorant of, context-dependence. The *homo economicus* assumption underlying rational choice has not proved very helpful in sussing out the nature, aims and resilience of sustained insurgencies. Rationalist reward–punish models misunderstand the history, motives and strategies of shabby opponents.[105]

A Vietnam era critic discerned that rationalist analysts 'were unable to recognize that a government that was totally dependent on a foreign power is inherently lacking in legitimacy' and so they resort to 'a systematic distortion of the facts.' Technocratic policy legionnaires were 'more concerned with order than with participation, more with techniques of governing than with the consent of the governed, more with stability than with change.' People became the 'mere objects of policy.'[106] When optimism about COIN doctrine was resurrected so too were these attendant attitudes.[107] Rick's positive assessment in Iraq of a switch to counterinsurgency techniques after 2005 is belied by the consistent testimony of his cited soldiers saying they no longer blow away every imaginable threat.[108] That's surely a gain but not a transformative change. In 2006 a RAND report actually recommended Phoenix as a model for implementation in Iraq and positively cited Moyar's account of Phoenix in Vietnam.[109]

Reasons Why

A 'can-do' spirit has its place in the military but in scholarship and intelligence analysis it is a sure source of seductive distortions.[110] The case for counterinsurgency in Vietnam relies on highly suspect data such as the *Hamlet Evaluation Survey* conducted over 1970–1971.[111] That evaluations rely on agencies catering to counterinsurgency objectives, and information extracted under duress, is curtly acknowledged and never mentioned again. The Hamlet Evaluation System rated letters A, B and C as 'secure,' while D and 'E were 'contested.' V was 'enemy controlled.' Who prefers the lattermost ranking when instant bombardment awaits? The incentive structure was clear; the way local agents respond to incentives was not. When the NLF 'lost' a village due to pacification it maintained a foothold nearby, tenaciously working for its chance for revival, which for most eventually came.[112] What authorities got was 'surface control of a seemingly passive population,' which was good enough for reports.[113]

A buttressing argument revived by implacable revisionists is that a 'Land to the Tiller' program was successful. The premise of the strategic hamlets 'was that the peasants wanted to resist communist infiltration but were powerless to do so,' a European correspondent noted. 'Unquestionably, many peasant wanted security from the Vietcong because they knew that the moment they fell into the hands or submitted, the government would strike back.'[114] The populace had no reason to trust a government so consistently careless with their lives and livelihoods. The 'Tiller' story ignored three facts: first, great swathes of South Vietnam were already under NLF control; second, the NLF land had been redistributed; and thirdly, the Thieu reforms were not redistributively aimed to benefit the poor but rather loyal cronies. In the 1950s 80% of peasants in the Mekong Delta were tenants; 1% owned 44% of the land. The first land 'reforms' of the Diem government restored to landlords the properties parceled out by the Viet Minh before the 1956 partition.[115] The 'Tiller' program featured a Stolypin-like emphasis on creating a class of 'middle' peasants. However, the distribution of uncultivated land in insecure areas, littered with unexploded ordnance and trigger-happy patrols, required capital if the land was to be restored to use, for which only usurious private loans were available.[116] This exploitative situation invited a reconcentration of control of property.

Under accelerated pacification cadres 'holed up in briar patches, recuperating and waiting for better times,' which came in 1971 and again in the Spring offensive of 1972. Tax revenues for the NLF fell in 1969 and 1970 but then rose again.[117] NVA forces across the DMZ were heavily dependent on NLF guidance, and guerrilla forces critically tied down several ARVN divisions in the officially 'pacified' Mekong Delta in Spring 1975.[118] In pacified areas a modus vivendi often obtained where villages escaped punitive action while GVN agents wielded apparent daytime authority. One had to 'question if so many enemy personnel had rallied [defected to the Southern regime] or been eliminated, how could the [Viet Cong] continue to pose a permanent threat to the pacification effort,' a former ARVN General, who deplored a 'live and let live' attitude in rural areas, asked afterward.[119] 'Indeed if statistics were useful, they strongly indicated the enemy's capability to recruit and replace surpassed everything we usually attributed to him.'

The reports pacification enthusiasts relied upon were more equivocal than advertised. Moyar concedes flaws in the HES system while insisting nevertheless that it 'did track a positive trend.'[120] Elliot instead found that the Mekong Delta was 'strongly pro-VC' in 1969–1970, long after the Tet offensive supposedly killed off most guerrillas, not to mention subsequent ferocious Phoenix forays and 9th Infantry division sweeps. Elliot noted that few locals 'defected from the war effort.'[121] Studies by Bergerud, Trullinger, Pace and Werner and Hunt likewise attest that the districts they studied remained pro-NLF throughout the war.[122] The NLF was undeniably hit hard during and after Tet.[123] CORDS director Robert Komer admitted that, even if granted the best case regarding NLF losses, 'we were never able to translate this into positive and active rural support for the government of Vietnam.'[124] What then was the point?

High on the list of boasted counterinsurgent achievements are the local Territorial Forces, the Regional Forces/Popular Forces (RF/PF), called ruff-puffs, who comprised half of South Vietnam armed personnel. A South Vietnamese general recalls that one of his 'constant headaches came from requests for reinforcements from field commanders who always asked for more and never seemed to be happy to settle for less.' This was perhaps another telling indication of the RF and PF ineffectiveness.[125]

I got the impression that pacification was like a leaking tank. No matter how much manpower you put in it, it never seemed to be enough for the task. ARVN was spread thin in its attempt to fill in the void where territorial forces were incapable of maintaining security. The enemy was given the chance to infiltrate local activities because many areas were left undefended for lack of forces … In the Mekong Delta the VCI was successful in transforming several RF and PF soldiers into turncoats. As for GVN cadres, 'the abuse of power and for personal benefit and the pursuit of worldly pleasures were widespread.'

Other ARVN generals affirmed that 'those enemy units which had been destroyed were surfacing again. Apparently they had been regrouped, refitted, and reorganized in base areas with manpower and equipment from North Vietnam. The maintenance of area security thus became a frustrating task, for no matter how dense our outpost system or how well motivate our troops were, the enemy could always find loopholes to penetrate and weaknesses to exploit. Ups and downs in village security were an inevitable reality we always had to face...'[126]

What exactly changed such that revisionists detected the attitudes of villagers becoming favorable toward US/GVN forces? The argument essentially is that, after many fits and starts, and once property was handed over, peasants transformed into contented market-oriented individualists. Yet the few land reform specialists who operated independently of Southern authorities observed instead 'a class-oriented program' at work and deduced that 'no amount of wishful or ideological thinking could turn Diem, Kah, Ky or Thieu into champions of the laboring poor.'[127] The hope inside the Palace in Saigon was that 1.5 hectares sufficed to create a loyal 'middle' peasant out of an aggrieved tenant. Yet the evidence indicates that middle peasants actually were more likely to provide NLF recruits since they had the surplus resources, time and ability to participate.[128]

Two ARVN generals confess that 'village elections were only valid to the extent that they provided rural areas with a coating of democratic veneer, other than that they often served no useful purpose. as far as the people were concerned. That village officials were compelled to undergo training and indoctrination at Vung Tau often caused concern and even suspicion among some of our people about the democratic system.'[129] General William DePuy lamented that it 'is difficult for this democracy of ours to deal with the political dimensions of insurgency,' the 'arbitrary and often undemocratic controls required' do not 'go down well back here at home.'[130] Algerian war strategist Trinquier advocated the logical next step that French society be realigned to fit the needs of the counterinsurgency—a martial variation on Brecht's sardonic advice that a displeased government ought to dissolve the people and elect another.[131]

In 1971 the GVN was in 'firm control' of hamlet security, claiming that 85.13 percent of hamlets were secure. 'These results were obtained at a moment when VCI activities were at their lowest level and when Communist main and local forces were avoiding engagement in preparation for their next big push,' an ARVN ranking officer explained. 'The security attained was not a guarantee that it would be immune to enemy spoiling actions and that the trend was irreversible. Pacification setbacks could occur anytime the enemy chose to strike.[132] Underlying grievances were never ever addressed. Grievances get dismissive treatment in the *Manual* as 'perceived injustices.'[133] While grievances don't matter, people doing something about them do attract attention. A clinical census-taking attitude meant that opinions were taken at face value. Long points out that for people living under a cruel authoritarian regime, the questions 'Do you believe the people should be masters?' and 'Do you believe in democracy?' were understood as more resonant of the NLF than of Saigon, but affirmative answers were coded to endorse the latter.

The *Pentagon Papers* acknowledged the post-Tet Systems Analysis finding that while 'we have raised the price to NVN of aggression and support of the VC, it shows no lack of capability or will to match each new US escalation. Our strategy of attrition has not worked.'[134] In sum: 'Despite a massive influx of 500 thousand US troops, 1.2 million tons a bombs a year, 400 thousand attack sorties per years, 200 thousand enemy KIA in 3 years, 20,000 US KIA, etc. our control of the countryside and defense of the urban areas is essentially at pre-August 1965 levels. We have achieved stalemate at a high commitment. A new strategy must be sought.'

After Tet

Revisionists argue that Tet was a military victory but a political defeat, which is a misleading distinction in the schema of total war. 'From the first the Viet Minh knew this was a political war fought for political objectives,' Fall noted. 'Its troops, unlike the South Vietnamese or the Americans, are specifically geared toward that task' and intervening powers 'have nothing on our side to counter that kind of theory of war.'[135] Insurgent forces often took heavy losses but experienced little wavering of local support.[136] The US high command during Tet conceded that insurgents regained control of the countryside as US and ARVN troops were diverted to defend cities—and admitted most cities were none too secure.[137] Statistics do not offset NLF losses during Tet against thousands of freed prisoners.[138] Generals Westmoreland and Earle Wheeler privately conceded that Tet was no victory.[139] In ensuing actions such as 'Mini-Tet' in April,' Willbanks writes, 'Communist forces had clearly demonstrated that they had not been destroyed during the earlier Tet fighting.'

The *Manual* claims that by 1970 over 90% of rural South Vietnamese resided in 'relatively secure villages.'[140] Hunt, however, found 'US/

GVN sweeps and mass killings seem to have pushed fence-sitters over the edge' so that more young people were volunteering for the NLF. Blaufarb rues 'violation of the local norms to the extent that it appeared to the villagers to be a threat to them in the peaceful performance of their daily business.' American analysts 'erred in not appreciating the extent to which the pathology of Vietnamese society would distort an apparently sound concept.'[141] It was precisely this 'pathology' that the US/GVN troops defended. The rationalist depiction of loyalty for the sake of gain cannot explain why the NLF was far more successful than the GVN, despite incurring immense punishment. If strict rational criteria informed the NLF's operating code, the Southern insurgency would easily have been stamped out.[142]

A practical rule of thumb in counterinsurgency is that carrot and stick, at the first experience of resistance, becomes mostly stick.[143] Over 1970–1972 government agencies split in their appraisals of pacification, depending on whether they understood the Vietnamese concept of protracted war.[144] In contrast to 'conventional warrior mentality,' a central committee member attests that for the NLF and NVA, 'every military clash, every demonstration, every propaganda appeal was seen as a part of an intelligible whole: each had consequences far beyond its immediate apparent result. It was a framework that allowed us to view battle as a psychological event and to undertake negotiations in order to strengthen the military posture. The Americans seemed never to appreciate fully this strategic perspective... It was after all a traditional Vietnamese approach to warfare, a technique refined over centuries of confrontation with invaders more powerful than ourselves.' [145]

The celebrated gains in control of the South Vietnamese countryside after November 1968 were far more tenuous than authorities allowed.[146] MACV estimated that VC strength fell from 189 to 120 thousand in 3 years after Tet. The consequence was that the VC adapted its tactics so that small-unit actions increased from 1374 in 1968 to 2400 by 1972.[147] This may be a better situation than brigade-strength actions but hardly augured victory. Davidson cites a drop-off in attacks on US/GVN forces from 32,362 in 1968 to 27,790 in 1969 and then 23,760 in 1970 as proof of declining resistance. A mere 23,760 attacks had become something to cheer about.[148] According to the office of the Assistant Secretary of Defense, in 1972, 4405 people were assassinated as insurgents abducted 13,119.[149] This assassination figure was higher than in 1971, but lower than in 1968, 1969 and 1970; not so, abductions.

Was it safe for uniformed personnel to wander around unarmed?[150] Absolutely not.

'Pacification in the broadest sense—for which the reform of the GVN and PVANF [was needed]—would never occur, but its narrow victory… was a resounding success.' Another General judged that while 'they changed at the village level, at upper levels they did not, and short of a respite of many years, could not change.'[151] A nation-state that cannot stand up to its own population, or retain the loyalty of a considerable majority, is inconceivable in the COIN universe. While the Manual expresses staunch faith in the support of populations in foreign climes where the USA intervenes, it is intensely suspicious of folks back home. Regarding Vietnam the *Manual* reverts to a stab-in-the-back motif; the enemy after Tet is portrayed as shifting 'from defeating US forces in Vietnam to weakening US will at home, and succeeded.'[152] Lyall uncritically takes this view as his baseline assumption regarding public attitudes, and their capacity to constrain elites in the conduct of warfare.[153]

THE HOME FRONT

It is worth asking what was really so successful about acclaimed successes. The 'Malayan emergency' outlasted national independence by 3 years, although the elites who obtained power were preferable to insurgents for Britain. During the Kenyan insurgency eleven thousand Kikuyu were killed (total deaths ran to six figures) against less than a hundred European deaths.[154] Of one and a half million Kikuyu the 'strategic hamlet' variant uprooted a million. A similar number of Chinese Malayans were forcibly relocated to 'New Villages.' Examples of coerced 'resettlement' (Angola, Mozambique, Rhodesia, Algeria, Burma, the Mizo hills in India) are legion. A glum French critic remarked that 'a more favorable ground for subversion could hardly be imagined.'[155] The armed insurgency was crushed but imprisoned leader Jomo Kenyatta was released to become an albeit conciliatory President of an independent nation in 1963.

Clinging to Algeria until 1962 required almost half a million French troops, most of the military budget, 18 thousand soldiers' lives and somewhere between 300 thousand to 1 million local deaths in an ordeal that engendered a coup attempt in France.[156] El Salvador's bloodshed subsided with a bargain in the early 1990s that local elites and US authorities resisted for a decade. In Northern Ireland, a ceasefire was agreed in 1994, faltered and renewed in 1996 (but for diehard splinters). Tallying Northern Ireland as a counterinsurgent victory would make sense if the IRA started the fray, which it did not. A movement for 'equal rights for British citizens' arose among Catholics in the 1960s, which was thwarted violently by police-backed sectarian mobs. The *Manual* mangles the sequence of events by portraying armed loyalists as 'arising in reaction' to the IRA. Once armed resistance gets under way the expeditious rule is to ignore everything except the isolated fact of insurgency. The *Manual* counsels that if a government cannot provide adequate protection, people themselves will organize militias to provide this service.'[157] That is exactly why the IRA revived, to protect the Catholic community from a sectarian police force and lethal loyalist militias. In 1969 the British Army arrived 'in aid of the civil power,' that is to say, in aid of a government whose misrule was the issue.

The peace process in Ulster, as in El Salvador, is a phenomenon the *Manual* writers could not have foreseen, desired or permitted.[158] The IRA was 'reactive, not remounting a war for reunification at first.'[159] The Catholic community subsisted in difficult straits in the six counties, eventually reacted, and in the course of doing so became the 'problem,' instead of the problem being the mini-state's flagrant discriminatory mechanisms. Given this distortion of the conflict, one cannot be heartened by the *Manual*'s bromide that 'the better learning organization usually wins.'[160] Learning is curved, or curbed, according to organizational needs and biases.

The revisionist view of concern here is a *faux* redemptive narrative that policy makers embrace in order to preserve coercive instruments. The archetypal predicament, according to such authorities, is the public's inability to endure losses during a counterinsurgency, not the inability of such an operation to withstand scrutiny that losses of life and treasure tend to bestir. What major power sets out to initiate a long war with the dangerous internal strains that such an enterprise risks? Is the protecting the host regime and local social structure worth it all?

Host regimes 'develop vested political and economic interests in sustaining a controllable conflict.'[161] 'A regime facing an armed insurgency is normally under less outside pressure for economic and political reform. It can justifiably demand more of its citizens and, conversely, postpone meeting their demands' as well as eviscerate civil liberties. The small groups that Collier identifies as predatory elements profiting from war are a critical problem in embattled nations. Hence, 'one approach is therefore to weaken these groups as rapidly as possible by reducing their profits.'[162] The advice is not meant to apply to superpowers or regional powers, though they are not immune to experiencing an 'asymmetry of interests' between those of elites and the national interest as non-elites may see it.[163] This 'small group takeover' thesis is well worth pondering inside the counterinsurgent state too but American IR analysts have never been eager to pry open their own black box of a state.

Conclusion

A rehabilitation of counterinsurgency has been under way since the end of the Vietnam War, rejigged for applicability to 'failed state' disarray. International relations scholars largely accept this rehabilitative narrative, retaining as it does coercive instruments that a superpower sees fit to use.[164] Whether deployed against Naxalites in India or against the 'unusually invertebrate insurgency' in Iraq, counterinsurgency has been an enabler of the firepower option under the guise of lesser force and an enabler too of extended occupations.[165] As COIN proponents note, an inherent ambiguity regarding how much force a 'hearts and minds' approach allows can slide swiftly toward the coercive end of the continuum.[166] If the 'line between global anti-terrorist action and counterinsurgency is growing blurred,' it has to do so since the latter is subordinate to the ambitions of the former.[167] COIN has its best chance to work if the insurgents cannot maintain growing support and if the intervening counterinsurgent does not mean to stay, but both often do.

The counterinsurgents' remedy is tinkering: 'Failure is ascribed to inadequate integration among the military advisory group, CIA, AID and the Embassy; or inapplicable or inadequate training of American personnel; or unpredictable funding of security assistance, for instance. The solutions prescribed are invariably programmatic while the promises upon which counterinsurgency doctrine are based remain inviolate.' Perhaps in a post-Cold War world governments that cannot act so as to retain popular support ought to be allowed to fall. Perhaps 'failed states' ought to be free of outside military intervention except where genocidal furies threaten.

The impression is widespread that Iraq's insurgency was avoidable if only George W. Bush's administration had made shrewder moves. Presumably Iraqis of all stripes would have sat still while the West reconfigured their society and resources. Given the stakes, the difference between hard-core enemy and 'accidental guerrilla' shrinks drastically.[168] The neoliberal regime imposed on Iraq—privatizing everything from public health to security—was itself a *casus belli*.[169] Obama's initial withdrawal plan to maintain tens of thousand troops in Iraq was viewed there as a permanent military presence, a counterindicator for counterinsurgency success. Nouri al-Maliki's government thwarted US intentions by insisting all uniformed troops depart. An indispensable aspect of successful counterinsurgency is a credible promise of withdrawal of foreign forces. American troops usually try (and sometimes fail) to set up permanent shop wherever they go, which begs questions regarding how COIN figures in American grand strategy.

Defence Secretary Robert Gates in 2009 optimistically stated that the USA had mastered counterinsurgency techniques. Like Gates' pronouncement, the *Manual* seems to have been more calculated for domestic consumption than for the US military, which displayed its flexibility when buying off the Sunni insurgency during the 'surge.' This flexibility implies that COIN was not really an operative doctrine. Sunnis during the Awakening joined with Americans 'against the nihilistic-Islamist terrorist Al Qaeda'—a heartening development except that there was no lethal Al Qaeda presence until after the invasion. Iraq soon became, in Petraeus's words, a 'competition among ethnic and sectarian communities for power and resources.' The rub is that this plight was not the cause but the result of the invasion, an unforeseen 'aftershock' that COIN was rolled out to quell. In Afghanistan the Obama 'surge' arguably appears, however, to have been set in motion more to justify the approaching pullout date than to accomplish COIN goals.[170]

Debates about COIN in IR journals tend to focus on the exact mix of coercion and consent that a 'hearts and minds' strategy can deploy and still retain the name of counterinsurgency.[171] A predictable thematic offshoot is the urging of a kinder regard for the merits of pure coercion.[172] Analysts instead would do well to look uninhibitedly at the wisdom of counterinsurgency doctrine and at the nature of their own state.[173] No procedure seems better geared to improving the bets the USA, or any other nation, decides to lay down in potential interventions than for researchers to turn around the analytical apparatus, 'reversing the gaze,' and apply it to the motives of the counterinsurgent too.

Addendum: Counterinsurgency Chic

Counterinsurgency never goes out of style, no matter how much its ardent fans bemoan it doing so, although the *styles* of counterinsurgency shift swiftly so as to sooth civilized sensibilities. The customary underlying COIN aims are (1) to gull the domestic public about the actual cruelties of counterinsurgency, (2) to bolster foreign allies no matter how indelibly corrupt they are and (3) to rub out supposedly small fry enemies abroad and, eventually, at home too. 'Bring the war home' is a silly slogan that the Weatherman faction promoted in the late sixties, silly because long dirty wars always come home anyway, as we witness in the steady erosion of US civil rights and breakneck militarization of police forces.[174] For policy elites in major powers there can be no such thing as a popular insurgency (unless those same elites sponsor it) so one must expect them to deploy carelessly calculated medleys of soft words and hard killers to stamp out designated nuisances.

Ever on tap is an ample supply of coldblooded functionaries eager to carry out the brutal and usually futile neoimperial task of shoving round pegs endlessly into square holes. No matter how often the dubious doctrines and cheery accounts of COIN are proved flat wrong, a new batch of steely gazed, semi-sober, task-oriented enablers arises to revive it whenever an anxious superpower puts out the call. Even if most counterinsurgencies do flop, punitive examples must be made of insolent insurgents. Noam Chomsky is correct that Vietnam, though a delirious defeat, served as a stern warning of the mighty price that disobedient actors abroad will pay for tangling with a leviathan.

The so-called COINdistas take it as an article of faith that the endangered population in any target country stands immaculately apart from 'bad insurgents,' who, as it usually happens, are family and neighbors of the same people the counterinsurgents profess to protect. Lt. Col. John Nagl, of *Eating Soup with a Knife* fame, obligatorily views appointed foes as all 'terrorists that leech off of disaffected indigenous populations for recruits and support for their extremist ideologies.'[175] The sneaky inscrutable populace, however, may back the insurgency, and even if they are not supporters at the start then clumsy COIN activities can transform them into rebels via routine rough treatment escalating all the extremely tempting way up to pure mayhem.

Authorities are well aware of the acute dilemma that arrogant and errant COIN actions only stoke local resistance, but they cannot restrain themselves from doing it anyway. As editor Hannah Gurman notes in her valuable collection *Hearts and Minds*, COIN is the thinly disguised descendant of earlier imperial ventures by cynical European powers and so prim American proponents cannot bring themselves to confess to anything like similar motives. In the Philippines (twice), Vietnam, Central America (many times), Iraq and Afghanistan, not to mention the frankly genocidal nineteenth century Indian Wars, the gruesome task—also dubbed pacification or irregular warfare or low intensity operations— was dutifully framed as liberating the proles from oppressive *Soprano*-like hoodlums, not imposing a new gang of thugs who serve American elites' interests, as poorly conceived as those interests may be.

Defense intellectuals, if that is quite the term for hired word-slingers, cling to the handy notion that moral qualms must not pollute the objective scientific enterprise of subjugating wayward populations. The phenomenon of the 'accidental guerilla,' of naive natives turning rebel after experiencing counterinsurgent abuses, which David Kilcullen lamented in his book of that title, is a by-product of bloody intervention, especially third-party intervention. Yet deciding not to meddle is virtually ruled out as a reasonable choice in official policy menus. So, in quagmire situations abroad, the COIN feedback loop gets stuck in reverse gear, which comes to be viewed by annoyed authorities as a form of progress. Why? Because generating more insurgents fuels the venerable self-serving argument that the remedy is higher doses of the same medicine. In *The Failure of Counterinsurgency* Ivan Eland of the Cato Institute denounces this slick syndrome as fiercely as do Gurman's group of left-liberal critics. So too does Colonel Gian Gentile, an Iraq combat veteran who (I am glad to learn) now teaches at West Point, in his short, sharp shock of a book *Wrong Turn*. These three dissenting volumes, which pretty much span the American ideological spectrum, converge on the need to bury COIN, not to 'improve' it.

Gurman's worthy collection is a 'response to the grand narrative of US counterinsurgency,' one nestled within cozy groupthink confines where the perpetrators agree to misunderstand or misstate facts to each other's satisfaction. Gurman's contributors offer a 'glimpse into the history of insurgency and counterinsurgency from "below," from the vantage points of ordinary people caught in the maelstrom of these conflicts.' So they attempt to 'detail the different segments of the population, their often complex and always evolving relationship to the "insurgency," and the impact of counterinsurgency campaigns on their communities and their lives.' Gurman also cannot help but observe that ongoing domestic espionage and surveillance efforts designed to separate American communities into desirable and undesirable elements is a local manifestation of COIN. The police today in Ferguson, Missouri, as some astounded veterans remarked, look better equipped than were many vulnerable soldiers patrolling Iraq and Afghanistan. One might lazily call this outcome 'ironic,' except that amping up repressive apparatuses at home is an entirely predictable part of coping with the fallout from pursuing expensive military expeditions abroad.

Karl Hack, examining the 'Malayan emergency' of 1948–1960, scrupulously defines 'people's history' as allowing voice for victims of insurgency as well as of COIN. Well and good—if only COIN advocates scrupulously counted both categories of victims too. Malaya, Hack argues, is misread as a stirring counterinsurgency success, as also is the Philippines Huk rebellion in the 1950s (though few enthusiasts probe too deeply into the Philippines horrors circa 1900). Authorities, you see, don't just want to crush foes, they want to be applauded for doing so in an angelically legitimate manner. Give our canny leaders credit for caring enough to lie about what they do. What happened in Malaya was not a touchy-feely 'hearts and minds' campaign, but lawless brutality and mass deportation conducted largely to serve rapacious British plantation and mining interests. The roots lay in post-war repression of labor as well as nationalist aspirations. Hack does not really try to distinguish between provocation and reaction, a *faux* evenhandedness. So when labor resists employer-sponsored violence, they seem to be loony villains. Ultimately, an ethnic split between a Chinese minority who formed most of the insurgency (and earlier resistance to Japanese occupation) and the Malay majority worked decisively in authorities' favor. Still, Malaya was an extraordinarily costly venture that the British could only 'win' by reluctantly ceding independence.

For US Cold Warriors both Malaya and the Philippines (where advertising exec-turned COIN guru Ed Lansdale became a legendary spook) resemble successes to be plumbed for profound lessons, but Gurman's contributors pry past the press clipping facades. Without women's support, for example, Vina Lanzano argues, there would have been no Huk rebellion, which stemmed from a radical shift in landlord–tenant relations.[176] She demolishes the assumption, necessary for COIN to seem plausible, that 'it was not a community and solidarity and strong kinship relations but communist agitation that explained the success of the Huk movement.' She also zeroes in on a crucial 'masculinized conception in which both peasants and guerrilla appear as free agents, manipulated, and, in the end, acting only for themselves and their own personal interests.' Hence, in a crude rational choice board game universe, insurgents get categorized as gangsters and gun molls. Here the lab-coated analysts impose a congenial explanation upon the mysterious environment. COIN tactics, Lanzano finds, 'deploy conservative strategies toward gender and women that, in the end, exploit and marginalize women and reinforce masculine ideologies of conflict and power.' The intent was the breakup of the communities themselves in order to suppress resistance. Eland points out the inescapable paradox that, even if we accept authorities' highly skewed assumptions, COIN cannot work until the population feels safe enough to collaborate but they can only do so when the insurgency is broken.

Vietnam's lesson, in the cookbook recipe phrase, is first catch (or select) a government the populace believes is worth defending.[177] The Saigon regime, a round-robin of authoritarian cabals, was devoutly corrupt and just as devoutly depicted in US propaganda as a frail democracy under threat. One rather admirable Marine officer in 1966, determined to win distrustful hearts and minds, wound up having to order his platoon to level its weapons at South Vietnamese officials who tried to pillage what the earnest Yanks helped to build[178] (his Marines behaved as nearly like Boy Scouts as Marines are capable of, which one suspects is not very much). The officer was aghast that he had to resort to force to protect villagers from their predatory government, but do you imagine the villagers were surprised? And what happened when the Marines departed? The COIN prognosis, to say the least, was not a promising one in so fundamentally inhospitable a climate. Gian Gentile, by the way, contrary to some giddy revisionists, detects no difference in the COIN aspect of the war in the changeover from Westmoreland's leadership to Abrams.[179]

B-52s are wretched ambassadors, but so too are nosey foreign soldiers poking around strange neighborhoods figuring out whom to scribble onto kill lists (which is one of many problems arising around the Human Terrain System).[180] Creating refugees also is no means for winning hearts and minds, though the USA counted mass relocations as a net plus. The real goal was to pacify domestic sources of opposition, for the 'people inside were being protected from the threat of their own potential disloyalty.' Thank goodness for any scrap of candor. The 'accelerated pacification campaign' (including the notorious Phoenix program) from late 1968 onward was unsparing and indiscriminate under the guise of precision. Guerrillas reeled, or backed off, for a while but rapidly recovered. So, after the war, the Pentagon quietly downgraded, if not ditched, counterinsurgency. It became the preserve of Special Forces. General David Petraeus, chief instigator of the best-selling COIN *Manual*, later helped to summon this zombie doctrine forth from its dioxin-laced coffin to torment Iraqis and Afghans too.

Regarding El Salvador Joaquim Chavez finds that terrified ordinary people in the 1980s had little choice but to fight the elites exploiting them. Implacable anticommunism was invoked to justify US intervention. American corporate interests aligned with the designs of rapacious Salvadoran elites. So the military-oligarch leaders treated intellectuals, unions, students and opposition politicians as mortal threats, 'portraying social activism as the same as guerrilla action.' Salvadoran leaders inflicted a sadistic counterinsurgency ordeal that generated the very leftist threat they feared and loathed. Fear of popular voice and reforms united local *jefes* and their paranoiac US enablers. During the Reagan years concessions were offered as matters of image management and so as to undercut or split the opposition. Yet the strategy failed to snuff out the FMLN and instead during George H. W. Bush's term the armed conflict came to an unwanted negotiated end.

Finally, in Gurman's volume, Rick Rowley's and David Enders' essays examine Iraq, where COIN was plucked from the vasty deep to bail out Dubya's hubris, while essays by Jeremy Kuzmarov and Jean Mackenzie ably sort through the 'scorched earth in slow motion' that is Afghanistan. The USA invaded Iraq, disbanded the army, privatized oil and added to these bad first impressions by shooting protesters in numerous street incidents. Ultimately, the celebrated Sunni 'awakening' led to the rise of ISIL today. Hooray. Kuzmarov aptly cites Gabriel Kolko's observation that in warfare, and especially wars of conquest, 'the functions, actions, and values of officers and men are the inevitable consequences of the kinds of societies they are seeking to create or defend'—neocolonial marionettes, in the case of Paul Bremer's Iraq and Hamid Karzai's Afghanistan, which could not stand.

In Iraq in the mid-2000s Lt. Col. Gian Gentile's *Wrong Turn* turned up few 'fence-sitters' waiting to be charmed by kindly counterinsurgents, of whom there were probably even fewer. The myth nonetheless was cultivated that the 'surge' under COIN auspices suddenly mollified the deadly place. Yet it really was bags of bribery cash and expert exploitation of sectarian tensions that redirected ferocious resistance away from American troops. The ballyhooed resurrection of COIN was a gambit to rescue a failed enterprise and ultimately just a garish cover for withdrawal.[181] Gentile attests that many young American officers used COIN techniques before Petraeus but they did so to little avail in a milieu that non-negotiably wanted Yankees to go home.

Gentile slams the 'deep-seated American military assumption that by getting organization, systems, and procedures working correctly wars can be won.' Gentile judges the USA 'failed at strategy,' but it may be somewhat more accurate to infer that US schemes failed at inception in their lethal little neocon cradles. What imaginable strategy could have succeeded in Vietnam, El Salvador, Iraq or Afghanistan anyway? 'The blunt answer,' replies Gentile, 'is that heart-and-minds counterinsurgency carried out by an occupying power in a foreign land doesn't work unless it is a multigenerational effort.' Maybe Nazis can get away with it, though their record was a bit mixed, and they didn't quite last a thousand years.[182]

COIN remains a respectable topic because a superpower can afford to keep every ugly option open and because no apparatchik brewing it up ever suffered for it. I recently heard a scholar I respect tumble into the trap of talking airily about US interventionist disasters as not really doing harm to 'us,' though by 'us' he meant the Ivy League-ish policy elites (whose Iraq invasion mania he opposed) who hatched the hubristic plans. The USA suffered in many ways but not these Teflon pundits who still infest our airwaves. The swamp of COIN concepts needs to be drained but good luck with that in the Trump era. The only unconventional attitude toward this entrancingly counterproductive form of warfare is to shelve it for good. Counterinsurgency, as Gentile and everyone else here grasps, 'is a recipe for perpetual war,' and that objective suits schemers who shouldn't be let anywhere near the levers of power.

Notes

1. *The U.S. Army/Marine Corps Counterinsurgency Manual* (Chicago: University of Chicago Press, 2007), p. 73. Hereafter, the '*Manual.*'
2. Steven Metz, *Rethinking Insurgency*. (Carlisle, PA: Strategic Studies Institute. June 2007), pp. 2–11; Bruce Hoffman, *Insurgency and Counterinsurgency in Iraq* (Santa Monica: RAND, 2004) p. 15.

3. Harry G. Summers, preface to Mark Moyar, *Phoenix and the Birds of Prey* (Omaha: University of Nebraska, 2007, 2nd ed.), p. xii, and Benjamin Valentino, *Final Solutions* (Ithaca: Cornell, 2004), p. 5.
4. Schell, in Christian Appy, ed. *Vietnam* (New York: Ebury Press, 2006), p. 204.
5. '(which were about zero to begin with).' Ibid.
6. Lorenzo Zambernardi, 'Counterinsurgency's Impossible Trilemma' *Washington Quarterly* (July 2010) p. 22. On 'this bitter trade-off,' see Jason Lyall and Isaiah Wilson III, 'Rage Against the Machine: Explaining Outcomes in Counterinsurgency War' *International Organization* 63, 1 (January 2009), pp. 104–106. Also David Kilcullen, *The Accidental Guerrilla* (New York: Oxford University Press, 2009), John A. Nagle, *Learning To Eat Soup with a Knife* (Chicago: University of Chicago Press, 2005), Andrew Exum, *This Man's Army* (New York: Gotham, 2005), and David Galula, *Counterinsurgency Warfare* (New York; Praeger, 2006).
7. See, regarding the UK, David Miller and Tom Mills, 'Counterinsurgency and Terror Expertise: The integration of Social Scientists into the War Effort' *Cambridge Review of International Affairs* 23, 2 (June 2010).
8. On this enterprise see David H. Ucko, *The New Counterinsurgency Era* (Washington DC: Georgetown University Press, 2009) and Jason Lyall, 'Do Democracies Make Inferior Counterinsurgents?' *International Organization* 64 (Winter 2010). The latter title stirs the questions: Why should democracies want to be 'better' third-party counterinsurgents, and what do they gain by it?
9. As counterexamples, respondents cited political comparativists, regional specialists and historians, but never specialists writing in IR journals. See historian David Hunt's 'Dirty Wars: Counter-insurgency in Vietnam and Today' *Politics & Society* 38 March 2010), historian Marilyn Young, 'Counterinsurgency, Now and Forever' in Lloyd Garner and Marilyn Young, eds, *Iraq and The Lessons of Vietnam* (New York: New Press, 2007), and Frank Frost, *Australia's War in Vietnam* (Sydney: Allen & Unwin, 1987).
10. *Manual*, p. 73.
11. Galula, *Pacification in Algeria, 1956–1958* (Santa Monica: RAND, 1963) p. xvii. For a superb critical overview see Peter Paret, *French Revolutionary Warfare from Indochina to Algeria* (London: Pall Mall Press, 1964).
12. Jeffrey Race, 'Vietnam Intervention: Systematic Distortion in Policy Making' *Armed Forces and Society* 2, 3 (May 1976), p. 4.
13. Lyall, 'Do Democracies Make Inferior Counterinsurgents?' p. 186. It is odd to grade insurgents' achievement of political voice

('power-sharing') as a draw when they often fight to achieve that voice. It is a gain. Nor is it a draw when the counterinsurgent aimed at the outset to stamp out the insurgency completely.
14. Walter Laqueur, *Guerrilla* (Boston, Little, Brown, 1976), p. 409. On US counterinsurgent practices under Carter and Reagan see Michael McClintock, *Instruments of Statecraft* (New York: Pantheon, 1992) and Author.
15. Thomas Ricks, *Fiasco* (London: Allen Lane, 2006), p. 70.
16. John T. Fishel, Letter to editor, *Perspectives in Politics* 7 July 2008.
17. See the exceptional insider critique by Benjamin C. Schwartz in his *American Counterinsurgency Doctrine and El Salvador* (Santa Monica: RAND 1991), p. 1.
18. Vanda Felab-Brown, *Shooting Up: Counterinsurgency and the War on Drugs* (Washington: Brookings 2010), p. 156.
19. See Lyall, 'Do Democracies make Inferior Counterinsurgents?' Lyall and Wilson, 'Rage Against the Machine' Andrew Kydd and Barbara Walter, 'Strategies of Terrorism.' *International Security* 31, 1 (Summer 2006), p. 68. On 'labor-intensive' COIN solutions, Jonathan Caverly, 'The Myth of Military Myopia' *International Security* 34, 3 (Winter 2009/2010), p. 153. Also see Kevin I. Sepp, 'Best Practices in Counterinsurgency' *Military Review* (May/June 2005), p. 12.
20. Wendy Brown, 'Review Symposium: The New U.S. Army/Marine Corps Counterinsurgency Field Manual as Political Science and Political Praxis' *Perspectives in Politics* 6, 2 (June 2008), p. 354.
21. Lt. Col. Robert M. Cassidy, 'Winning the War of the Flea' *Military Review* (Sept–Oct 2004), p. 41.
22. Lyall and Wilson, 'Rage Against The Machine,' pp. 63–67. Chinese peasants had a saying: 'Bandits come and go. Soldiers come and stay'— which hardly sounds like the welcome mat is out. Max Hastings, *Retribution* (New York: Knopf, 2008), p. 210. French activity in Algeria closely approximated Lyall and Watson's recommendations but the French experienced severe divisiveness between garrison forces and elite formations and pulled out anyway. Paret, *French Revolutionary Warfare*, p. 39.
23. Bernard Fall, *Street Without Joy* (Harrisburg, PA: Stackpole Company, 1966), pp. 11, 353–354.
24. Manual, p.xix. See David Galula, *Pacification in Algeria 1956–1958* (Santa Monica: RAND, 1963).
25. Colonel Alexander Alderson, 'US COIN Doctrine and Practice: An Ally's Perspective' *Parameters* (Winter 2007–2008), p. 43.
26. David Elliot says that 'interviewing these "simple peasants" was a transforming experience. I was astounded by their political sophistication

and analytic skills (that would put most American graduate students to shame).' David Elliot, *The Vietnamese War* Vol. 1. p. xiii. He does not always sustain this respect. For a perceptive rejoinder see David Hunt, *Vietnam's Southern Revolution* (Amherst: University of Massachusetts Press, 2008), p. 9.
27. Trinquier declared, 'The right organization can turn the trick.' Roger Trinquier, *Modern Warfare* (London: Pall Mall Press, 1964), p. 4.
28. Critiques of this stance include Noam Chomsky, *American Power and The New Mandarins* (New York: Pantheon, 1967), Gabriel Kolko, *Anatomy of a War* (New York: Pantheon, 1985), James William Gibson, *The Perfect War* (New York: Atlantic Monthly Press, 1986), Jonathan Schell, *The Real War* (New York: Pantheon, 1987) and Michael Shafer, *Deadly Paradigms* (Princeton: Princeton University Press, 1988).
29. Max Abrahms, 'Why Terrorism Does Not Work' *International Security* 31, 2 (Fall 2006), p. 42.
30. Fall, *The Two Viet-Nams*, pp. 344–345.
31. I. F. Stone in 1961 observed: 'In reading the military literature on guerilla warfare now so fashionable at the Pentagon what rarely comes through to them are the injured racial feelings, the misery, the rankling slights, the hatred, the devotion, the inspiration and the desperation. So they do not really understand what leads men to abandon wife, children, home, career, friends; to take to the bush and live gun in hand like a hunted animal; to challenge overwhelming military odds rather than acquiesce any longer in humiliation, injustice or poverty.' This passage appeared in the *Small Wars Journal* blog. What is noteworthy is that a veteran felt his seasoned associates still needed to hear this revelation. See http://smallwarsjournal.com/blog/2009/09/a-few-random-thoughts-on-coin/
32. Rather than bridle at the problem of Vietnamese corruption, defense analyst Herman Kahn saw it as part of the solution of making 'all of the population dependent on the US' and thereby more tractable. Frances Fitzgerald, *Fire in The Lake* (New York: Little Brown and Company, 1972), p. 352.
33. Shaher Ameiri, 'Global Governance, Local Rule: Counterinsurgency in Iraq and Afghanistan as Territorial Politics' Asia Research Centre, Murdoch University, Working paper 164 (April 2010), p. 10.
34. Schwarz, *American Counterinsurgency Doctrine and El Salvador*, p. 8.
35. Interservice rivalry is also blamed. The faith in sheer technique is echoed in most critiques. Ricks laments that in Iraq 'the US wasted a year by using counterproductive tactics that were employed in unprofessional ignorance of the basic tenets of counterinsurgency warfare.' Ricks, *Fiasco*, p. 4.

36. Quoted in Cassidy, 'Winning the War of the Flea' p. 46.
37. A recent setback is a video of Marines in Afghanistan urinating on corpses. Dan Murphy, 'Marines Urinating on the Dead? This is War.' *Christian Science Monitor* 13 January 2012.
38. Stephen Biddle, 'Review Symposium: The New U.S. Army/Marine Corps Counterinsurgency Field Manual' p. 348.
39. Robert M Chamberlain, 'With Friends Like These: Grievance, Governance, and Capacity building in COIN' *Parameters* (Summer 2008), p. 89.
40. *Manual*, p. 17.
41. 'It is clear that the absence of direct PIRA involvement in certain forms of criminality is imperative for the development of Sinn Fein's political successes.' John Horgan and Max Taylor, 'Playing the Green Card; Financing the IRA' *Terrorism and Political Violence*. Vol. 11, 2 (Summer 1999), p. 1. Also see Christopher Fettweis, 'Freedom Fighters and Zealots: Al Qaeda in Historical Perspective' *Political Science Quarterly* 124, 2 (2009), p. 280.
42. Stathis Kalyvas, 'Review Symposium: The New U.S. Army/Marine Corps Counterinsurgency Field Manual as Political Science and Political Praxis' p. 351. On greed seeming 'more important than grievance.' see Paul Collier, 'Doing Well out of War' in Mats Berdal and David Malone, *Greed and Grievance: Economic Agendas in Civil Wars* (London: Lynne Rienner, 2000).
43. Christopher Bayly and Tim Harper, *Forgotten Wars* (London: Penguin, 2007), p. 182.
44. Ibid., pp. 180–181.
45. See Alfred McCoy, *The Politics of Heroin* (Chicago: Lawrence Hill, 2003, 2nd rev. ed). McCoy reports that Trinquier, to fund his hill tribe counterinsurgency force in Northeast Laos and Tonkin, connived in the transport of opium.
46. Chamberlain, 'With Friends Like These' p. 83.
47. Alan J. Vick, et al., *Air Power in the New Counterinsurgency Era* (Santa Monica: RAND, 2006), p. 39.
48. Marx Moyar, Phoenix, p. 3–35. In this vein, apart from works discussed below, see Mark Woodruff, *Unheralded Victory* (New York, Harper Collins, 1999) and Michael Lind, *Vietnam: The Necessary War* (New York, Free Press, 1999).
49. Moyar, *Phoenix*, pp. 28, 303.
50. Ibid, p. 300. Compare Trinquier: 'People who know our adversaries will not protest in submitting to inconveniences they know to be necessary for the recovery of their liberty.' *Modern Warfare*, p. 48.

51. See Mai Elliot, RAND In Southeast Asia (Santa Monica: RAND, 2101), pp. 116–195. General Westmoreland, to his credit reckoned Goure 'overplayed the presumed low state of Viet Cong morale.' (p. 172). See Leon Goure, 'Some Impressions of the Effects of Military Operations on Viet Cong Behavior' (Santa Monica: RAND, RM-4517-I-ISA March 1965).
52. Moyar, *Phoenix*, p. 375.
53. Ibid. p. 394.
54. *Covert Action Information Bulletin* (now Covert Action Quarterly) Summer 1982, p. 52.
55. Neil Sheehan, *A Bright Shining Lie* (New York: Vintage, 1988), p. 732.
56. Mark Mazower, *Hitler's Empire* (London: Penguin, 2008), p. 487.
57. Fall, *Street Without Joy*, p. 169 fn.
58. Lyall, 'Do Democracies make Inferior Counterinsurgents?' p. 169 fn 9. Again, why should Democracies seek to be 'superior counter-insurgents,' and what would they gain by it?
59. Douglas Blaufarb, *The Counterinsurgency Era* (New York: Free Press, 1977, p. 276.
60. Ibid, p. 389.
61. Marilyn Young, *The Vietnam Wars, 1945–1990* (New York: Harper Perennial, 1991), pp. 222–223.
62. Brush, 'Civic Action: The Marine Corps Experience in Vietnam,' Part I. downloaded from Texas Tech Vietnam archive.
63. Loren Baritz, *Backfire* (New York: Morrow, 1985), p. 275.
64. Kuno Knoebl, *Victor Charlie* (New York: Frederick Pager, 1967), p. 130. Ricks, *Fiasco*, p. 339, 341.
65. Moyar, *Phoenix and the Birds of Prey*, p. 379; Vick, *Air Power in the New Counterinsurgency Era*, p. 33. Brendan Nicholson, 'Insider Attacks on The Increase' The Australian 1 September 2012.
66. Ricks, *Fiasco*, pp. 339–341.
67. Fortini and Semple invoke an 'Afghan logic of siding with the winner' in 'Flipping the Taliban' p. 44. The catch, and not the only one, is that they presume to understand how local people calculate who is going to win.
68. Robert K, Brigham, ARVN (Topeka: University of Kansas, 2006), p. 7.
69. Ngo Vinh Long, 'Vietnam: The Real Enemy' *Bulletin of Concerned Asian Scholars*, 21, 2–4 (April–December 1989), p. 26.
70. Zalin Grant, *Facing the Phoenix* (New York: Norton, 1991).
71. Lewis Sorley *A Better War* (New York: Harcourt Brace & Company 1999), p. 14.
72. Ibid, p. 383.
73. An aide to both commanders detected no major changes in combat operations in the 2 years after Tet. Andrew Krepinevich, *The Army and*

Vietnam (Baltimore: Johns Hopkins University Press, 1986), p. 257. In 1966 Westmoreland did entertain a pacification approach which was rejected in Washington because of potentially unlimited troop levels it entailed. Caverly, 'The Myth of Military Myopia' p. 151.
74. Thomas L. Ahern, *Vietnam Declassified* (Louisville: University of Kentucky Press, 2010), p. 306.
75. Elliot, *RAND in Southeast Asia*, p. 331.
76. George W. Allen, *None So Blind* (Chicago: Ivan R Dee, 2001), p. 265.
77. Konrad Kellen, *Conversations with Enemy Soldiers in Late 1968/Early 1969* (Santa Monica: RAND 1970), pp. 105–106.
78. Moyar, *Phoenix and the Birds of Prey*, p. 394.
79. Schwatrz, *Counterinsurgency*, p. 55. Gimmicky civic action programs never aspired to redistribute land, wealth or power in favor of the target populace, or protect their rights. See Race, *War Comes to Long An*, p. 176.
80. Bayly and Harper, *Forgotten Wars*, p. 443. Also comparing Malaya and Vietnam, see Bernard Fall, *The Two Viet-Nams* (London: Pall Mall Press, 1963), pp. 372–376.
81. Margaret Shennan, *Out in the Midday Sun* (London: John Murray, 2000), pp. 261, 316.
82. C. C. Chin and Karl Hack, eds. *Dialogues with Chin Peng* (Singapore: Singapore University Prss, 2004), p. 43.
83. In December 1978 a British Defence Intelligence Staff appraisal of the IRA was leaked, which affirmed the Provos were an intelligent, capable and patriotically motivated organization with considerable popular support. Peter Taylor, Provos, *The IRA and Sinn Fein* (London: Bloomsbury, 1997), p. 217.
84. Shennan, *Midday Sun*, p. 522. Karl Hack contends that the insurgency 'as a large scale campaign' was broken between 1950 and 1952. 'The Malayan Emergency as Counterinsurgency Paradigm,' *Journal of Strategic Studies* 32 (June 2009), p. 384. By 'broken,' Hack explains, 'I mean counter-insurgency achieved a trend of improvement which the insurgents were no longer able to reverse, not that the latter's activity levels were at a low level' (fn. 6). If the security option worked, then why was the campaign so protracted?
85. Ibid, p. 526. Briggs' plan in 1951 had deployed 67,000 police, 300,000 home guard and 23 infantry battalions to confront 8000 guerrillas.
86. Moyar, *Phoenix*, p. 317.
87. Ahern, *Vietnam Declassified*, pp. 313, 363.
88. Shennen, *Midday Sun*, pp. 321, 322. For exceptions see Ucko, 'Counterinsurgency and Its Discontents,' Hack 'The Malayan Emergency as Counterinsurgency Paradigm,' and Author 2009.

89. Daniel Ellsberg and Vu Van Thai, 'On Counterinsurgency.' RAND document No. 19136 (July 1969), p. 2. They note 'As in the strategic hamlets, when the troops leave, cooperation stops.'
90. Austin Long, *On 'Other War'* (Santa Monica: RAND, 2006), pp. 8–9.
91. John M Gates, *The U.S. Army and Irregular Warfare*, Chap. 7, accessed from Texas Tech Vietnam Archive.
92. William Colby, *Lost Victory* (Chicago: Contemporary Books, 1989). p. 355.
93. Ibid p. 331.
94. Ibid p. 31.
95. Ibid pp. 260, 268.
96. Victor Marchetti and John D. Marks, *The CIA and the Cult of Intelligence* (New York: Knopf, 1974), p. 207.
97. On the inception of data networks during the Philippines insurgency and inevitable spillover into American society see Alfred McCoy, *Policing America's Empire* (Madison: University of Wisconsin Press, 2008), pp. 15–58, 99–124.
98. Kydd and Walter, 'Strategies of Terrorism,' p. 61.
99. Michael T. Klare, *War Without End* (New York: Vintage, 1972) p. 265.
100. Colby, *Lost Victory*, p. 348.
101. ibid, p. 238.
102. Ibid, p. 373.
103. 'What Alsop didn't know was that they actually had a large military escort. Armed teams and helicopters preceded and followed the car just out of sight.' Appy, *Vietnam*, p. 322.
104. Robert W. Chandler, *War of Ideas* (Boulder: Westview Press, 1981), p. 205.
105. The input–output model originates with Charles Wolf's *Insurgency and Counterinsurgency* (Santa Monica: RAND, 1965), which superfluously advises authorities to eschew any concern with legitimacy.
106. Eqbal Ahmad, 'Theories of Counterinsurgency' *Bulletin of Concerned Asian Scholars*, 1970, p. 77.
107. See John Kelly, Beatrice Juaregi, Sean T. Mitchell and Jeremy Walton, eds, *Anthropology and Global Counterinsurgency* (Chicago: University of Chicago Press, 2009).
108. Ricks, *Fiasco*, p. 415.
109. Long, *On 'Other Wars'*, p. 64.
110. See Andrew Bacevich, 'The Unmaking of a Company Man' accessed at http://www.commondreams.org/view/2010/08/26-6.
111. On systemic HES distortions see Elliot, *RAND in Southeast Asia*, p. 381, 412.
112. Ibid, p. 408.

113. David Halberstam, *The Making of A Quagmire* (New York: Random House, 1965), p. 195.
114. Knoebl, *Victor Charlie*, p. 254.
115. Mark Selden, 'The NLF and the Transformation of Vietnamese Society' *Bulletin of Concerned Asian Scholars* 2, 1 (October 1969), p. 36.
116. Ngo Vinh Long, 'Land Reform?' *Bulletin of Concerned Asian Scholars* (February 1971), p. 50.
117. ibid.
118. There are 'ironic' historical echoes: in the American Revolution a 'symbiotic blend of guerillas and General Nathaniel Greene's forces enabled ultimate victory in the Carolinas and contributed to overall victory.' Anthony James Joes, *America and Guerrilla War* (Lexington: University Press of Kentucky, 2000), p. 48.
119. Tho, *Pacification*. p. 74.
120. Moyar, *Phoenix*, pp. 258–259. Yet in June 1971 US estimates show VC activities in two-thirds of the villages. Thomas C. Thayer, *War Without Fronts* (Boulder: Westview Press, 1985), p. 206.
121. David Hunt, Review of David Elliot, The Vietnamese War,' *Critical Asian Studies* 35, 4 (2003), p. 600. 'Large-unit sweeps, conducted with conventional resources within a framework similar to that of conventional warfare, and invariably limited in time, temporarily disperse guerrilla bands rather than destroy them,' Trinquier writes. *Modern Warfare*, p. 58.
122. James Trullinger, *Village at War* (New York: Longman, 1980), pp. 1233–147; Jeffrey Race, *War Comes to Long An* (Berkeley: University of California 1972; David Hunt and Jayne Werner, *The American War in Vietnam* (Ithaca: Cornell University Press 1993.
123. Young, *The Vietnam Wars*, pp. 224–225.
124. Komer, quoted in Thompson and Frizzel, eds. *The Lessons of Vietnam*, p. 108.
125. Tho, *Pacification*, pp. 166, 175, 177, 179.
126. General Cao Van Viem and Lt. General Dong Van Khuyen, 'Reflections on the Vietnam War' (Washington, DC: US Army Center of Military History, 1980), p. 68.
127. Robert K Brigham and Martin J, Murray 'Conflicting Interpretations of the Vietnam War' *Bulletin of Concerned Asian Scholars* 26, 1–2 (January–June 1994), p. 117.
128. Robert D. Schulzinger, *A Time for War* (Oxford: Oxford University Press, 1997), p. 201.
129. Viem and Khuyen, 'Reflections on the Vietnam War.' p. 63.
130. General William DePuy, 'What we might have done and why we didn't do it' ARMY February 1986, p. 31.

131. Andrew Mack, 'Why Big Nations Lose Small Wars: The Politics of Asymmetric Conflict.' *World Politics*, 27, 2 (January 1975), p. 89.
132. Tho, *Pacification*, p. 164.
133. *Manual*, pp. 99–100.
134. *Pentagon Papers*, Gravel edition, Vol. IV, p. 557.
135. Fall, *Two Viet-Nams*, p. 343.
136. James H. Willbanks, *The Tet Offensive* (New York: Columbia University Press, 2007), p. 82.
137. *Pentagon Papers*, Vol. IV, p. 556. Also Richard A. Hunt, *Pacification* (Boulder: Westview Press, 1995), pp. 136–138.
138. Bruce Franklin, *Vietnam and Other American Fantasies* (Amherst: University of Massachusetts, 2000), p. 95.
139. Robert Buzzanco, *Masters of War* (New York: Cambridge University Press, 1996), p. 96.
140. *Manual*, p. 75.
141. Blaufarb, *The Counterinsurgency Era*, p. 275.
142. See Kellen, *Conversations with Enemy soldiers*.
143. Welsh, 'Pacification in Vietnam' p. 293.
144. Truong Nhu Tang, *Viet Cong Memoir* (New York: Harcourt, Brace, Jovanovich, 1985), pp. 86–87.
145. Ibid, pp. 212.
146. 'But without sustained political efforts in urban and rural south Vietnam between 1968 and 1975 aimed at rebuilding the revolutionary infrastructure, and retraining political support, the final communist victory might not have come as speedily and completely as it did.' Kevin Ruane, *War and Revolution in Vietnam 1930–1975* (London: Routledge, 1998), p. 116.
147. Hunt, *Pacification*, p. 253.
148. Davidson, *Vietnam at War*, p. 633.
149. Lewy, *America in Vietnam*, p. 10.
150. 'The true state of security was revealed by the fact that travel by road beyond their outskirts was often impossible without a heavily armed escort.' Milton Osborne, *The Mekong* (Atlantic Monthly Press, 2000), p. 199.
151. Philip P. Davidson, *Vietnam at War* (New York: Presidio Press, 1988), p. 63.
152. Manual, p. 14. On this drumbeat theme note Jeffrey Record and W. Andrew Terrell, 'Iraq and Vietnam: Differences, Similarities, and Insights' (Carlisle PA: Strategic Studies Institute May 2004), p. 4.
153. Lyall, 'Do Democracies make Inferior Counterinsurgents,' p. 170. Democracies are 'hobbled' by international and domestic opinion, which 'are cost-intolerant.' Kull and Ramsey find in 'Korea and Vietnam

it is more likely that support diminished as the public came to *question the purposes of the wars* and their likelihood of success.' Steven Kull and Clay Ramsay, 'The Myth of the Reactive Public' in Philip Everts and Pierangelo Isernia (eds.) *Public Opinion and the International Use of Force* (London: Routledge, 2001), p. 20.
154. Caroline Elkins, *Britain's Gulag* (London: Jonathan Cape, 2005), p. 354.
155. Paret, *French Revolutionary Warfare*, p. 51.
156. Alistair Horne, *A Savage War of Peace* (New York: New York Review of Books, 1977), pp. 505, 538.
157. *Manual*, p. 113.
158. See Kurt Jacobsen, 'After the Docklands: The Irish Peace Process and The American Connection' *Brown Journal of World Affairs*. Winter-Spring 1996.
159. Ed Moloney, *A Secret History of the IRA* (London: Penguin 2002), p. 84 and John Newsinger, *British Counterinsurgency* (London: Macmillan Palgrave, 2002), pp 131–158.
160. *Manual*, p. 1.
161. Metz, 'With Friends like These.' p. 44.
162. Collier, 'Doing Well out of War.'
163. See Richard K. Betts, 'Interests, Burdens, and Persistence: Asymmetries Between Washington and Hanoi' *International Studies Quarterly*, December 1980.
164. John J. Mearsheimer, 'Hollow Victory' *Foreign Policy* 2 November 2009.
165. See Anuj Chopra, India's Failing Counterinsurgency Campaign' *Foreign Policy* 14 May 2010.
166. Paul Dixon, 'British Counterinsurgency from Malaya to Iraq' *Journal of Strategic Studies*, 2009, pp. 366, 379.
167. Vick et al. *Air Power in the New Counterinsurgency Era*, p. 5.
168. Kilcullen, *The Accidental Guerrilla*, p. 263.
169. Wendy Brown, 'Review Symposium' p. 355.
170. 'Biden Told Obama Military's Afghan Plan Flawed, According to Leaked Memo,' Associated Press. 25 June 2012.
171. Dixon, 'British Counterinsurgency from Malaya to Iraq,' p. 367.
172. This is the upshot of Hack's work on Malaya and of Christopher Griffin, 'Major Combat Operations and Counterinsurgency Warfare: Plan Challe in Algeria 1959–1960' *Security Studies* 19, (2010), p. 587.
173. As Hunt observes regarding Vietnam: 'Rand staffers misrepresented themselves to subjects, edited the transcripts, and vainly labored to understand a popular movement whose ethos surpassed the limits of their imaginings.' *Vietnam's Southern Revolution*, p. 229.
174. Radley Balko, *The Rise of the Warrior Cop* (Washington DC: Public Affairs, 2013) and Kristian Williams, William Munger, and

Lara Messersmith-Glavin, eds. *Life During Wartime: Resisting Counterinsurgency* (AK Press, 2013).
175. John A. Nagl, Foreword to David H. Ucko, *The New Counterinsurgency Era* (Washington DC: Georgetown University Press, 2009), p. viii.
176. Benedict J. Kerkvliet, *The Huk Rebellion: A Study of Peasant Revolt in the Philippines* (Lanham: Rowman & Littlefield 2002), pp. 22–25.
177. According to Kaplan's account, David Kilcullen eventually confronted the following confounding syllogism: 'We shouldn't engage in counterinsurgency unless the government we're helping is effective and legitimate: a government that needs foreign help to fight an insurgency generally isn't effective or legitimate; therefore we generally shouldn't engage in counterinsurgency.' Fred Kaplan, *The Insurgents David Petraeus and the Plot to Change the American Way of War* (Simon & Schuster, 2009), p. 290.
178. William Corson, *The Betrayal* (New York: W. W. Norton, 1968). Bing West's *The Village* (New York: Pocket Books, 1972) was a more gung-ho and less circumspect version of the combined action platoon experience in Vietnam and therefore much more acceptable for military reading lists.
179. In this redemptive militarist vein see any book by Lewis Sorley or Mark Moyar.
180. See Kelly, *Anthropology and Global Counterinsurgency*.
181. For a rosey-hued look at the surge see Thomas Ricks, *The Gamble* (New York: Penguin, 2008).
182. See Mark Mazower, *Hitler's Empire* (London: Penguin, 2009).

Why Freud Matters: Psychoanalysis and IR Revisited

Scholars of politics, not just IR, long have neglected psychoanalysis. The attacks on Freud and his followers over the last generation evidently discouraged political scientists from exploring psychoanalytic methods.[1] An earlier generation of scholars—Paul Roazen, Fred Alford, Michael Rogin, Fred Greenstein, Lloyd and Susanne Rudolph, and others—had taken a deep interest and produced many works of distinction. That interest is long gone, except for a very minor and embattled presence in the subfield of political psychology. Even there, little has changed in three decades since a volume entitled *Psychological Models in International Politics* appeared, devoid of even a single token reference to psychoanalysis.[2] Freud, as Paul Roazen lamented long ago, 'has remained throughout political science something of a spook.'[3] Roazen referred to American political science. Critics of this summation combed political science to cite at best a few marginal forays (usually British or Commonwealth in origin) into psychoanalysis, which is of interest only insofar as a particular analyst thereby buttresses their paradigmatic preferences in constructivism or post-structural discourse analysis.[4]

A major methodological objection to psychoanalysis is that an investigative means devised for individuals is inadvisable to apply to collective entities. States cannot possess egos, ids or superegos—although a case has been made by Zizek, and Erich Fromm long before him, for the palpable influence of an 'institutional unconscious.'[5] Freud was alert to the perils of overstepping domains when he pondered whether civilizations could be said to be neurotic.[6] Psychoanalysts, an eminent analyst cautions, are 'uniquely qualified to understand, analyze and assist the patient on the couch, but as soon as they move away from this personal confrontation (or the modification of a small group) to comment on matters outside their training and experience, the value of their comments would appear to depend on their knowledge and wisdom, not on their qualification.'[7] While some scholars draw upon cognitive frameworks to analyze otherwise overlooked political phenomena, psychoanalysis remains firmly on the fringes of IR where Lacanian discourse analysts treat us to such illuminating sentences as: 'It then endeavors, via constructing fantasies, to use transitive discourse objects to sustain the desire for the constructed dichotomies, which hankers for discursive closure.'[8] Psychoanalysis, contrary to Freud's proponents, neither begins nor ends with the semiotic allurements of Lacan.

Few scholars deny that psychological factors exert a significant effect upon politics. Hans Morgenthau wrote that international politics was primarily psychological in character and that the personal inclinations and oddities of leaders can at crucial times matter a great deal.[9] If anarchy is 'what we make of it' (and the rise of Athenian power created *anxiety* in Sparta), then it pays to ask who we are in our inner worlds as well as in our outer guises when we make something out of whatever we behold.[10] At what point in an explanation do psychological factors— from personal quirks to group dynamics to mass perceptions—become important? From the very beginning of our lives, is the psychoanalytic answer. Indeed, psychoanalysis aims to change where the beginning is reckoned to begin in any explanatory probe.

In the 1930s radical analyst Wilhelm Reich was really rather restrained when arguing that psychoanalysis had a role in explaining why actors pursue what to the external observer are irrational, blinkered and self-injurious actions.[11] Reich's intent was not only to explain 'deviations from rationality' but to inquire into the adequacy of our notion of rationality, especially as this seductive and problematic concept is buffeted by changing contexts and personal interests.[12] Misperception is a widely accepted phenomenon in IR now, as is the imputed sway in decision-making circles of analogical reasoning, such as the domino theory.[13] But important differences exist between Freud's depth psychology and, to use shorthand for a bundle of related practices, 'cognitive psychology.'[14] The purpose of psychoanalysis is to pry into our unconscious drives and defenses to illuminate their influence over the motives and behavior of the beholder as well as the beheld.[15] Cognitive psychology, unlike psychoanalysis, usually exempts practitioners from being prey to their own forms of unexamined irrationality, which may be one reason for its relative toleration in the field.

This essay reconsiders, long after Lasswell's heyday, whether psychoanalysis, beyond discourse analysis, can be a useful interpretive approach in international politics. What is the significance in human behavior of the unconscious, that is, of motives and forces of which we are largely unaware?[16] (extremely significant, Freud says, because unconscious forces, if unexposed, tend to make our decisions for us). The first section examines Freudian analysis and its uneasy relation to political analysis. I then examine key issues raised by psychoanalysis regarding the efficacy of IR models, the concept of self-interest and the waging of war. Finally, to appraise the 'value added' of this approach, I examine psychoanalytic understandings of intervention in Vietnam and, more briefly, the 'war on terror.' The argument is that psychoanalytically attuned approaches yield important insights into the wielding of power.

Psychoanalytic Triggers

Psychoanalysts regard human emotional life as a continuum in which we share every feeling and impulse to some degree, and indulge or capitulate to them if the combination of internal and external conditions is right. Violent emotions are universal, as much so as love, though they usually are channeled in muted ways that avert harm in everyday life. One is only is tempted to summon the psychoanalyst when excesses form a profoundly damaging pattern. The same rule of thumb goes for bringing psychoanalytic perspectives, or psychological predilections of leaders, to the fore in inquiries. Do so when behavior is very much out of keeping with observable circumstances. Freud, while shying away from direct applications to politics, always intended that psychoanalysis contribute to the social sciences and even to public health.[17] At minimum, such exploratory expeditions demand considerable knowledge both of psychoanalysis and of the social scientific field into which one introduces analytic concepts.

One may well ask whether we need to know what, for example, the youthful years of leaders have to do with their professional lives. Their actions surely are over-determined.[18] Methodological humility, a rare enough trait anywhere, is called for. In 1965, after the long-distance 'analysis' of candidate Barry Goldwater, the American Psychiatric Association president rebuked those who diagnosed political personalities from afar.[19] Psychological reductionism is a tempting pitfall, though anyone trained in political science, with its overvaluation of quantitative methods and formal theory, is unlikely to stumble into it.[20] One thereby would underestimate familiar tangible forces that shape political decisions. Still, seasoned scholars cannot credibly deny that international politics is at best only *partly* a rational enterprise. If so, IR is a valid arena for psychoanalytic inquiry.

What some players within IR deem rational—'thinking about the unthinkable,' 'brinksmanship' or 'winning hearts and minds' through supposedly selective violence—will appear irrational to beholders who apply different standards. 'You can't be too careful.' is a bromide that counterproductively spurs dangerous imbroglios, such as the security dilemma.[21] Rationality often is what we choose to make of it, under institutional pressure, disciplinary habits and unexamined personal traits. Mercer notes how rational choice notions, supposedly stripped of emotion, consistently lead to distorted depictions of human action, although this insight harks back half a century or more in Freudian annals.[22] Consider too Mannheim's classic distinction where what is functionally rational is not always substantively rational.[23] Ellul captured this significant divide acutely when he defined technology as the application of increasingly refined means to ever more carelessly considered ends.[24] Rationality is conceived as rationalization, a defense mechanism cloaking other motives, which may or may not be conscious.

Psychoanalysis is applied not only to the leadership but also to relations between elites and the citizenry. Rose notes that actors must be understood not only in terms of their material interests and institutional constraints but also of their images (of reality) and identifications.[25] This venerable formulation sets up interestingly porous dichotomies between inside and outside (private and public), and between the social and psychic. A lack of personality and group psychology studies only deprives us of useful ways to burrow into the 'agentic,' which is, after all, where the 'mutual constitution' of agency and structure that constructivists are so concerned about occurs.

As for realists, the political murderers in a Brecht play apologize to their victim: 'Sorry-force of circumstance'—a sentiment realists readily understand. But one trouble with halting inquiry here is that Freud demonstrated how often, to quell a conscience or to fool an outsider, we attribute to circumstances what are our own impulses. 'A common psychodynamic mechanism is to convert desire so that it appears an external necessity,' Bakan explains. 'It is thus an open question in each instance whether what appears to be external necessity really is that, or simply a facet concealing some internal pressure.'[26] Hence, even when interests seem to do the trick in explaining behavior, actors may resort to pleasing or exculpating rationales to justify callous aims. Acknowledging this slippery fact of political life is useful to understanding and even anticipating what actors do.

The story that the US elites invaded Iraq because they feared a WMD threat does not play so well anymore despite interesting but extremely tenuous defenses.[27] If key actors say they were misled by faulty intelligence that they had a strong hand in purveying then one is well advised to look elsewhere for an explanation. Typically, we can come up with a plausible answer based on material interests such as oil (ridiculed in mainstream circles at the time). Typically too there are 'multiple equilibria' in any policy choice. Why did these leaders select this course of action when force of circumstances was not determinative? Why impute credence to what is 'in actors' heads' when imputation of material factors or structural forces can do the job? The reason is that although social structural forces operate apart from individual human agency they remain dependent on the character of human beings to carry them out. 'It is precisely at this juncture that Freudian theory proves so suggestive,' Lichtman argued.[28] 'For the conjunction of individual intentions and social structures is embedded dialectically in the alienated institutions of social life and in the repressed unconscious of specific social agents.' How does this apply in international relations?

FREUD AND THE THREE IMAGES

Waltz' 'first image' is an obvious locale for Freudian theory, with international politics driven by the flawed and myopic leaders of an even more flawed and myopic *hoi polloi*.[29] Few psychoanalysts dispute that institutional structures (second image) within which we grow up and take our places are powerful determinants interacting with our drives and intentions. Nor would they disparage the influence of economic and global systems (third image) surrounding us. These 'images,' of course, are heuristic ones and actually interpenetrate. In Waltz' reckoning, though, the system forces individuals of whatever mettle, and units of any measure, to fall into line with its demands. So structural realism and psychoanalysis seem opposites, in that the former wants to exclude all but external influences while the latter has been inclined to downplay or even exclude external influences.

Yet, following Lichtman's cue above, it is difficult to ignore instances where players respond not to an unequivocal stimulus but, in part, to projected images of their internal turmoil, indoctrination, mistrust or disowned motives. Projection is the attribution to others of unsavory motives that one denies within oneself. One might term this phenomenon as the generation of 'surplus fear,' a level beyond that warranted by circumstances—hence the 'security dilemma,' the 'conflict spiral' and other renowned rationalist follies.[30] This 'surplus fear' is almost irresistible for leaders to play upon to gain consent for foreign adventures. Lasswell urged elites to manage the 'direction of discharge of insecurities' and speculated as to how an aspirant ruling group can go about 'capturing attention and guiding mass insecurities,' which he thought for the good of all.[31]

It goes both ways. The 'appeasement' scenario on which the Munich analogy is based centers on overidealistic statesmen who were not fearful enough of a goose-stepping threat. Bullitt's and Freud's controversial study of Woodrow Wilson details the life of a leader who consistently underestimated, and underwhelmed, relevant counterparts. The sources, and management of 'surplus fear' (orange alert, anyone?), seem fair game for a psychoanalytic approach. Unlike the first image (human nature) in Waltz' framework, psychoanalysis—like liberal institutionalism and constructivism—anticipates that transformative experiences can usher an afflicted party into the realm of sober 'ordinary unhappiness.' That is to say, learning takes place, a learning that is 'worked through' by the individual, and culminates perhaps in beneficial rules of thumb, such as the bent but not broken 'Vietnam syndrome.'

Psychoanalysis indicates that if the rulers, or the citizens who vote in rulers, become self-aware and savvy, they then can change the dynamics of the institutions and systems they operate within or, at least, alter their own reactions to them in beneficial ways. Booth and Wheeler in IR recently made a similar argument with respect to defusing the security dilemma.[32] Thereafter, emotional buttons aren't so easy to push. One commendably self-aware psychoanalyst speculates that a tendency to resort to psychoanalytic explanations of political actions is a sign that the more naïve practitioners are compensating for a correctly perceived lack of political efficacy.[33] If, however, policy is governed by irrational phenomena, then politics—in Crick's sense of a deliberative and reflective public process by which policies are generated and changed—sinks into a feeble condition.[34] Constructivists and discourse analysts, coming several generations late to this fray, have insisted that they say similar things, which is a most peculiar reason for disparaging psychoanalysis, except as an embarrassingly prescient competitor.

Rycroft defines psychoanalysis as 'a biological theory of meaning' that 'interprets human behaviour in terms of the self that experiences it and not in terms of entities external to it, such as other-worldly deities and leaders, and that it regards the self as a psychobiological entity which is always striving for self-realization and self-fulfillment.'[35] While this implied prohibition is prudent for clinicians who usually cannot perform reality checks on what clients tell them, there is every reason for non-clinician investigators to account for the influence of entities external to the 'client.' 'The theories of resistance and repression, of the unconscious, [and] of the etiological significance of infantile experiences,' Freud wrote, 'form the principal constituents of the theoretical structure of psychoanalysis.'[36] If so, it may be hard for some scholars to discern what use psychoanalysis is for illuminating the dynamics of international politics.

Self and Society

Human beings 'live in a field of transferences,' that is, transferences of earlier emotional relations onto later ones of which we are more or less aware and more or less in control—though usually less.[37] Slavoj Zizek, a Lacanian, and Jacquelyn Rose, a Kleinian, focus on the collective and structural aspects of psychological influences that pervade, constrain and even generate the political field, as individuals experience it. The dichotomy between subjectivity and objectivity, they argue, ought to be discarded. 'All perceptions of the world are refracted through the prism of our inner life,' Loewenberg notes. 'No phenomena has an inherent meaning. It becomes a datum by being assigned a frame of reference which confers meaning [so that all] research is unconsciously self-relevant.'[38] There is a sense in which everything we perceive is liable to contain an element of projection. Samuels further argues that mental imagery 'that looks like a psychological response to a social situation is also a facet of the construction of the social situation.'[39]

So can such a psychoanalytic theory of personality illuminate Stalin's alleged paranoia, Richard Nixon's resentments or Robert Mugabe's intransigence, and the effect of these respective conditions on the play of power? These leaders operated within states, replete with bureaucratic apparatuses with their own operational codes, and festooned with highly pedigreed advisers holding ideological worldviews. They were socialized and channeled within structures (second image) and systems (third image). After all 'political figures matter to history not because of their psychic conflicts but because of what they managed to accomplish in spite of these problems,' Roazen acknowledges.[40] So one must tread carefully in terrain where what is mad or bad for a single human is deemed meritorious for leaders engaged in economic rivalries or military conflicts. The minimal definition of sociopath—an exploitive person without conscience—fits all too snugly with behavior dictated by what realists regard as the common sense creed of realpolitik.[41]

Zizek and Rose instead promote a psychoanalytic approach for assaying events. Their approach is neither individual analysis (providing a critique of irrationality through the rational method) nor is it social psychology, in which the complex of conflicting forces and determinations is illuminated (as Freud aimed to do). Perhaps the best shorthand concept expressing the result of interplay of self with collective milieu is 'structured subjectivity.' In other words, the moment of subjective freedom is structured by objective alternatives—and within that space neurosis (or healthy autonomy) works itself out. This interplay, or dialectic, between external and internal forces must be kept in mind whenever we suss out how actors interpret the environments they operate in. Freud demonstrated that we are not 'masters in our own house,' which is no more welcome an insight now than in his day.[42] People are not always aware of psychical factors swaying perceptions. Freudian considerations therefore confute neat rational choice portraits of decision-making. Indeed, those who focus only on rational processes may be seeking any seemingly calm port in the storm, away from untamed complexities roiling within themselves or others. The reasons why personalities gravitate to formal models and rational choice—and others do not—would itself be an intriguing object of investigation.[43] Of course, this game can be turned around smartly on the diagnostician too.[44]

Psychoanalysis and the 'Problem' of the External

Freud's 'anti-political bias' is exemplified by his view that emotions 'begin privately and are rationalized outward' and that politics 'can be traced along a chain of projections to the individual.'[45] But, as Rieff noted, if politics ceases to stem from or appeal to the 'neurotic side of personality,' the citizen becomes a better viewer and perceiver. What Rieff calls the 'medicinal taste of modern liberalism' is apparent in Lasswell's injunction that the problem of a leaders-know-best democracy 'is equivalent to the development of social health.' So 'protest against society is explained away as a morbidly neurotic symptom.'[46] Those who do what they are told by properly invested authorities, and the authorities themselves, are, by contrast, perfectly rational and mature adults. Really?

Freud seemed most elitist in *The Future of an Illusion*, where the 'masses are lazy and unintelligent, they have no love for instinctual renunciation, they are not to be convinced of its inevitability by argument.'[47] Yet Freud's reputation as a political conservative is quite misplaced.[48] Freud gave Marxism its due 'for what it reveals about how economic circumstance influence other elements.'[49] Freud cautioned, like the Frankfurt School critics, that it 'cannot be assumed that economic motives are the only ones that determine the behaviors of human beings in society; for not only were these reactions concerned in establishing the economic conditions, but even under the domination of these conditions, men can only bring their original instinctual impulses into play—their self-preservative instinct, their aggressiveness, their need to be loved, their drive towards obtaining pleasure and avoiding unpleasure.' Then there are 'also the claims of the super-ego, [which] represent tradition and the ideals of the parents, [and] will for a time resist the incentives of a new economic situation.' Freud here identifies key causes of cultural lag.[50] Cultural development is 'a process influenced by other factors but able to influence them independently too.'[51]

Freud, after the First World War, 'sympathized with progressive reforms proposed by the Socialist party.'[52] In 1927 he endorsed the Social Democratic Party: an easily understood choice given the alternative of a reactionary coalition of Pan-Germans, National socialists and Christian Socials.[53] Freud was indeed skeptical of the then opaque social experiment in the Soviet Union. Many analysts in Freud's inner circle, however, were socialists and social democrats.[54] Few were oblivious to their fraught milieu.[55] The view of Freud as a conservative arises not from partisan ties but from an inclination of psychoanalysis to favor interior explanation.[56] Freud himself was keenly alert to the interaction of the environment with the developing psyche. If blame lies within, though, as it can seem in certain analytic writings, the social order is let off the hook.

One finds this exculpatory mechanism at work in Lasswell's volumes on America and in Nathan Leites' treatment of bolshevism, depicting revolution as a revolt against the father image.[57] The Johnson and Nixon White Houses, those shining repositories of mental hygiene, were overjoyed during the Vietnam War to have their foes derided by some analysts as 'obsolete youth' set on clashes with authority for no good reason.[58]

Far from favoring intrapsychic explanations, Freud 'recognized that ego and superego are continuously enmeshed with outside forces—family, politics, religion.'[59] Despite that measured stance, the earliest Freudian formulations, Rappaport writes, 'may at times have given the impression that the organism is totally autonomous from its environment.'[60] Many early psychoanalysts showed 'little regard for social influences' until ego psychology, spurred by Heinz Hartmann and Erik Erikson, came to the fore by the 1960s, viewing 'man in the context of his society.' Ego psychology recognized that reality (environment) can shape the ego and drives and that the ego had its own initiative. Under Freud's earlier drive theory, one beheld society's function in a Hobbesian way as inhibiting hostility, or else channeling it. Freud later softened this position, writing 'we suggest one can ameliorate the condition of civilization imposing such costs for renunciation and to avoid suffering that is indeed avoidable, though not all of it is avoidable.'[61] The same holds true for the sources of fear.

STIMULUS AND CONDITIONAL RESPONSE

'Each stimulus is not transparent,' psychoanalytic writers caution, 'having an obvious significance.'[62] Indeed, the meaning of any behavior 'is not primarily a property of the behavior itself, but of the relation between the behavior and the context'—and that connection is made, and meaning conferred, by the behaver.[63] The upshot is that 'the stimulus that reaches the individual does not register directly but are first internally reconstituted in such a way as to give them personal, even idiosyncratic meaning' so that, among other things, there 'is no direct of necessary connection between one's social condition and one's subjectivity.'[64] This insight was well understood by Freud and a philosophically sophisticated group of early followers.[65]

From this point—beholding the stimulus, and making something of it—the beholders' interests, operational codes, professional experience and psychological predilections all come into the fray. Psychoanalysis, far from viewing people as passive receptors of cues or as analogical dupes, interposes 'psychic reality' between subject and social order, thus 'making possible the pursuit of the feminist project of revealing the construction of the subject, without necessitating a mirroring relation.' Indeed, to affirm instincts is to 'range oneself squarely against domestication.'[66] Feminists in psychoanalytic ranks oppose a 'direct, unmediated, and uncontested translation and transference of patriarchal values'—or any other kind of value.[67] Therefore, one ought to be wary of yielding to interiorizing inclinations, or to caricatures. Reducing social events to psychological ones is as misleading as 'ascribing all psychological phenomena to the impact of societal forces.'[68]

Some analysts venture out anyway to locate the primal causes of organized human conflict.[69] These included Erich Fromm, Frankfurt School scholars, Reich in the 1930s and R. D. Laing.[70] In the Baskin-Robbins emporium of psychoanalysis, where a Lacan or a Klein figures as just one of thirty-some flavors, the Kleinians are especially interested in aggression and its infantile sources, concentrating on the phenomena of projective identification, envy and paranoia. For Freudians the infant wants to kill the father and monopolize the mother while for Kleinians the infant wants to kill the father and murder the (disappointing) mother too.[71] One can imagine why IR specialists especially like Kleinians, when they like analysts at all.

In *Group Psychology and the Analysis of The Ego*, Freud applied analytic concepts to explain irrational cohesion and conformity, to be found in inner circles of every kind. Freud moved gingerly out of the consulting room, aware of hazards in doing so, which does not mean any were avoided. The couch exacts its solipsistic revenge. This inbuilt uncertainty induces some clinicians to throw their hands figuratively in the air. So how would Freudian analysts answer the perennial query whether, for example, Stalin was paranoid?[72] The customary surmise is that he may have become so, but even paranoiacs have enemies. The key indicator for Freud as to whether unconscious motives and drives were operative is 'excessiveness.' Symbolism too can be carried too far. Scanning a symbolic account of Gandhi's march to protest the salt tax, Coles sensibly observes that 'in the immediate context of the chronic semi-starvation that has undermined the vitality of the Indian masses and considering the periodic threat of widespread death by famine, it would seem appropriate, first of all, that salt means salt.'[73]

In political science, psychoanalysis has been confined largely to personalities. From the armchair analysis of Woodrow Wilson to psychohistorians of varying merit, to *Bush on the Couch*, most psychoanalytic work smacks of *ad hominem* argument.[74] The analyst may discuss symptoms but the imputed symptoms are borne by individuals. Yet is it not worth asking why certain policy makers, and not others, exaggerate or underplay threats? It's advisable to exhaust 'situational' explanations before turning to psychology for aid. There is the rational cynicism of leaders to examine before one probes unconscious motives. The psychic depths are not the first place to go when material interests readily account for policy inclinations. Yet such study can provide information we need to understand why a 'trigger,' so to speak, was pulled.

Freud's social psychology is shot through with ambivalence. Man 'is rapacious and self-centered [but] Freud recognizes as well the natural sociability of man, his permanent emotional need for community,' Rieff writes.[75] For Freudians to argue solely from expediency and mutual advantage is to treat the matter in 'far too rational a matter,' and implies what is plainly untrue, that social cohesion does not outlast 'the immediate advantage gained from the other people's collaboration.' So explanations of social unity based purely on 'economic interest and political expediency' are going to be inadequate.

At one psychoanalytic extreme, interest is read as manifest content, while the other end is that of psychological motives being privileged as 'more real.' So the flip side of seeking insight into psychological motives and mechanisms, and their dodges and feints within rational decision-making, is a belief that social relations play to psychological needs. All authority is derivative of the *Totem and Taboo* patriarch while dissent is described as puerile or neurotic. That won't do as a menu. The abiding question is how do we square rationalist explanations with inquiries into the role of irrational forces, or decide in what instance which approach should be regarded as uppermost. A final caveat is that rancor between psychoanalysis and its enemies pale in comparison to conflicts between rival schools. The Georges remarked that critics told them the 'Kohut approach or Erikson approach or Karen Horney approach would be more illuminating'—an experience everyone in the field undergoes.[76] In the writer's experience with critics the Lacanian approach monopolizes illuminative capacity nowadays.

Psychiatrists, Theologians and Constructivists

Henry Kissinger in 1999 wagged a finger at non-*realpolitik* rivals for their naive 'tendency to divide foreign policy into two schools of thought. One that identified foreign policy as a subdivision of psychiatry and another treated it as a subdivision of theology.' The psychiatrist, he stated, 'thinks relations among nations are like relations among people and you bring peace through this strenuous exercise of goodwill.' The theologians, on the other hand, 'believe that all foreign policies are a struggle between good and evil and the thing to do is to destroy the wrongdoer once and for all, after which normalcy returns.'[77] Theologians, by this definition, occupied Washington in 2000, which did not diminish Kissinger's willingness to work with the breed.

If Kissinger imagined psychiatrists act only with gentle good will, he knew little about the profession. In retrospect, some psychiatric knowledge might have come in handy when dealing with Nixon's behavior.[78] Then again, maybe not. 'We're up against an enemy, a conspiracy,' Nixon, who devised the illegal Houston Plan, COINTELPRO, secret bombings of Cambodia and Laos and the Watergate break-in, told his subordinates.[79] What might one make of this projection? Yet spotting an erratic leader does not mean one ignores the system in which they operate and the rivals he/she is up against. The guideline is to look to psychoanalytic factors when people are not behaving as informed outsiders reckon they should, not acting rationally either in the rational choice sense or in a common sensical mode.

No one can put a president on the couch (except in a movie). The nearest thing to a psychiatrist making a difference in international affairs is the White House plumbers raiding the office of Daniel Ellsberg's psychiatrist, triggering a cascade of events that led to Nixon's downfall. Given his 1972 reelection landslide, few can fathom why Nixon risked his presidency by placing it in the hands of the reckless plumbers (called such because their task was to stop leaks). So there are grounds for probing deeper into personality structure than is customary for social scientists—though never forgetting the structural components of the subject's situation.

Freudian psychoanalysis, at its best, sticks to a person's subjectivity without losing sight of the biological basis of social life.[80] Against radical constructivists, Gay notes, 'psychoanalysis reminds us that there are indeed universal problems—the relationship between love and hate, men and women, and individuals and groups—that everyone negotiates.'[81]

To contend, like Wendt, that individuals 'formulate their actions only as a rational response to particular situations, is as much a statement about their nature as to suggest that they behave according to innate drives,' a British critic acutely observes. Here the state, like the individual, is a 'blank sheet,' but 'if human behavior merely mirrors other human behavior, where does source behavior come from?' In constructivism, in sum, there is no 'core of recalcitrance to human conduct' (despite Wendt allowing that there is value in a psychoanalytic approach).[82] Is such a formulation realistic?

For Freudian psychoanalysts, 'there is deep within man an unbreakable nucleus, a central portion of the self ineluctably in opposition to society.'[83] Freud found 'every individual is virtually an enemy of culture' because instinctive needs are at war with social restrictions.[84] Inner conflicts remain, regardless of repression. Freud cannot settle for a portrayal of people as purely rational calculators. Constructivists (and most cognitive psychologists) see states, and people, as summations of reflected appraisals, with no combative core. Constructivists contend that states have 'identities' and can be 'persons'; although, probing these identities, one finds nothing like the conflictual process of maturation that psychoanalysis investigates.[85] The problem here is that constructivists mistake what psychoanalysts call a 'role' for an 'identity' or conflate the concepts. Erikson's 'ego identity,' for example, is 'the accrued confidence that the inner sameness and continuity prepared in the past are matched by the sameness and continuity of one's meaning for others.' An achieved identity is solid, resilient and more or less balanced, which is what constructivism asserts about state 'identities,' but which states plainly cannot possess. Indeed, a role is what is played by a disturbed patient who lacks an identity—'an identity based upon a role disintegrates when the role collapses under the stress of real life situations.'[86] The person who is playing a role is performing, and he requires a receptive audience. So when Wendt says that, like 'any collective intention, state persons can only be real as long as individuals accept and participate in their existence' he is not talking about something psychoanalysis views as an 'identity' at all.[87] The term 'identity' is divested of its former content in order to fit what Wendt wants to make of the state, a strikingly shallow person.[88]

Sucharov's study of Israeli-Palestinian relations insists on 'the ontological possibility of a group self in the form of a state identity.'[89] Sucharov believes states 'share some elements of human psychology' to the extent that 'powerful unconscious fears can plague an actor (state) which has strayed from the action path suggested by her identity.'[90] This imputed identity is formed through internalization of norms over time, and through guiding narratives that actors tell themselves about the state's *raison d'etre*. Hence, states, not just leaders and functionaries, suffer cognitive dissonance from clashes between a cherished identity (self-image) and uncongenial roles they undertake. Yet is there any evidence at all that George W. Bush and his team experienced qualms about violating international norms that the American state is known for promoting? Can the Israeli state, as opposed to individuals or groups within it, feel remorse or guilt such that it explains why Israel 'sought peace' with the PLO after the second intifada (a highly contested assertion in some quarters)? Political parties, and lower-level organizations, may boast identities that they then impose on the state when they take power. To claim there is an 'overarching group self' to the state is stretching things.

PSYCHE, SELF-INTEREST AND WARFARE

Updating Thucydides, 'what made war inevitable was the presence of WMD in Iraq and the fear this caused in the United States.' There is ample room here for interpretive work.[91] What is at stake is not only a possible shift in relative capabilities but also what a powerful actor was inclined to see the other's actions as portending. Freud, after the outbreak of war, remarked in a proto-realist way, 'Psycho-analysis has inferred from dreams and parapraxes of healthy people as well as from the symptoms of neurotics, that the primitive, savage and evil impulses of mankind have not vanished in any of its individual members, but persists, although in a repressed state, in the unconscious [and] It has further taught us that our intellect is ... a plaything and tool of our instincts and affects. If you will observe what is happening in this war—the cruelties and injustices for which the most civilized nations are responsible, the different way in which they judge their own lies and wrong-doings and those of their enemies and the general lack of insight which prevails—you will have to admit that psychoanalysis has been right in both these theses.'[92]

World War I spurred Freud's death instinct hypothesis, of an aggressive, destructive drive independent of sexuality.[93] Waltz likely approves Freud's point that 'war cannot be abolished so long as the conditions of existence among nations are so different and their mutual repulsion so violent, there are bound to be wars' but, more utopianly, Freud noted 'war will only be prevented with certainty if mankind unites in setting up a central authority to which the right of giving judgment upon all conflicts of interest shall be handed over.' Freud declined to attribute war to instincts running amok; he espied room for improvement in realizing one's 'enlightened' self-interest. How did war tally with self-interest— whether from the vantage point of individual or state—anyway?

Historians and social scientists rarely examine the 'psychological status of self-interest or to trace its actual incidence in human life,' Gay charges.[94] The 'cold calculations that shape actions are less interesting (and often in the long run less important) than the passions that produced the calculations in the first place.' So psychoanalytic researchers study how 'individuals and groups internalize [socially induced] deceptions and take them to be their own ideas' (strongly akin to the Marxist notion of false consciousness). He contends: 'Much like a neurotic symptom, self-interest is a compromise formation: and much like the ego, an interest must cope with three generally hostile forces: the outside world (the depository of competing interests), the superego (which pours out distressing reminders that others too have valid claims and that one's own claims are at best suspect) and the id (which incessantly generates wishes). That is why the ideas of a self-interest wholly rational, clearly perceived and consistently pursued, is largely an abstraction.'[95] So the serrated boundary line between material interest and intrusive psyche really runs thin in most cases and therefore is open to psychoanalytic forays.

Fornari highlighted a vital aspect of the legitimation of war as it being based on the group defending itself against acute internal anxieties [and] 'in this manner we arrive at the paradox that the most important security function is not defend ourselves from an external enemy but to find one.'[96] The mechanism here is projective identification: 'If I project aggression on to the other, he or she is likely to become—in reality—the mirror or embodiment of the aggression I am trying to displace into him or her.'[97] If this is old news it is because psychoanalysis earlier unveiled it.[98] Winnicott and Fromm contended that people more often go to war because they are afraid of freedom, and its uncertainties, than in order to extend freedom to others, as Bush claimed. Fromm found no 'cruelty and viciousness which has not been rationalized individually or [presented] as being motivated by good intentions.'[99] This process gets especially complex when leaders display a deft ability to believe whatever is expedient, and in this ruse intrapsychic mechanisms and external motives mingle. As Brooks and Woloch put it, psychoanalysis fosters 'an attitude of suspicion toward human behaviour and ostensible motives, a semiotic postulate that in all actors [there are] messages to be read, a genealogical undermining of claims to unalloyed virtue, disinterestedness and civilization.'[100] What would such beholders make of the Vietnam War, or the 'war on terror'?

Two, Three, Many Vietnam Syndromes

The Vietnam War is not usually regarded as ripe stuff for couch analysis.[101] Psychoanalysts shied away, instead of taking on related issues such as PTSD.[102] However, at least one analytical account probed 'narcissistic personality disorders' in Lyndon Johnson and Richard Nixon—a disorder that seems a job requirement.[103] The question why these leaders, and LBJ's 'best and the brightest' advisers, went so awry in Southeast Asia remains intriguing and inadequately understood. Free world leadership, institutional inertia, anti-communist ideology, bureaucratic politics, leaders' personal reputations, the military-industrial complex, misplaced optimism in counterinsurgency techniques are all among the factors driving the USA deep into the 'big muddy.'

Cognitive psychology has scoured this irresistible subject. 'From a cognitivist point of view, all causal inferences and policy lessons are the product of mental constructions of what would, could, or might have happened had a different set of antecedent conditions held or policies been tried,' explain Goldgeier and Tetlock.[104] 'There is, in principle, an infinite number of possible background factors that one could enter as antecedents in one's counterfactual constructions of alternative worlds.' So 'observers must rely on draconian simplifying rules that reduce the number of scenarios to be entertained to a humanly manageable number.' The price exacted by reliance on 'draconian simplifying assumptions' can be very high. Parsimony isn't always a virtue.

Policy makers, according to this tack, became mesmerized by 'analogies' in the form of falling dominoes or Munich-like appeasement. These analogies matter because 'policy makers routinely turn to the past for guidance.'[105] Such 'schematic processing' made it 'difficult for policymakers to appreciate the local forces at work in Vietnam.' So policy inertia chugged on. In this regard too, Elster, who scolds psychoanalysis for concocting 'meaning where none exists,' cannot account for why people adopt 'cold mechanisms, these cognitive logics so rigid and naïve that they systemically lead people into error'—errors that can be 'individually farcical and collectively tragic.'[106] Perhaps, contrary to Elster, one is entitled to probe 'inside' in order to understand underlying reasons?

The supreme problem for Khong is a 'breakdown of consensus' because a 'consensus' is deemed a good thing even though it ushered the USA into Vietnam. Perhaps policy makers were ensnared in an axiomatic tangle of their own making, but it is clear from the *Pentagon Papers* that this was a system for which they had a strong 'elective affinity' inasmuch as particular analogies were chosen as the most likely ones that the public would swallow.[107] *The Pentagon Papers* show that McGeorge Bundy invoked domino theory, but only after he 'rejected even the subtle argument, offered by some long-time Asian experts, that the uniqueness of the Vietnamese case, particularly its extraordinary lack of political structure, invalidated any generalization of our experience there to the rest of Asia.'[108] If 'domino theorists' did not know that the theory was disputed, it was not because they were unaware. Hans Morgenthau in debates with Bundy poured scorn on domino theory.[109] Cabinet naysayer George Ball, citing Japan, ridiculed domino theory at high-level meetings.[110] There was 'no shortage of Southeast Asian specialists in the foreign affairs and intelligence wars of the US government,' a former CIA analyst states, but the 'consumers did not want what they were producing.'[111]

This ample latitude of choice undermines the cognitivist case that policy makers had become hapless prisoners of analogical reasoning. Morton Halperin noted that Defense Secretary Clark Clifford on a trip to South Asia 'discovered to his amazement that none of the countries in the region shared our view about the dominos.'[112] A cognitive psychology account, if anything, is likely to furnish convenient if inadvertent 'cover' for policies pursued for other reasons (and irrational reasons are reasons too.) Khong's argument seems true in the same manner as is Viennese satirist Karl Krauss's acid sally that 'diplomats lie to journalists and then believe those lies when they see them in print.'

Another stellar example is the MACV underestimate (by several hundred thousands) of insurgents available to the National Liberation Front in the run-up to the Tet offensive when US officials were boasting of progress in pacification.[113] This underestimate was doubtless deliberate; the only question was the motive. A motive far stronger than 'simplifying and filtering operations of human cognitive processing' was at work when deciding who counts as an enemy guerrilla at a time when authorities were under severe pressure to deliver good news.[114] An abiding flaw in the cognitive psychologists' 'trust-building approach' is that when policy makers 'ignored or misinterpreted evidence of the other's desire for an accord' (regarding arms control, an economic treaty or a peace agreement) the motive need not be 'guiding beliefs' at all but rather the decision-makers' calculations that they could succeed on their own terms anyway. Only if that familiar possibility is found wanting can unconscious processes credibly come into consideration as significant factors.[115]

Puzzling over LBJ's escalation in Vietnam over 1964–1965, Kaiser sees the inadvisable series of decisions as a matter of 'personality and choice,' goaded by a 'GI generation' of advisors who experienced nothing but success in all earlier endeavors.[116] Yet the Rural Affairs Office in Vietnam reported in 1963 that the pacification campaign was 'a will-o-the wisp'—a failure.[117] Senator Mike Mansfield and others counseled Johnson to avoid a catastrophic commitment to shore up a flimsy South Vietnam regime.[118] LBJ and close aides had many well-documented reasons to be wary about the sinuous course of events. Former defense secretary Robert McNamara later stirred a furor with a *mea culpa* book on Vietnam, but his claim that he didn't know until long afterward that the Vietnamese liberation movement was nationalist is, to say the least, extremely dubious.[119]

'McNamara now says we didn't know anything about Vietnam and what was really happening was not understood,' complained a State Department analyst. 'That's a lot of garbage. We would come out with papers showing that things were going very badly indeed.'[120] Dissent contradicting official optimism was assiduously ignored. This response constitutes denial in both the everyday and psychoanalytic senses of the word, and it runs up and down bureaucratic organizational ladders. Hence, a social worker in 1969 reported that co-workers treated reports of the My Lai atrocity as 'obviously delusional.'[121] They found it impossible to believe Americans committed war crimes.

Psychoanalytic relevance again is triggered by excessiveness, as in an encounter between LBJ and Moyers on 1 July 1965.[122] Moyers was troubled by the President's 'paranoia' and had been contacted by high officials who were 'deeply concerned' too. One day the 'President would be in severe depression' and '24 hours later, no one who had seen him this way would ever have suspected it.' LBJ, by selective uptake of intelligence input, quelled his doubts that the USA could salvage the South

Vietnam regime.[123] Yet whenever Johnson returned to Vietnam the 'cloud in his eyes' and 'predictably unpredictable behavior' reappeared. Moyers and Goodwin went so far as to speak to psychiatrists about LBJ. The President informed Goodwin 'that since he couldn't trust anyone anymore he was going to get rid of everybody who disagrees with his policies.'[124] The classic paranoiac impact was to transform Goodwin into someone LBJ couldn't trust either.

Was the US fighting in Vietnam to maintain its global credibility, as a key justification goes? The 'doctrine of credibility,' Logervall notes, 'is a psychological rather than territorial domain theory.'[125] Against assertions that 'American credibility was on the line,' Logervall cites DeGaulle's plea in 1963 to cease intervention in the South and permit a coalition compromise.[126] Only a handful of nations supported, or could be induced to support, the growing American misadventure. 'What allied and non-aligned government questioned was not America's will, but its judgment,' Logerval tartly observes.[127] LBJ operated 'less out of concern for American credibility, I believe, than out of fear for their own personal credibility; it became a 'question of manliness for LBJ.' Doris Kearns recorded LBJ's 'recurring dream' early in the war that pulling out of Vietnam would bring hordes of hawks (including *bête noir* Robert Kennedy before his turnaround) down on him as a 'coward. An unmanly man. A man without a spine.'[128]

> Oh I could see it coming, all right. Every night when I fell asleep I old see myself tied to the ground in the middle of a long open space. In the distance I could hear the voices of thousands of people. They were all shouting and running toward me: 'Coward! Traitor! Weakling!'

Unless circumstantial necessity can be demonstrated, Logerval's suggestion is a compelling hypothesis. Moyar too viewed Johnson as able to go either way in 1964–1965 on Vietnam.[129] Moyar quotes LBJ's tragic plea that he had 'the choice to go in with greater casualty lists or to get out with disgrace.'[130] Here is an emotive plight, roiling with idiosyncratic personal predilections, that it would be very odd for analysts to ignore. Deputy Secretary of Defense John McNaughton, by 1967 too concluded the 'US objective in Vietnam is to avoid humiliation' in 'an escalating military stalemate.'[131] The scare word 'humiliation,' attests a *Pentagon Papers* researcher, reverberated up and down executive branch corridors. Curiously, by contrast, President Reagan later did not feel, nor was in any way made to feel, 'humiliated' for pulling Marines out of Lebanon after the massive barracks bombing in 1982.

Steinberg identifies pivotal moments for LBJ in 1965 and for Richard Nixon in 1969–1970 when force of circumstance was not operative and both presidents retained the option of backing off commitments to a predicament that they viewed with misgivings. Steinberg detects the clinching clues in the inner worlds of LBJ and Nixon, leaders 'prone to shame and humiliation when thwarted,' or about to be, and who therefore unwisely escalated.[132] Even Kissinger, despite a renowned distaste for psychiatry, wondered what Nixon would have been like had somebody loved him.[133] Steinberg's 'control group' here is Dwight Eisenhower who by her reckoning was a well-balanced personality who declined military intervention at Dien Ben Phu (Eisenhower, out of office, nonetheless advised Johnson and Nixon to 'go all out' once bogged down in Vietnam).[134] Unable to live up to their own idealized standards, LBJ and Nixon 'externalize the punitive unconscious self-criticism,' which then comes back to them magnified, and malevolently so.[135] In layman's terms, both presidents responded to perceived challenges to their brittle masculinity by acting rashly when the actual situation, and the institutional dynamics in play, did not remotely warrant it. What opens up here are opportunities for prying open not only the 'black box' of the state but of political agents too in those important instances where neither the domestic political environment nor structural exigencies dictate reactions.

9/11 AND THE MISMANAGEMENT OF FEAR

Realpolitik proponents blanch at the post-9/11 neoconservative *Project for a New American Century* agenda, an agenda featuring a grandiosity worthy of a distinct DSM-IV category. Whether the Bush administration strategy for Iraq, and all the wishful thinking therein, is describable as 'rational' is a matter for debate, but one can allow it for the moment. Cognitive explorations of 9/11 cannot explain why Americans— 'unaided' by the drumbeat of incessant insinuations—came to identify Saddam Hussein as culprit when the evidence to the contrary was abundant. No matter how much weight scholars attribute to the role of emotions, a vengeful US public did not drive a reluctant Bush administration into war in Iraq. Granting the post-9/11 sense of national peril, the next step is to look at the tactics used by US and UK leaders to persuade citizenries to 'disarm' Iraq. Bush and Tony Blair deployed propaganda blitzes. To rephrase Thucydides again, 'What made war inevitable was the presence of WMD) in Iraq and the fear this caused in the United States.' Even champions of the invasion of Iraq at the time now admit there is a great deal wrong with that sentence. We are no longer concerned with shifts in relative capabilities (between Iraq and the West anyway) but with whatever one set of players (state A) was inclined, indeed determined, to see the actions by a counterpart player (state B) as portending, and why.

One doesn't need a Freudian to show that by stirring fear a central authority can win acquiescence to radical schemes purporting to protect the citizenry. Lasswell discussed how elites manage the 'direction of discharge of insecurities' and about how a group can go about 'capturing attention and guiding mass insecurities.'[136] Politicians who have little else credibly to offer ordinary citizens readily resort to this maneuver. Security is a 'bewitchment' word, in Wittgenstein's sense, which induces beholders to mistake the word for the thing it promises to provide, when the authorities' actions produce the opposite of the announced effect. It may be impeccably rational, from the authorities' 'nested' vantage point, to behave aggressively abroad because blowback redounds to their benefit insofar as it is interpreted as evidence of need for more of the same coercive medicine, which augments their power.

Psychoanalysts have contributions to make in parsing out these complex motivations. A psychoanalytic approach is warranted in circumstances where one has reason to believe that, because of asymmetric power, 'oppression gets psychologically inverted: the oppressor is the victim who is defending himself.'[137] It is a truism in international relations that the attacker never deems itself the aggressor, but rather a wounded party. Why should the weak not suffer what they must, with Thucydidean fatalism, and national leaders leave it at that, with Thucydidean realism? Clearly, no one ever leaves it at that. Psychoanalysis aids efforts to explain why.

A strong case can be made for applying psychoanalytic method even in instances where interest-oriented models seem to do the job. One may have good cause to suspect that realpolitik functions as an excuse for doing what one wants for less 'rational' reasons. Morgenthau reproved McGeorge Bundy, and other, on this score regarding Vietnam.[138] 'These disastrous policies consistently pursued served the self-protection of by those who have initiated or inherited them,' Morgenthau wrote. 'We are here in the presence of an issue not of foreign policy or military strategy, but of psychopathology.'[139] Indeed, political figures believe they rarely can go too far in pleading for security and its accompanying dilemma. 'Getting tough' plays well at home and even politicians who know better played along, as in the 2003 vote authorizing action against Iraq. Yet, as Page and Bouton, among others, attest, surveys disclose a public that is less belligerent, and more conciliatory, than their leaders (which overturns hoary Lasswellian caricatures).[140]

Did George W. Bush invade Iraq due to unresolved Oedipal conflict?[141] The problem for psychoanalytical explanations is twofold: first, nearly every move Bush made can be explained in rationalist terms; second, Bush's advisers encouraged his foreign policy venture. 'In trying to understand the frequently unconscious aims of individuals it often helps to ignore what they say, to themselves as well as to us, and to look as ingenuously as possible at what they seem to be trying to do,' a veteran psychotherapist advises, 'in which case the aims may become surprisingly obvious.'[142] Few IR specialists will contest the view that the weight assigned to psychological (or structural) factors needs to be tempered by attention to deeds, to what actors 'are trying to do.'

CONCLUSION

Psychoanalysis offers analytical added value in cases especially where ideational analysis can be said to apply, and where pivotal decisions depart from what observers reasonably agree is rational action. Multiple equilibria invite deeper looks at the motivational bases of the participants. Past applications of psychoanalysis either tended to cleave to 'top-down' elite theory or else applied individual methodology uncritically to collective phenomena that really are the hybrid product of many factors. State managers certainly can behave irrationally in ways that do not require depth psychology for an explanation.

Psychoanalysis requires an investment in time, resources and sometimes clinical training. Psychoanalysis does not begin and end with Lacan, as one might infer from the discourse-oriented IR practitioners parsing this realm (indeed, the hermeneutical element of Lacan's work that intrigues IR specialists often has little to do with the clinical psychoanalysis of dreams, drives, ambivalence, relationships and unconscious forces). Will an academic knowledge pay off in insight for scholars or even policy makers? One obvious danger here is mere indulgence in formulaic dead-end 'parlor analysis.' But, apart from guidance in investigating puzzling policy decisions, psychoanalysis urges us to examine the motives behind the models we deploy. Still, the field of IR, and political science generally, tends toward quantitative and formal modeling.[143] Even those who are historical in approach usually do well enough without depth psychology. What then is to be gained?

The force of the circumstances and institutions ('operational codes') in which leaders find themselves override personal considerations—but not always. Structural forces, and institutional constraints, need not press the decision-maker to take one particular course of action. The 'sufficient' decision based on material factors may seem adequate from one angle and question-begging from another. One doesn't need a sadistic personality structure to launch a war, but it seems to help. It may be instructive to wonder what would have happened if, instead of Kennedy, Nixon or a grown-up George W. Bush had been President during the Cuban missile crisis? In any case, the task of parsing the interaction of agency and structure, of their 'mutual constitution,' too rarely is approached from the 'agency' end, perhaps because few in IR circles are disposed to try.[144]

Finally, the 'sunk cost fallacy,' encountered in Vietnam, is a descriptive term, and requires an explication of the personal psychodynamics underlying the decision rules invoked to account for it.[145] Why does one person, or group, 'stay the course' in a hazardous situation but another counsel against it? Emotional states, character structure and defenses help us to understand how leaders process what they behold. Even in cases where material circumstances seem overwhelmingly powerful, psychoanalysis still can illuminate our studies of decision-makers and group psychology and thereby 'open up space for human agency.'[146] What can we get away with not knowing when we analyze politics?, is not a compelling slogan to emblazon on a scholarly banner, Occam notwithstanding.

Addendum: Eli Zaretsky's Freud

Is psychoanalysis *kaput*? If not, ought it be put out of its misery? Sigmund Freud and his notorious 'problem child' have fallen on hard times and for reasons having virtually nothing to do with their real merits, argues historian Eli Zaretsky in his book *Political Freud: A History*.[147] Though a collection of five previously published articles, *Political Freud* musters a telling assault on a legion of critics who accuse Freud of straying recklessly from the truth, meaning truth as reckoned by diehard positivists, Big Pharma, and those obliging shrinks who want nothing more than to help clients to 'fit in' the social disorder. That's the neoliberal spirit.

Was Freud a political animal? Yes, Zaretsky answers, from the very first and in important ways. That Freud sympathized strongly with the Social Democrats of 'Red Vienna' is the least of it. Zaretsky, the author of the splendid *Secrets of the Soul*, among other works, resurrects political Freud 'to reaffirm the critical element in Freudianism' and to trace out why this dynamic radical core became all but eclipsed. Since the rampant denigration of psychoanalysis in the 1970s onward, Zaretsky argues, we have taken a 'huge step backward' in explaining the mysteries and the slippery grip of irrationality in our lives.

In an achingly ironic fashion Freud, that exquisite connoisseur of ambivalence, should appreciate, the very success of psychoanalysis in the early to mid-twentieth century generated a milieu that hastened its own decline in an ever more individualistic epoch. Zaretsky 'highlights two seemingly antithetical moments: a critical moment when political thinkers and social movements looked to psychoanalysis to clarify the irrational sources of domination and an affirmative moment when Freudianism became submerged in a larger history and appeared to become obsolete.'[148] Zaretsky briskly embarks on his mission of integrating 'psychoanalysis into the broad matrix of modern social and cultural history,' which he persuasively says 'has barely begun.'

The first essay reconsiders Max Weber's analysis of the role of the Protestant ethic in capitalism, which requires a motivating spirit (if only as a cloak) for its remorseless acquisitiveness. This 'spirit' changes roughly as the economy develops, so Calvinist discipline 'helped generate the utopian ideology of individuality that accompanied mass consumption.'[149] In a liberal vein Daniel Bell, among others, pondered the implications of this shift in his *The Cultural Contradictions of Capitalism*. This shift entailed a freeing of individuals from the chafing authority rooted in family life, which is in turn rooted in, and reflective of, society. Hence, one cannot speak validly of the inner world in isolation from external events. That essential insight alone makes Freudian psychoanalysis inescapably political. Individuality in the dawning twentieth century became 'the governing norm,' and for navigating our murky inner worlds psychoanalysis became 'a theory and practice of those new aspirations for a personal life [and] encouraging an inward development that is the only secure basis for progress.'

What was relished in this early psychoanalytic heyday was the freedom not to discover 'universally valid moral rules' but rather 'what one wants to do with one's life,' although these were hardly mutually exclusive activities. I am reminded of future prominent psychoanalyst Editha Sterba, who as a teenager would bask on a beach poring over a volume of Kant, which was not unusual for youngsters of her strata at the time. 'For psychoanalysis what matters was not worldly success but the state of one's soul.'[150] Psychoanalysis, with its 'charismatic, anti-institutional origins,' was indelibly subversive, or so it seemed. As Freud recognized, 'a bit of unconquerable nature lurks' inside all of us and is ever poised to upset any old institutional apple cart. The eroding of awareness of this crucial and subversive reality is at issue throughout the volume.

Zaretsky's complains that in the post-war phase the rapid rise of ego psychology, with its conformist 'maturity ethic,' arose to dilute and distort the radical crux of Freud's work. Psychoanalysis purported to study the 'durable, unique individual personality,' Zaretsky laments, even as a host of new 'intersubjective theories and practices insisted that no such thing ever existed.' The notion of a 'personal life interior to the individual was repudiated in favor of an emphasis on flexibility, sociality and sensitivity to difference.'[151] Why? Because in a new era of slick managerial capitalism 'image, personality and interpersonal skills, not autonomy, have the highest commercial value.' Mass diffusion, especially in post-war America, 'democratized and banalized a newly psychological way of thinking.' This is pretty much what Erich Fromm, who I suspect Zaretsky might lump among the ego psychologists, long ago diagnosed as the blight of 'other-directedness.'

Zaretsky's second essay is a fascinating probe into psychoanalysis as an illuminator of, and ingredient in, the transforming of blacks' self-image through the Harlem renaissance, the Popular Front and the Cold War eras. The 'achievement of genuine subjectivity' by urban blacks 'had to pass through a recognition of degradation,' and psychoanalysis became a valuable means for addressing and rectifying 'internal submission' and an unmastered past. The blues were 'a triumph over a shaming culture,' which "yearned for 'emancipation, including from the racial community itself," just as many Jews sought a way out of ghettoes imposed not only by hostile others but by tribal Jews themselves. W.E.B. Dubois, Frantz Fanon, Richard Wright, Ralph Ellison and other notables were preoccupied with the plight of 'double consciousness between self and gaze of others,' defining oneself through the eyes of others, although this tack ultimately seems to have had more to do with G. H. Mead's superficial social psychology than with Freudian analysis.

If there was no sex before the 1960s, as poet Philip Larkin averred, there apparently was no 'self' before the industrial age either. 'Self,' in this parched rendering, was the human being stripped of volcanic Freudian core and made up instead of little more than the 'reflected appraisals' of others—a conceptual recipe for abject or, for that matter, sly conformity. One can imagine why the corporate world warmed to resolutely hollow men and women. Ralph Ellison palled around with neo-Freudian Harry Stack Sullivan whose blunt essay, 'The Illusion of Human Personality,' sums up the stance nicely and icily. Richard Wright, though, recognizing 'mental states had a historical and social basis,' tried to combine Marx and Freud, and Zaretsky sees this quest pervading the later years of the Popular Front.[152] The remarkable Lafargue clinic in Harlem was attentive to social conditions creating neurosis, and its research into segregation as a public health problem contributed to the 1954 Supreme Court school desegregation decision. Meanwhile, in mainstream America, where medical schools and naive empiricism reigned, the Freudian canon slowly but steadily was recruited into 'the cold war synthesis as a supposed critic of utopian ideas and advocate of maturity.'

Zaretsky next tackles Freud's *Moses and Monotheism*, detecting that Freud's acute concern with Jewish identity, as an annihilatory World War loomed, was as much about the survival of psychoanalysis and, in turn, the survival of our collective spiritual and intellectual accomplishments. The Nazis were keen to obliterate it all. Today when genial greed *uber alles* is prized (behold Herr Trump) and civilizational and planetary reversals seem under way at breakneck, we might sympathize with Freud's attunement to the fragility of higher values. For Freud, monotheism was an advance that offered 'freedom from subordination to the senses and deepens the inner world.'[153] Monotheism and psychoanalysis, however, were 'difficult and even ascetic practices subject to vulgarization and distortion as they took a popular form.'

Like Moses confronting golden calf worshippers, Freud edgily faced Adler, Jung and other dissidents. What was at stake for Freud, Zaretsky explains, 'was the subjectivity or inwardness of *geistigkeit*, through which the mind rose above the instincts and encompassed its own ambivalence.'[157] *Geistigkeit* connotes spirituality in a not necessarily religious sense, and it aligns with the strictly secular meaning of soul in Bruno Bettelheim's splendid *Freud and Man's Soul*. The dissidents, who were well-meaning enough folks, let everyone off easy with palliatives geared to the tempo of glossy, quick fix-obsessed American life. The path to *geistigkeit*, toward a better-integrated and morally sound human being, was through resistances, which had to be worked through, not sidestepped. To get to what Lincoln called the better angels of our nature, one has to acknowledge and integrate the hellish aspects of that same nature. No shortcuts.

The fourth essay, 'The Ego at War' is a critique of Judith Butler's take on 9/11 in *Precarious Life*, but also of what Zaretsky regards as the vogue-ish and inadequate view that 'the ego is formed through object relations and language.' Freud over time moved to 'analyzing the ego's defenses rather than interpreting unconscious wishes directly,' but Melanie Klein and others of the object relations school went much further. This is a technically abstruse debate for most readers but Zaretsky carefully lays out what matters in it for the wider culture. Freud wanted to 'strengthen the ego while Klein wanted to strengthen personal relations.' Zaretsky pinpoints this latter trend, which will make some readers bridle, as the source of a 'weakening of concern with reason and justice and more on intersubjective relations.'

For Kleinians the relationship to the mother—curiously termed an 'object'—is the key to ethical responsibility so that the inception of the British welfare state then is attributed to the necessity to protect mothers and children (as if one needed a certified psychoanalyst to vouch for such a motive). Arising from this is a 'maternalist iconography of social democracy' so that a distinguished British Kleinian in June 1940 winds up condemning what she terms a 'Munich complex,' which is a manifestation of 'the son's incapacity to fight for mother and country.' This formulation is daft on so many levels that only Kleinian acolytes (and not all of them) could buy it. The kindest thing to say is that this explanatory mode is seriously incomplete. All experience is hyper-individualized and society is lost sight of.

Judith Butler, an object relations theorist, asks why after 9/11 the collective emotional make-up of America 'led away from intersubjective sadness and deliberation and toward vengeful, blind reaction.' Wrong question. While there is much to say in favor of Butler's analysis of the 'precariat,' despite oblique prose getting in the way, Zaretsky notes that Butler treats 9/11 as if every single American slavered for a lashing out in blind revenge. Anyone ever heard of the neocon *Project for a New American Century* gleefully kicking into gear? Butler commendably urges us toward a broadened circle of solidarity, Zaretsky notes, but this can go in two directions: one is benign and progressive; the other churning out more neoliberal 'free thinking' Ayn Rand fans. A Marxist critique is an essential supplement if we are to comprehend our elites' post-9/11 high jinks. Unlike Butler, the political Freud tradition refuses to treat 'dependence and independence as if they were antitheses [and] demonstrates rather the ego reaches down to its earliest, most primal, and essentially immortal dependencies precisely when it is strongest and most independent.'[155]

Zaretsky picks up momentum in his final essay which reappraises the New Left, feminism and a 'return to 'social reality.' In the 1960s Herbert Marcuse, especially, re-politicized Freud with an analysis of surplus repression. By the 1970s radical feminism and gay liberation, taking aim (rather understandably) at visible power imbalances, give a Freud they misunderstand the bum's rush. Psychoanalysis still 'embodied powerful sexual and other emancipatory currents that key socializing institutions, above all the family, could not contain,' but this mutinous aspect was muted or ditched as analysts too gradually were enlisted in a project that 'weakened traditional authority but substituted the adjustment, labeling and manipulation that the New Left criticized.' Psychoanalysis thereby lost analytical depth. Juliet Mitchell criticized fellow feminists for reducing everything to power relations and promoting culture over biology, which, Zaretsky correctly (I think) accuses, only 'paved the way for accommodation with neoliberal thought.' These erstwhile rebels were suckered into a 'rights revolution' focused on discrimination against individuals while downplaying structural reform. Thus, again ironically, viewing 'the past in terms of power has left men and women powerless' before our worst enemies. Abandoning a notion of authority as entailing an unconscious or intrapsychic dimension was 'a gift to neoliberalism.'

How liberated are we anyway? 'Can we honestly say,' Zaretsky rhetorically asks, 'that a society that is based on release of the instincts, on gratification and on a turning away from guilt, at least at the conscious level, is a freer, more just and more civilized society than the repressive one it replaced?' Zaretsky draws our attention to our blind spots and to the most peculiar ways in which we have colluded in blinding ourselves. A dangerously neglected value of psychoanalysis is that it 'enables radicals to look at internal sources of woes, class exploitation within, violence internal to liberalism, misogyny internal to family and violence internal to nation state.' Readers will emerge from *Political Freud* with a clearer sense of what is lost and must be recovered in the much-maligned psychoanalytic tradition.

NOTES

1. See Kurt Jacobsen, *Freud's Foes: Psychoanalysis, Science, and Resistance* (Lanham, Md: Rowman and Littlefield, 2009) and Paul Robinson, *Freud and His Critics* (Berkeley: University of California Press, 2003).
2. Lawrence Falkowski (ed.), *Psychological Models in International Politics* (Boulder: Westview Press, 1979). A decade later one essay in a political psychology volume mentions Freud. See Eric Singer and Valerie Hudson (eds.), *Political Psychology and Foreign Policy* (Boulder, Colo: Westview, 1992). A decade later authors discuss psychology and IR without reference to psychoanalysis. J. M. Goldgeier and P. E. Tetlock, 'Psychology and International Relations Theory', *American Political Science Review* 95(4) 2001. Another decade and also Freudless is Vaughn P. Shannon and Peter Kowert (eds.), *Psychology and Constructivism in International Relations* (Ann Arbor: University of Michigan Press, 2012). An exception containing 3 essays regarding analysts is British. See Jenny Edkins and Nick Vaughn-Williams (eds.), *Critical Theorists and International Relations* (London: Routledge, 2009).
3. Paul Roazen, *Freud: Political and Social Thought* (New York, Vintage, 1968), p. 5.
4. Cynthia Weber delivered a feminist slant on policy in *Faking It: American Hegemony in a Post-Phallic Era* (Minneapolis: University of Minnesota Press, 1999). Other exceptions are Europeans or are not political scientists: Jenny Edkins, Charlotte Epstein, and Badredine Arfi. Richard Schuett, author of the 2010 Palgrave Macmillan volume *Freud, Human Nature, and International Relations*, is housed in a psychology department. I rest my case.
5. Powerful institutions have 'obscene, disordered undersides'. Slavoj Zizek, *Violence* (London: Profile Books, 2008), p. 142. Erich Fromm describes a 'social unconscious' as 'that specific part of human experience which a given society does not permit to reach awareness. ...' Fromm, *Beyond The Chains of Illusion* (New York: Continuum Books, 1962), pp. 103fn16.
6. 'I would not say that an attempt of this kind to carry psycho-analysis over to the cultural community would be absurd or doomed to be fruitless. But we should have to be very cautious and not forget that, after all, we are dealing with analogies and that it is dangerous, not only with men but also with concepts, to tear them away from the sphere in which

they have originated and been evolved'. Freud, *Civilization and Its Discontents* (New York: Norton, 1962), p. 91.
7. Geoffrey Gorer, 'Psychoanalysis in the World,' in Charles Rycroft, ed, *Psychoanalysis Observed* (London: Constable, 1966), pp. 28–29.
8. Badredine Arfi, 'Fantasy in the Discourse of Social Theory of International Politics,' *Cooperation and Conflict* 45, 4 (2010), p. 428.
9. Hans Morgenthau, *Politics Among Nations* (New York: Knopf, 1973, 5th ed), p. 7. Morgenthau wondered if psychology and psychiatry could construct 'a counter-theory of irrational politics, a kind of pathology of international politics.'
10. Neta C. Crawford, 'The Passion of World Politics: Propositions of Emotion and Emotional Relationships.' *International Security* 24(4), 2000), p. 156.
11. Wilhelm Reich, *Sex-Pol* (New York: Random House, 1972), pp. 3–37.
12. Jonathan Mercer, 'Rationality and Psychology in International Politics.' *International Organization* 59(1), 2005, p. 81.
13. Robert Jervis, *Perception and Misperception in International Politics* (Princeton University Press 1976): Deborah Larson, *Origins of Containment* (Princeton: Princeton University Press, 1985); Rose McDermott, *Political Psychology in International Relations* (Ann Arbor: University of Michigan Press, 2007 rev.) and *Anatomy of Mistrust* (Ithaca: Cornell University Press, 1997), and Yuen Foong Khong, *Analogies at War* (Princeton: Princeton University Press, 1992).
14. Rifts *within* psychoanalysis are legion and legendarily bitter. See Clara Thompson, *Psychoanalysis: Evolution and Development* (New York: Grove Press, 1950) and J.A.C. Brown, *Freud and the Post-Freudians* (London: Penguin, 1961).
15. 'What [psychoanalysis] aims at and achieve is nothing less than the uncovering of what is unconscious in mental life.' Freud 'The Common Neurotic State,' in *Introductory Lectures* (New York: Norton, 1977), p. 389.
16. Roazen, *Freud*, p. ix.
17. See Elizabeth Danto, *Freud's Free Clinics* (New York: Columbia University Press, 2005).
18. Erik Erikson dismisses as 'originology' the 'habitual effort to find the "cause" of a man's whole development in his childhood conflicts.' Erikson, *Gandhi's Truth* (New York: Norton, 1969), p. 98.
19. Heinz Kohut, 'Psychiatric Opinion in the Political Realm,' *Journal of the American Psychiatric Association*, 13(2) 1965, p. 450.
20. Freud disliked interpretations from afar: 'The general public is right in rejecting this type of analysis.' Cited in Joseph Schwartz, *Cassandra's Daughter* (New York: Viking, 1999). p. 103.

21. George W. Bush told reporters that there might be nuclear weapons in Iran. He can't prove it but 'Who knows?'—and therefore who wants to take chances? Editorial, *Chicago Sun-Times* 24 March 2008.
22. Mercer, 'Rationality and Psychology,' pp. 97–98.
23. Karl Mannheim, *Man and Society in an Age of Reconstruction* (New York: Harcourt, Brace and Company, 1951).
24. Jacques Ellul, *The Technological Society* (New York: Knopf, 1964), p. 6.
25. Jacqueline Rose, 'Where Does the Misery Come From?' in Rose, *Why War?* (Oxford: Basil Blackwell, 1993), p. 89.
26. David Bakan, *Disease, Suffering & Sacrifice* (Boston: Beacon Press, 1968), p. 117.
27. The most surprising quarter is Robert Jervis, *Why Intelligence Fails* (Ithaca: Cornell University Press, 2010). In caustic response see Fulton Armstrong, 'The CIA and WMDs,' *New York Review of Books* 19 August 2010.
28. Richard Lichtman, *The Production of Desire* (New York: Free Press), 1982), p. x.
29. Kenneth Waltz, *Man, The State and War* (New York: Columbia University Press, 1959), p. 3.
30. The term is inspired by Herbert Marcuse's concept, 'surplus repression.'
31. Harold D. Lasswell, *World Politics and Personal Insecurity* (New York: McGraw-Hill, 1935), p. 8.
32. Ken Booth and Nicholas Wheeler, *The Security Dilemma: Fear, Cooperation and Trust in World Politics* (London: Palgrave Macmillan, 2008), p. 80.
33. Adam Rosen, 'On Psychoanalysis and Political Theory,' *The Psychoanalytic Quarterly* 76(3), 2007, p. 976.
34. Bernard Crick, *In Defense of Politics* (London: Pelican, 1964).
35. Rycroft, 'Introduction,' in Rycroft, *Psychoanalysis Observed*, p. 21.
36. Freud, *An Autobiographical Study*, p. 67
37. Peter Loewenberg, *Decoding the Past* (Berkeley: University of California Press, 1985), p. 58.
38. Loewenberg, *Decoding*. pp. 12, 58.
39. Andrew Samuels, *The Political Psyche* (London: Routledge, 1993) p. 283.
40. Roazen, *Freud: Political and Social Thought*, p. 22.
41. Hervey Cleckley, *The Mask of Sanity* (New York: New American Library, 1982, rev. ed.), p. 382.
42. On intellectual repercussions see H. Stuart Hughes, *Consciousness and Society* (New York: Knopf, 1958).
43. Alfred North Whitehead 'sees science as one-sided, as one aspect of a total cultural situation—"a dull affair, soundless, scentless, colourless;

merely the hurrying of material endlessly, meaninglessly." Norman O. Brown, *Life Against Death* (New York: Vintage, 1959), p. 316.
44. For intriguing psychoanalytic insights into academic life see Loewenberg, *Decoding the Past*, pp. 67–80.
45. Philip Rieff, *Freud: The Mind of a Moralist* (New York: Viking, 1959), p. 240.
46. Ibid., p. 243.
47. Freud, *The Future of an Illusion*, p. 7.
48. On Freud's flexibility see Paul Roazan, *How Freud Worked* (Northvale, NJ: Jason Aronson, 1995).
49. Joseph Wortis, *Fragments of an Analysis with Freud* (New York: Simon & Schuster, 1954), p. 120.
50. 'The child's superego is constructed on the model not of its' parents but of its parents superego ... It seems likely that what are known as materialistic views of history sin in underestimating this factor. They brush it aside with the remark that human ideologies are nothing other than the product and superstructure of their contemporary economic conditions. That is true, but very probably not the whole truth. Mankind never lives entirely in the present.' Freud, 'The Dissection of Personality', *New Introductory Lectures*, p. 60.
51. Freud, 'A Weltanschauung?' *in New Introductory Lectures*. p. 157–158.
52. Ernest Jones, *The Life and Work of Sigmund Freud* (New York: Doubleday Anchor, 1957) p. 353.
53. Edward Timms, *Karl Krauss* (New Haven: Yale University Press, 2005), p. 250.
54. Russell Jacoby, *The Repression of Psychoanalysis* (Chicago: University of Chicago Press, 1983), p. 12.
55. Kurt Jacobsen, 'Escape From the Treadmill: Education, Politics and the Mainsprings of Child Analysis,' in Stephen Bronner and Peter Wagner (eds.), *Vienna: World of Yesterday* (Atlantic Highlands: Humanities Press, 1997).
56. 'Freud's subversiveness is derived from his concepts and not from his stated political opinions. This disjunction is absolutely crucial to recognize.' Russell Jacoby, *Social Amnesia* (Boston: Beacon Press, 1975), p. 25.
57. Lasswell, *Psychopathology and Politics* (New York: Norton, 1948); Nathan Leites, *A Study of Bolshevism* (Glencoe: Free Press, 1953).
58. Blema Steinberg, *Shame and Humiliation: Presidential Decision-making on Vietnam* (Pittsburgh: University of Pittsburgh Press, 1996).
59. Peter Gay, *The Naked Heart* (New York: Norton, 1995), p. 9.
60. David Rappaport, *Psychological Issues* (New York: International Universities Press, 1960), p. 58.

61. Freud, *Civilization and Its Discontents*, p. 62.
62. Peter Brooks and Alex Woloch, *Whose Freud?* (New Haven: Yale University Press, 2000), p. 105.
63. Thomas Scheff, *Being Mentally Ill* (New York: Aldine, 1984), p. 175.
64. Robert Wallerstein, 'Psychoanalytical Perspective on the Problem of Reality,' *Journal of the American Psychiatric Association*, 21(1), 1973, p. 7.
65. Larson, *Origins of Containment*, p. 22.
66. Jacoby, *The Repression of Psychoanalysis*, p. 158.
67. Lisa Appignanesi and John Forrester, *Freud's Women* (New York: Basic Books, 1992), p. 461.
68. Joost A. Meerlo, *That Difficult Peace* (Great Neck, NJ: Channel Press, 1961), p. 51.
69. Rose, *Why War?* p. 15.
70. R.D. Laing, *The Politics of Experience* (New York: Pantheon, 1967). p. 7.
71. Klein was 'deeply committed to instinct theory, assuming that the problems stem from infancy where an "excess of aggression" either innate or in response to frustration is experienced, [rendering analysts] blind to the life circumstances of the patient.' Lomas adds, 'there is no reason both the intrusion of the environment and the projection of undesired emotional states should not combine in the production of symptoms'. In Rycroft, *Psychoanalysis Observed*, pp. 128–129.
72. But paranoia 'need not be incapacitating.' John Lewis Gaddis, *We Now Know* (Oxford: Clarendon Press, 1997), p. 8.
73. Robert Coles, 'Erikson's Search for Gandhi,' in Fred Greenstein and Michael Lerner (eds.), *A Sourcebook for the Study of Personality and Politics* (Chicago: Markham Publishing, 1971), p. 149.
74. See Justin A. Frank, *Bush on The Couch* (New York: Regan Books, 2004).
75. Rieff, *Freud*, p. 309.
76. 'Writing Psychobiography,' in Alexander L. George and Juliette L George, *Presidential Personality and Performance* (Boulder, Colo: Westview, 1998), pp. 55–56.
77. Henry Porter, 'Tyrant who stands between Peace and Catastrophe,' *The Guardian*, 6 August 2006.
78. Seymour Hersh, *The Price of Power* (New York: Summit Books, 1983), p. 87.
79. Stanley Kutler, *Abuse of Power* (New York: Free Press, 1997), p. xvii.
80. Seymour Fisher and Roger P. Greenberg, *Freud Scientifically Appraised* (New York: John Wiley 1996), p. 8.
81. Gay, *Freud for Historians*, p. 167
82. Alaistair J. H. Murray, *Reconstructing Realism* (Keele: Keele University Press, 1997), p. 181.

83. Roazen, *Freud*, p. 159.
84. Freud, *Future of an Illusion*, p. 4.
85. On the state as person because it/he/she is an 'intentional system' see Alexander Wendt, 'The State as Person in International Theory', *Review of International Studies*, 30(2), 2004, p. 289–316.
86. Alexander Lowen, *The Betrayal of the Body* (New York, Macmillan, 1967), p. 233.
87. Wendt, 'The State as Person in International Politics,' p. 316.
88. Jennifer Mitzen, like Wendt, conflates 'identity' and 'role' into 'role identity.' See Mitzen, 'Ontological Security in World Politics,' *European Journal of International Relations* 12(1) 2008.
89. Mira Sucharov, *The International Self* (Albany: State University of New York, 2002), pp. 2, 12.
90. Ibid., p. 15. For a critique see Chap. 3.
91. 'Thucydides makes plain his assumption that emotions determined, or participated very significantly in determining, decisions of historic interests [and] such calculations—the desire for what wealth or victory or safety affords—give only an external, active form to deeper-lying urges.' Ramsey MacMullen, *Feelings in History* (New Haven: Regina Books, 2003), p. 13.
92. Freud 'Thoughts for the Times in War and Death' delivered at B'nai Brith club, Vienna. And Appendix to paper: Letter to Dr. van Eedan, 28 December 1914.
93. The 'death instinct' was unveiled in 1920 in Freud's *Beyond the Pleasure Principle*.
94. Gay, 'Human Nature in History,' in *Freud for Historians*, pp. 105–106.
95. Ibid. p. 111.
96. Franco Fornari, *The Psychoanalysis of War* (Bloomington: Indiana University Press, 1975), p. xvii.
97. Ibid.
98. 'The need for an enemy is transferable so long as it fulfills the personal function of a target for hate, which organizes one's life [while] for organizations it supplies the glue of cohesion and purpose.' David J. Finlay, Ole R. Holsti, Ricard R, Fagen, *Enemies in Politics* (Chicago: Rand McNally and Co 1967), pp. 13.
99. Erich Fromm, *The Greatness and Limitations of Freud's Thought* (London: Jonathan Cape, 1979), p. 24.
100. Brooks and Woloch, *Whose Freud?* p. 10.
101. See Paul Joseph, *Cracks in the Empire* (Boston: South End Press, 1981): Günter Lewy, *America in Vietnam* (New York: Oxford University Press, 1978), Leslie Gelb, with Richard K. Betts, *The Irony of Vietnam*

(Washington: Brookings Institution, 1979): and Noam Chomsky, *American Power and the New Mandarin* (New York: Pantheon, 1969).
102. See Robert Jay Lifton, *Home From The War* (New York: Simon and Schuster, 1973). On PTSD see Allan Young, *The Harmony of Illusions* (Princeton: Princeton University Press, 1995).
103. On Nixon see Bruce Mazlish, *In Search of Nixon* (London: Penguin, 1973) and Garry Wills, *Nixon Agonistes* (Boston: Houghton Mifflin, 1970).
104. Goldgeier and Tetlock, 'Psychology and International Relations Theory,' p. 83. 'These simplifying rules are generally drawn from the shared understandings of epistemic communities.' For a critique of epistemic communities see Kurt Jacobsen, 'Much Ado About Ideas: The Cognitive Factor in Economic Policy,' *World Politics* 47(2), 1995.
105. Khong, *Analogies at War*, p. 252.
106. Elster, *Political Psychology*, pp. 14, 82.
107. See volume 4 of the *Pentagon Papers* (Boston: Beacon Press, 1971) Mike Gravel edition.
108. Ibid. p. 89.
109. Morgenthau, *Vietnam and The United States* (Washington: Public Affairs Press, 1965), pp. 77–78.
110. Brian Von DeMark, *Into The Quagmire* (New York: Oxford 1991), p. 170.
111. George W. Allen, *None So Blind* (Chicago: Ivan R Dee, 2001), p. xi.
112. Appy, *Vietnam*, p. 404.
113. See Sam Adams, *War of Numbers* (Royalton, VT: Steelforth Press, 1994) and Kurt Jacobsen, *Pacification and Its Discontents* (Chicago: Prickly Paradigm Press, 2009).
114. Larson, *Origins of Containment*, p. 11.
115. Larson, *Anatomy of Mistrust*, p. 4.
116. David Kaiser, *American Tragedy* (Cambridge, Mass: Harvard University Press, 2000), pp. 3, 89.
117. Ibid. p. 208.
118. Michael H. Hunt, *Lyndon Johnson's War* (New York: Hill and Wang. 1996), pp. 103–104.
119. Kurt Jacobsen, 'The Passion of Robert McNamara, or Sympathy for the Devil?' *New Politics*. 10(1) 2004.
120. Evelyn Colbert, in Appy, *Vietnam*, p. 83.
121. Ben Shephard, *A War of Nerves* (Cambridge: Harvard University Press, 2001), p. 369.
122. Michael Beschloss, *Reaching For Glory* (New York: Simon and Schuster, 2001).
123. 'Like almost all who followed him, LBJ liked the agency's work only if it fit his thinking. When it did not, it went into the wastebasket.' Tim Weiner, *Legacy of Ashes* (New York: Doubleday, 2007), p. 248.

124. A C. Langguth, *Our Vietnam* (New York: Simon and Schuster. 2000), pp. 367–368.
125. Fredrik Logervall, *Choosing War* (Berkeley: University of California Press, 1999), p. 31.
126. Ibid, p. xiii.
127. Ibid., pp. 380, 393.
128. Doris Kearns, *Lyndon Johnson and The American Dream* (New York: Harper and Row, 1976), pp. 251–252.
129. Mark Moyar, *Triumph Forsaken*, (New York: Cambridge University Press, 2006), p. 292.
130. Ibid. p. 409.
131. *Pentagon Papers*, Vol IV, p. 47.
132. Steinberg, *Shame and Humiliation*, p. 4.
133. Jeffrey Kimbel, *Nixon's Vietnam War* (Topeka: University of Kansas, 1998), p. 11.
134. Brian Von DeMark, *Into the Quagmire* (New York: Oxford University Press, 1991), p. 172; Lloyd C. Gardner, *Pay Any Price* (Chicago: Ivan R Dee, 1995), p. 215.
135. Steinberg, *Shame and Humiliation*, p. 9.
136. Lasswell, *World Politics and Personal Insecurity*, p. 8.
137. Noam Chomsky, *Imperial Ambitions* (London: Hamish Hamilton, 2005), p. 166.
138. Donald W. White, *The American Century* (New Haven: Yale University Press, 1996), pp. 363–364; Louis B Zimmer, *The Vietnam War Debate* (Lanham Md: Lexington Books, 2011), pp. 41–76.
139. Morgenthau, *Vietnam and The United States*, pp. 18–19.
140. Benjamin Page and Marshall Bouton, *The Foreign Policy Disconnect* (Chicago: University of Chicago Press, 2006) and Paul Joseph, *Are Americans Becoming More Peaceful?* (Boulder, Colo: Paradigm Publishers, 2007).
141. See Frank, *Bush on The Couch*.
142. David Smail, *Why Therapy Doesn't Work* (London: Robinson, 1997), p. 259.
143. 'The more formal thinking becomes the more likely it is to provide short cuts from one area of ignorance to another.' Vladimir Nabokov, in Brooks and Woloch, *Whose Freud?* p. 10.
144. Daniel Maliniek and Michael J Tierney, 'The American School of IPE.' *Review of International Political Economy* 16(1), 2009, p. 21.
145. Elster, *Political Psychology*, p. 10.
146. Booth and Wheeler, *The Security Dilemma*, p. 79. 'In clinically treating children the corresponding rule is 'even when there is ill-treatment, it

is still important to disentangle reality from the child's interpretation of events.' Julia Segal, *Melanie Klein*, (London: Sage 1997), p. 29.
147. Eli Zaretsky, *Political Freud: A History* (New York: Columbia University Press, 2015).
148. Ibid., p. 12.
149. Ibid., p. 18.
150. Ibid., p. 28.
151. Ibid., p. 38.
152. Ibid., pp. 55, 62.
153. Ibid., p. 32.
154. Ibid., p. 90.
155. Ibid., p. 147.

The Mystique of Genetic Correctness

> REASON, v.i. To weigh probabilities in the scale of desire
> - Ambrose Bierce, *The Devil's Dictionary.*

The advent of Dolly the cloned sheep in 1996—RIP 2003—left many an onlooker feeling both celebrative and queasy.[1] With irrepressibly manic ingenuity the biological sciences were dissolving supposedly fuddy-duddy moral boundaries so that many scientists soon found themselves ensnarled in debates they would rather avoid as to the wisdom of playing cavalierly with genetic material. If one believes the headlines, resistance is futile.[2] Genetic engineering erodes familiar norms and instead gives us (whoever 'us' is) 'the power to impose our own invented norms'—norms that arise from within the far from infallible scientific community itself.[3] Science, as an indispensable means of acquiring knowledge and manipulating nature, is lodged snugly inside the realm of production-for-profit. So scientific activities must be examined in the context of social processes, even if not—*pace* Alan Sokal—reduced to them.[4] In an economic system hell-bent on commodifying everything in its path there is ample cause for public concern about the conduct of bioengineering.

Scientists, despite comforting fables to the contrary, usually conform to the reigning values in the middle class milieus in which they usually grow up. The average nuclear physicist or molecular biologist is as likely to equate their self-interest with the interest of the community, national or local, as is a televangelist or stockbroker. So great care is needed when wielding tentative scientific findings and one is well advised to err on the side of generosity when it comes to rushing to judgments about human development because these verdicts can be self-fulfilling in their consequences.

One must step back at least a century to appreciate what is unfolding. The Victorians took hearty pride in looking hard facts about evolution in their hairy faces, which especially to *Punch*-subscribing British readers, looked awfully Irish. It was not quite clear to many respectable scientists at the time whether Greeks, Italians or Jews were fully members of the white—or human—race either. British South Africans, understandably piqued, imagined that rebellious Boers were not quite 'white' enough.[5] Not even pre-Israel Zionists were averse to eugenics as a means to churn out the 'perfect' Jews that the Nazis, with much the same aim for Aryans, elsewhere were mass murdering.[6] The social upshot of most research was that groups deemed low on the social scale also were designated biological problems foremost and then—to the extent they appeared a threat or nuisance—social problems too. While humanity, after Darwin, mostly managed to digest the news of its descent from apes rather than radiant angels, some groups, as always, were deemed less descended.

Biological value coincides so neatly with class and/or racial 'worth' because dominant groups do the observing, analyzing, interpreting and recording. This common arrangement yielded a tenacious legacy of determinist explanation, and its biological rendition was a stringent reductionism 'in which the arrows of causality run from genes to humans and from humans to humanity.'[7] How human beings think and behave is dictated by genetic structure to so complete a degree that nothing intervening between structure and action was reckoned to make a significant difference. Statistician Karl Pearson discerned through his impressive calculative techniques that 'the influence of environment was not one-fifth that of heredity' and that 'it was man who makes the environment, and not the environment which makes the man.'[8] And that was that. 'Nearly all the nineteenth century champions of statistics were laissez-faire liberals,' Menand explains, and so they were 'fierce opponents of state intervention' which only reflected their class upbringings where 'they had already decided that nature operated like a market.'[9] That is not the full harvest of social wisdom from statistical wizards. 'It is the great good fortune of mankind that there is a substantial positive correlation between intelligence and morality, including good will toward one's fellows,' deduced Edward Thorndike, a prominent number-cruncher in psychology. 'Consequently our superiors in ability are on the average our benefactors, and it is often safer to trust our interests to them than to ourselves.'[10] Well, it goes without saying.

Are we witnessing in the twenty-first century the resurgence of the scientifically intoxicating project of biological 'improvement?' Eugenics was a social engineer's dream of molding humanity to a prim perfection resembling nothing so much as the engineers themselves (or how they would like to see themselves). Scientists and/or sensationalist media routinely announce glorious discoveries of genetic causes for phenomena as infinitely intricate as homosexuality, shyness, homelessness, schizophrenia, manic-depression, autism and perhaps even for the gall to advance these extravagant claims. Only a century ago scientists proclaimed the single gene explanations for thalassophilia ('urge for sea-faring'), drapetomania ('irrational urge by slaves to run off'), Jewish facial expressions, 'shiftlessness' and chicken stealing.[11] On reflection, there are sound reasons not to consign public policy to scientists, their employers or politicians to whom employers strategically dish out campaign contributions.

Genetics research raises slippery little issues that scurry over, under and around specialists' boundaries. No scientist can instruct us as to whether we should clone living creatures, retrieve sperm from comatose men, treat genetic materials as corporate property or fix insurance premiums to gene test results. Identifying hereditary disease—or, for that matter, just how hereditary a hereditary disease—is a tough task that poses thorny moral issues. Behold 'designer children.' Surveys indicate 40% of American parents, with the best and blithely obsessive intentions, happily embrace genetic engineering if it will craft their kids into sharper, slicker competitors. (What's wrong with that 60% of parental slackers?) It is possible to find out in the eleventh week of pregnancy what sex the child is and to abort if you don't like what you learn. This is practically a traditional practice today in India (despite laws against sex selection as a daughter-preventer there and in China), but middle-class Americans and Europeans are more progressive, aren't they?

Parallels between Ye Olde Eugenics and thoroughly modern genetics are far stronger than scientists care to acknowledge.[12] A cultural amnesia about the history of eugenics is cultivated with the greatest of ease in commercial societies that prize short-term, amoral expeditious thinking. Why are our elites so tempted to assume humanity is 'hard-wired' for absolutely every trait? The answer lies in a far from solely biological predisposition to accrue power and, no less important, a desire, owing more to laziness than to selfish genes, to shirk responsibility for one's actions and for the welfare of others.

RAW EUGENICS

In late nineteenth century America a declining middle-class birth rate coincided with migrations North of recently freed blacks and the unseemly inpour of especially Eastern and Southern Europeans. These alien influxes, as they do, annoyed the locals. In 1913 arch-eugenicist Henry Goddard advised authorities that of the tired, huddled masses filing through Ellis Island: 83% of the Jews, 80% of Hungarians, 79% of Italians (especially the darker Southern ones) and 87% of Russians were feeble-minded. Maybe one could blame their backward environments.

The 'wrong' people were madly breeding. Weren't there enough lowlife immigrants already swarming around who could do the dirty work? No more need apply. In *The Clone Age* Andrews interviewed numerous Americans who expressed the same opinion, lamenting the sparse reproduction rates and falling sperm counts among full-fledged natives. Presidents Theodore Roosevelt, Grover Cleveland, Woodrow Wilson, Warren Harding and Calvin Coolidge unabashedly invoked eugenic tracts at public occasions. Eugenics, after all, promised to transfer political conflicts into a more serene biological realm where impartial 'science' held sway. All policy decisions flowed from this ineluctable truth. This contorted quasi-utopian ambition animated a middle-class movement determined to fashion an 'administrative state,' a state whose refined exponents intended that their expertise would displace coarse conflicts based on class, race and gender.[13]

In Britain Francis Galton published *Hereditary Genius*, which proclaimed that genius was inherited and that elites ecerywhere were elected by sagacious nature. That being the case, the objective was to upgrade the racial 'stock' swiftly through a judicious blend of negative measures (to discourage the 'unfit' from reproducing) and positive ones (to encourage the 'fit' to breed).[14] People of the lower orders were viewed very much like poultry or fruit flies, except that certain debased specimens, outrageously, could cast ballots.

The eugenics movement was based on the glib doctrine that mental characteristics (intelligence, diligence, sobriety) pass across generations as physical ones (eye color) do. Nature tramples nurture. Galton logically denounced philanthropy and the public health movement as hideous wastes of good money. Eugenicists merely were recognizing the cool dictates of science when they opposed old age pensions, public schooling, the minimum wage or prohibition of alcohol (although the lattermost, some eugenicists fretted, could impede the plunge of lower breeds to their genetically fated doom). Poverty was brushed aside except as a natural aid in culling a flock these sages rarely encountered (during evacuations of children from British cities after 1939, many rural families was shocked by the physical signs they saw of terrible poverty which many working class children also escaped—and many rural families campaigned for the children to be removal forthwith).[15]

If every inherited characteristic was a blend of traits of the parents and ancestors, as eugenicists argued, the unavoidable problem was that this implied a regression to the mean, portending loss of prized WASP characteristics over time. Not only did the best stock need to be shoved manfully into the boudoir to breed, they must cultivate 'desirable' traits too, which is a pretty tall order in a rude and disorderly world. The way out of this fix was to welcome the Lamarckian doctrine of inheritance of acquired characteristics, which Galton, ever the pragmatic optimist, decided to believe required no more than three generations to fasten in the genetic make-up. Galton willed his fortune later to finance London Eugenics laboratories where Pearson continued the biological crusade. Eugenics would not go away quietly, although it would strive—after all those *déclassé* Nazis got so carried away—to assume more pleasing shapes.

Tainted Breeds, Tainted Deeds

Enthusiasts beheld an enticing vision for improving one's fellow man, grounded in good hard statistics. Nothing could seem more sound. For capitalists, a social Darwinian theory of human evolution was a demonstration of the iron necessity of the free market; for a mechanistic strain of Marxist it proved the utter inevitability of desired social change. History was on your side whichever side you were on. Eugenics even was compatible with the fight for women's rights and with many socialist goals. George Bernard Shaw and H.G. Wells were beguiled, although Wells later came to scribble his admonitory *The Island of Doctor Moreau*.

In America a stream of sensationalist studies steadily stoked a sense of imminent apocalypse. From the sagas of the squalid 'Jukes' (1877) to the 'Kallikaks' (1912) stern WASP investigators imbued what they viewed as pure sociopathic rubes with every conceivable vice.[16] 'For the low grade idiot, the loathsome unfortunate that may be seen in our institutions, some have proposed the lethal chamber,' Goddard wrote regarding the Kallikak family saga. 'But humanity is steadily tending away from the possibility of that method, and there is no probability that it will ever be practiced.'[17] Here the Puritan conscience, unchecked and unconscious, contrives to crucify a former Revolutionary War soldier for the 'havoc caused by one thoughtless act' of sexual intercourse, thereby sowing the star-spangled land with defective degenerate rabble.[18]

The film *Deliverance* famously traded on this frightful image of slack-jawed hillbilly descendants for its dramatic kick while physicist William Shockley later cited the Kallikaks study as if it still were regarded as pristine social research.[19] The specter of the unrestrained tainted stock begetting like crazy in rough cabins in the Appalachian hills at taxpayer expense was ideally calculated to stir popular alarm.

Immoral acts summarily were viewed 'as evidence, not as a consequence, of mental defects.'[20] Eugenicists usually were much less agitated about assuring survival of the fittest than about reducing the odds for the survival of the unfit. Leonard Darwin, cousin of the *Beagle* voyager, explained that in eugenics the term 'fittest' designated who *ought* to survive in the evolutionary sense rather than who actually happens to survive. In other words, nature, the supreme arbiter, really would appreciate a helping hand. Never did so eminent and *consciously well-meaning* a social group strive so hard to achieve so vast and vicious an objective.[21] British scientist and scholar Joseph Needham impishly would challenge the birthright 'fitness' of rich shareholders of companies that relied for their profits upon unemployment, low wages and poor safety conditions inflicted on their fellow human beings.

Eugenicists, pleased at the advent of a congenial brand of Mendelian genetics, very much needed to believe that neuropathic characteristics were transmitted in a straightforward way. It was wholly self-evident to the brethren that a better body carried a purer spirit. The medical model, a view of life that presupposes a mystical correspondence between particular brain cells and particular thoughts, abetted this not so tacit assumption. The concomitant degenerationist view held that mental qualities were rooted in the brain's structure, and put 'considerable weight on physical stigmata, partial sight, deafness, dyslexia and left handedness.'[22] So, on the basis of partial and disputable evidence, public policies were urged which, if enacted, inflicted irreversible damage on targeted groups. Harry Laughlin urged what he called a gradual approach—immediate sterilization only of the lowest 10%, as infallibly demonstrated by their lack of means. Once this pruning was accomplished, he would go on to cull the next lowest decile. It was never clear just where this progressive decimation was supposed to stop.

Degeneration and Its Discontents

Although geneticists began to appreciate the full complexities of heredity by the 1920s, most biologists and geneticists still clung to eugenic ideas. Charles Davenport of the Cold Harbor eugenics research center invoked Mendelian genetics to claim that a single bad gene—because it would not blend—could ruin an entire 'stock,' that is, an entire nation. Until the Second World War many biologists 'agreed with, or at least did not publicly oppose eugenicist formulations and this attitude was shared by many prominent American psychologists and sociologists.'[23]

Yet scientists already had found that a stable genotype could correspond to a continuous variation in phenotype, that 'many symptoms regarded as pathological might only arise from interaction of genotype with surrounding conditions' and that 'a genotype cannot always be derived from phenotype.' These findings should have extinguished the theoretical basis of eugenics, if cutting-edge science were all that mattered. Danish geneticist Wilhelm Johennsen surmised 'the complexity of society made it impossible that one single human type should be the best. We need all different types of humanity.'[24] One could not draw a more democratic lesson or one more widely ignored. In 1930 a British study showed that mental defects occurred proportionately across social classes, not mostly among the poor. In 1933 the British Medical Association repudiated the notion of the inheritance of feeble-mindedness. In 1935 the American Neurological Association rejected eugenics as scientifically untenable. Yet none of these repudiations made the slightest dent in public attitudes. In 1937 Fortune reported 66% favored sterilization for mental defects, 63% for criminals. Only 15% opposed sterilization.

That same year British eugenicist R.B. Catell mournfully reiterated Galton's dreadful prophecy that '300 years from now half the population will be mentally defective.'[25] Indeed, if 'we really want to build an A1 nation we must take this matter to its logical conclusion, and employ the whole machinery of our medical services, not merely for "preventative medicine" in the narrow sense, not even for ante-natal hygiene but for large-scale efforts along eugenic lines—and just such an epic effort was going into action in Germany'—was it not?[26]

HOME OF THE FREE AND 'LIFE UNWORTHY OF LIFE'

The USA, Cattell found to his evident surprise, was the first country to approve compulsory sterilization. Indiana legalized it in 1907 and in another decade fifteen more states joined the valiant mission to preserve imperiled 'homo europaeus.' *Scientific American* editorialized in favor of compulsory sterilization. In 1927 the US Supreme Court approved sterilization for institutionalized inmates. As in the notorious *Buck vs. Bell* decision, eugenics regained ideological momentum on the pretext of preventing an outbreak of feeble-mindedness (in this sense it was indeed the disease for which it purported to be the cure). In Connecticut in 1890 a pauper—by definition, congenitally feeble-minded—having sex with a woman under age 45 was liable to a 3 year prison term. By the 1890s, incidentally, craniectomies emerged as a medical fad for 'curing' retardation, despite a 15–25% death rate.[27] The doctors who doughtily performed them doubtless remained pillars of their communities.

Sterilizers liked to report, after their prudential snipping, that patients were happier, healthier and grateful. California by 1927 sterilized 5000 patients a year. Harry Laughlin played a major role in lobbying for the restrictive 1924 Immigration Law by testifying that foreign-born and poor people disproportionately populated prisons—despite a snide Midwestern senator drolly pointing out to his honorable Southern colleagues that arriving Danes, Norwegians, Dutch and Germans were far more literate than the average Southerner. The US government tactfully suppressed findings during World War II that Southern blacks scored higher than Southern whites.[28]

Some thirty US states approved involuntary sterilization for criminals, epileptics and anyone clinically deemed promiscuous. Involuntary sterilizations occurred at much the same rate in states with no legislation. Yet the known facts even then were that retarded children mostly have normal parents while mentally retarded parents can and do have normal children. The incidence of mental retardation had not grown at all over time. The American Neurological Association noted in 1937 that MR people lived shorter lives with low (bordering on nil) marriage and fertility rates. The spreading panickiness was based on a thoroughly manufactured if sincerely believed myth. Fears of decline relative to other races made the technology of air power seem to 'buttress the dominant position of the white race' in the run-up to World War II.[29]

The Eugenics Society applauded innovative and daring Nazi programs. The 'model' Nazi law on Preventing Hereditarily Ill Progeny, though, was itself heavily influenced by American predecessors. A 1933 law mandated sterilization for the retarded, schizophrenics, manic-depressives, epileptics, the deaf, alcoholics and other unwanted afflicted persons. In Germany from 1933 to 1945 three and half million sterilizations were performed. The Third Reich inaugurated its campaign to purify the earth of unworthy life by murdering some 75,000 patients. Though parental-led protests in August 1941 brought the overt practice to a halt, it soon resumed secretly. Seventy to one hundred thousand infirm people were killed in Germany—and a quarter of a million more throughout Europe.

Racism of this fastidious medical sort was promulgated by credentialed professionals who by their self-understanding and rules were engaged in dispassionate scientific research. The German Medical Association was pleased to inform Nazi leaders at one point that they soon may devise a foolproof way to detect Jews, Gypsies and homosexuals through refined blood tests. Few professional groups (except perhaps for engineers) were more supportive of the Nazi blueprint than were physicians.[30] Deichmann points out that biologists enjoyed substantial state funding and, if they didn't make a fuss about dismissal of Jewish colleagues or about Nazi ideology, had 'substantial freedom of research,' including the golden opportunity to experiment on psychiatric patients and on concentration camp inmates: 'The fact that some of them made use of this option reveals the abyss of a science without a humane orientation,' Deichmann concludes, 'an orientation that cannot come from science.'[31] Science, in the crudely reductive but widespread rendition, made mass murder that much easier. Physicians on trial at Nuremberg for camp experiments were quick to cite American examples to prove that the onerous task of eliminating 'inferior elements' was not a mission unique to Germany.[32] Nuremberg prosecutors, many of whom were under sway of eugenicist notions picked up on home soil, never prosecuted Nazis for sterilizations, only for deaths.

Reilly judges that it was less revulsion at Nazi racial crimes than the wartime shortage of physicians which curbed American sterilizations.[33] The baby boom ended the entire racket about depopulation. Totalitarianism, not eugenics practices, plunged eugenics into disrepute. Research eventually demonstrated that many mental disorders stemmed as much or more from traumatic experience or deprivation as from inherited characteristics. Scientists also became more aware of race as a constructed category—though not so much as to avert abuses such as the Tuskegee experiments. This is the history that genetic engineering enthusiasts dismiss, ignore, downplay or deny is relevant to an understanding of what they are up to today. Everything is different. Leave it in their capable hands.

WHAT NEW WORLD?

While books on genetic engineering, pro and con, contain obligatory admonitory allusions to *Brave New World*, one wonders how many authors really have taken Huxley's point. The 'new' genetic determinism is accompanied in the press by precious little skepticism. Once again the media revels in reporting that 'research has tipped the scale overwhelmingly toward nature,' even though further examination always discloses back-pedaling as to what is thought, let alone proven, to be heritable. The handsomely funded Human Genome project, to much fanfare, created a 'complete' map of the nucleotide system for genes and was immediately followed by the ENCODE Project to decipher what the relations among the 3 billion base pairs actually might be. Andrews recounted dismaying experiences in the original Genome Project's Committee on Ethical, Legal and Social Implications, which was hamstrung, usually ignored and functioned as an in-house device to deflect outside criticism, thereby enabling scientists inside to do pretty much as they pleased. Genome project proponents, like nineteenth century statisticians, and for much the same reasons, opposed government 'interference,' preferring to place research under both scientific and corporate control, such as these categories are distinguishable. This is hardly a reassuring political inclination and only generates concern as to the social and ethical naiveté—or disingenuousness, as the case may be—rampant in the research community.

If corporations fail to choreograph the human gene pool it will not be for want of trying.[34] In 1991 the National Institute of Health announced a program of patents on human gene fragments—or 'express tag sequences'—on 2375 fragments representing about 5% of genes. Control of the fragments blocks any use of the full gene, even if the identity of the genes was unknown. The strategic use of patents raises the prospect of corporations owning our genetic material—an obscene prospect that is only lately coming to light. Why should genes be owned by whom ever possesses the technology to manipulate them? Physicians with major financial stakes in genetic research have great incentives to deceive their own patients. Will the very expensive products of genetic technologies be available only to the rich, or be made compulsory? More likely the former, but neither is anything to rejoice about.

All these issues, and how they are treated, hinge on cultural understandings and misunderstandings of science. The peculiarly pinched view that human beings are nothing but fleshy vehicles for genes rests on an artificially atomized view of the world. The trouble with it is that the properties of the parts can't be understood except in their context in the whole because the environment of the organism is constantly being remade by the life of the organism, Lewontin pointed out. There is no such thing as 'general genetic superiority—different environments bring out different degrees of superiority.'[35]

Disease now supplies the perfect moral justification to pursue a kinder and gentler and stealthier eugenics quest. What is control of reproduction for, except for 'improvement of the race'? Does a fetus with an 'unsound' genotype have a right to be born? Cystic fibrosis, Duchesne disease, muscular dystrophy, myotonic dystrophy, Huntington's disease, Tay-Sachs disease and Down's syndrome are single gene disorders but most are complex and are not related in any invariant ways to genes. Everyone carries probabilities and predispositions for diseases that may appear only in conjunction with certain environmental stimuli. Huntington's Chorea may not, as earlier assumed, result from a single gene.[36] Are all diseases transmitted genetically? Are misbehaviors acquired in response to unsupportive and even miserable milieus? There remains the statistically incalculable problem of sussing out how physiological dispositions blend with environmental cues to cause whatever behavior they cause.

Sensationalized reports of genetic causation emerge from the nebulous processing zone where researchers meet the media. It still is customarily front page news when a bold claim for a genetic cause is announced, and page 10 news when it is retracted, as the Breggins observed, for instance, about 'the' gene for alcoholism.[37] Nothing has changed. Claims for a manic-depressive gene have been loudly made and silently retracted; a gene for depression detected in Amish families turned out to affect a single extended family (which, by the way, reintroduces socialization as a more probable cause). The gene(s), if any, for schizophrenia is elusive as ever.[38] Genes for breast cancer are likewise very hard to locate, and even the implicated BRCA1 and BRCA2 genes alone by no means guarantee cancer, despite the well-publicized double mastectomy undergone by a major movie star in 2013 to preempt it.[39] The infamous 'gay' gene was never corroborated nor has any gene or genes for autism survived scrutiny. Most scientists do know better than to advance such 'gene for' explanations.[40] Yet ask someone not only on the street but in corridors of power and they most likely will reply that they heard that scientists have found genetic causes for all of the above. The allegation that an extra male 'Y' chromosome caused aggression in 'XYY syndrome' people also hit a dead end yet Andrews cites at least one case of parents of an XYY child deciding to abort just to be on the safe side.[41] People have been denied health insurance and/or employment either because of gene testing or for refusing to undergo it.[42] Direct to consumer (DNC) marketing of gene tests by private firms has been marked by scandals, with the General Accounting Office in 2010 all but dismissing them as modern patent medicine peddlers.[43] Getting into credit card debt is palmed off as a genetic malady, rather than as a predictable result of more than four decades of stagnating average worker wages, tax cuts for the wealthy and upward redistribution of income into the hands of a stratum that lends it back at what once were regarded as usurious rates.[44] Well, blame that on your genes, not on a ubiquitous system-boosting PR apparatus.

The gene for sickle cell anemia extends to peoples inhabiting malarial regions in Africa and the Middle East where it serves a protective function against the disease. Curing sickle cell raises the problem of pleiotropy wherein 'negative' genes that exert positive effects also will be lost if the 'cure' should work. The majority of diseases with a genetic component are polygenic disorders and involve significant interaction with the environment. This consideration raises a question as to which end—environmental or molecular—one should start in order to study a given problem. Genes are not enough. From shady Cyril Burt to the present, the tendentious misuse of 'twins studies' to prove predesignated conclusions on genetic causation is one of the dodgiest episodes in the history of science.[45]

I attended a university seminar a few years ago where hardly anyone objected when a presenter soothingly stated that genetic engineering by definition cannot be eugenic if the state is not involved.[46] So we presumably need not fear madcap market-driven genetic modification. Nothing could be more mistaken. Eugenics in the late nineteenth and early twentieth centuries was not a top-down phenomenon but rather emerged from a folksy blend of class bias, scientism and a cynical seeking of personal and professional advantage. Eugenicists lobbied very hard for their programs until states implemented them, or parts of them. Nor did it matter whether these policies worked or not, the fervent promoters went ahead anyway.

The future threatens the spectacle not only of coercive state-sponsored control but also of a 'eugenics of the free market.' Andrews relates a case of an HMO instructing a couple, who found through amniocentesis that their child-to-be possessed a gene for cystic fibrosis, that it would not pay for the child's care if the pregnancy came to term.[47] Parents want normal children, but what is 'normal' is determined both by the values current within their social circle and by the rules imposed by the institutional environment. Under Nazi eugenics we breed you aim to get steely SS officers; under modern genetics we breed to get *Beverly Hills 90120* clones and the prospect of a world populated by soap opera stars, presumably with ethics, sensitivity and compassion levels to match. For all the eugenic propaganda, a high IQ never has been the supreme quality for worldly success. Just behold President Donald Trump who, unlike many Oval Office predecessors, spouts his eugenic opinions only in private.[48] Rather, a passable intelligence will do nicely if one luckily is born into an affluent family and/or is willing to conform cunningly to reigning dogmas. Innovation is prized insofar as it does not ruffle gatekeepers or prove socially disruptive. Perhaps there are genes for conformity or cunning or bigotry or integrity? Even to ask this preposterous question about such qualities is to answer it.

Genetics, as popularly understood, is an embodiment of a reductionist methodology that doubtless can be useful as a research tool but is dangerous when depicted as all there is to the scientific enterprise and then applied to the world. Genetics as a discipline jettisons human beings as ends in themselves. Genes are 'selfish' only because a bright wordsmith like Richard Dawkins selects anthropomorphic adjectives and projects them onto isolated genes, stripped from their life world contexts, and informs you they are selfish. Genetics, leaning on a 'Lego model' of the genome and misapplied as a total philosophy, courts this dismal projected result. 'Rather than seeing genes as fixed entities in a static structure awaiting self-activation,' Krimsky updates us, 'the current conception views the genoma as more characteristic of an ecosystem—more fluid, more dynamic, and more interactive than the Lego model implies.'[49]

So the problem is not biology but rather the mindset of some of the manipulators. On the ample positive side one finds, for example, University of California at San Francisco researchers 'identifying signatures of ethnicity in the genome that appear to reflect an ethnic group's shared culture and environment, rather than its common genetic ancestry.'[50] 'Unlike the rest of the genome, which is only inherited from an individual's parents (with random mutations here and there), methylation and other epigenetic annotations can be modified based on experience,' the report goes on. 'These modifications influence when and where particular genes are expressed and appear to have significant impacts on disease risk, suggesting explanations for how environmental factors such as maternal smoking during pregnancy can influence a child's risk of later health problems.' It is not a one-way street.

Reductionist methods boast the resilience of Hammer horror film vampires—rising and beckoning ever again no matter how many wooden stakes are stabbed through their chilly hearts. We all like it when two plus two equals four, and those of us who haven't heard of Heisenberg (except in an HBO series) badly insist that the entire universe to behave accordingly. In the popular realm, unlike the scientific one, 'genetic' has become a synonym for 'immutable.'[51] In the 1930s the field of psychiatry resorted to somatic treatments such as electric and insulin shock due to a congenial assumption that mental disorders stemmed from organic defects, as yet unascertained. In the 1990s psychiatric geneticists 'began to propose genetic anticipation, the tendency of some illness-causing genes to expand in size when passed from generation to generation, as the mechanism behind the increasing severity of schizophrenia or manic-depressive illness as handed down by a family tree.'[52] Hence, the problem simply cannot be family conflict or lousy schools (both rooted in bad social conditions), the child instead is blamed—with the very best intentions—as carrier of disease or a misshapen gene, which supports the biopsychiatric inclination to 'reduce human conduct and social conflict to grossly sluggish neurotransmitters in a particular type of nerve cell.' It's not begging the question, you see, it's genetic.

Eugenics in all its subtle spiffed-up forms is propelled by an utterly anti-democratic worldview. It is just not possible to accept a reductionist mode of genetics and not be drawn into this stance. So science should always be a voice, usually several squabbling voices, but never be taken as the last word in policy making. One must beware of scientists pleading, like the inventor of the cloning process that yielded the short-lived Dolly, that the messy ethical and social implications were unimportant on the grounds that one is 'only a scientist.'

Many geneticists inertially (for lack of a better adverb) endorsed eugenics long after the 1940s. In 1970 67% of American physicians polled felt that 'forcible sterilization of criminally insane, retarded and feeble-minded was a desirable social policy.' The *Boston Globe* in 1982 found that half of those it surveyed favored sterilizations for the feeble-minded and criminals. Involuntary sterilizations continued in the US into the 1960s; in Canadian provinces until 1978; and in Sweden until 1975. You 'hear no hatred in the eugenical voice, just pragmatic selection,' Hilary Rose observes, 'The difference is that today there is a huge resistance.'[53]

The unsavory history of eugenics may work today as a sharp reminder of how flawed our rulers are and how fallible the scientific establishment, if not all scientists, may be. The eugenics story need to be retold and reviewed often so that the wider community weighs the risks in this costly research game and brings to bear the necessary degree of skepticism. 'Technically flawed and conceptually unsound models—no matter how often published or repeated,' Burt and Simmons, who demolish a raft of slipshod heritability studies, irritably write, 'do not by virtue of their number make for sound evidence.'[54] That remark remains more a hope than a reality. Doubling down is what genetic researchers do best. 'The current trend in psychiatric genetics,' Leo confirms, 'is to use enormous samples to find genes of miniscule effects.'[55] The trend is not one of great promise anymore but it is institutionally set, despite 'lowered expectations,' to continue, which makes a certain sort of sense.[56] To develop an indisputable refutation of genetic sources for schizophrenia, for example, there is no process better than to expand implicated genes—already up to the tens of thousands—to the point of encompassing the whole genome.[57]

NOTES

1. In February 2003 Dolly was euthanized. She suffered from progressive lung disease and earlier had developed arthritis. Sheep tend to live twice as long as Dolly lasted. Cloning, actually, is rife with glitches. See Tim Radford. 'Cloning, Deaf to the Warning: Society and Science are Not Ready.' *The Guardian* 8 August 2005.
2. Not so fast though. 'For evolutionary biologists there still are major controversies over the processes of evolution and the mechanisms of

speciation,' the Roses point out. 'Even the most basic questions—what evolves, what is adaptation and whether selection is the only motor of evolutionary change—remain under debate.' Hilary and Steve Rose, 'Darwin and After,' *New Left Review* 63 (May–June 2010), p. 85.
3. Bryan Appleyard, *Brave New Worlds: Genetics and The Human Experience* (London: Viking, 1999), p. 3.
4. On Alan J. Sokal's spoof article in the Spring/Summer 1996 Social Text see Stephen Hilgartnek, 'The Sokal Affair in Context' *Science, Technology and Human Values* 22, 4 (Autumn 1997) and Jennifer Daryl Slack and M. Mehdi Semati, 'Intellectual and Political Hygiene: The Sokal Affair' *Critical Studies in Mass Communication* 14, 3 (September 1997); and Nick Jardine and Marina Fraser-Spada, 'Splendors and Miseries of The Science Wars' *Studies in History and Philosophy of Science* 28, 2 (June 1997).
5. Susanne Klausen, 'For the Sake of the Race: Eugenics Discourses of Feeble-mindedness and Motherhood and the South African Medical Record' *Journal of South African Studies* 23, 1 (March 1997).
6. See the report on Stachlav Stoler-Liss' research on the influence of eugenics on the Zionist movement in the 1930s. Tamara Traubmann, 'Do Not have Children if they won't be Healthy.' *Haaretz* 16 June 2004. http://www.haaretz.com/hasen/pages/ShArt.jhtml?itemNo=437879. On the home front see Christine Rosen, *Preaching Eugenics: Religious Leaders and the American Eugenics Movement* (New York: Oxford University Press, 2004), pp. 106–109.
7. Leon J. Kamin, Richard C. Lewontin, and Steven Rose, *Not in Our Genes: Biology, Ideology and Human Nature* (London: Pelican, 1984) p. 18. 'The essence of the reductionist position is the assumption that a disorder is caused by a simple malfunction of a body region—or a biochemical substance—or a gene' (p. 189).
8. Eileen Magnelli, 'The Non-Correlation of Biometrics and Eugenics: Rival Forms of Laboratory Work in Karl Pearson's Career at University College London' *History of Science* 37, 2 (June 1999), p. 132.
9. Louis Menand, *The Metaphysical Club: A Story about Ideas in America* (New York: Farrar Strauss, 2001), pp. 194, 195.
10. Cited in Noam Chomsky, 'Intellectuals and The State,' in Chomsky, *Towards A New Cold War* (New York: Pantheon, 1982), p. 65.
11. William H. Tucker, *The Science and Politics of Racial Research* (Champaign: University of Illinois, 1994), p. 65.
12. See Kurt Jacobsen, *Technical Fouls: Democratic Dilemmas and Technological Change* (Boulder: Westview Press, 2000).
13. See Samuel Haber, *Efficiency and Uplift: Scientific Management in the Progressive Era* (Chicago: University of Chicago, 1964) and Dwight Waldo, *The Administrative State* (New York: Ronald Press, 1948).

14. Galton was nowhere more transparently naive than when interpreting photos of the children of Jewish immigrants to London in the 1880s: 'I felt, rightly or wrongly, that every one of them was coolly appraising me at market value, without the slightest interest of any kind.' This is what a Kleinian analyst would call a vivid instance of projective identification.
15. Clive Ponting, *1940: Myth and Reality* (London: Hamish Hamilton, 1992), p. 139; Angus Calder, *The Myth of the Blitz* (London: Pimlico. 1991), p. 79.
16. See Nicole Hahn Rafter, *White Trash: The Eugenic Family Studies 1877–1919* (Boston: Northeastern University Press, 1988 and J. David Smith, *Minds Made Feeble: The Mythical Legacy of the Kallikaks* (Rockville, MD: Aspen, 1985).
17. Henry Herbert Goddard, *The Kallikaks* (New York: Macmillan Press, 1931), p. 101.
18. Goddard, *The Kallikaks*, p. 103.
19. See Joel N. Shurkin, *Broken Genius: The Rise and Fall of William Shockley, Creator of the Electronic Age* (New York: Macmillan, 2006).
20. Matthew Thomson, *The Problem of Mental Deficiency: Eugenics, Democracy and Social Policy in Britain, 1870–1959* (Oxford: Clarendon Press, 1998), pp. 7, 20.
21. Perhaps the Nazis are comparable insofar as so many administered lethal occupation duties and the holocaust with clear consciences.
22. Thomson, *The Problem of Mental Deficiency*, pp. 7, 20.
23. Edward J. Larson, *Sex, Race and Science: Eugenics in The Deep South* (Baltimore: John Hopkins University, 1995), p. 30.
24. Hansen, 'Something Rotten in The State of Denmark: Eugenics and the Rise of the Welfare State' in Gunnar Broberg and Nils Roll-Hansen, eds, *Eugenics and the Welfare State: Sterilization Policy in Denmark, Sweden, Norway and Finland* (East Lansing: Michigan State University Pres, 1996), p. 24.
25. R. B. Cattell, *The Fight For Our National Intelligence* (London: P.S. King & Son, ltd., 1937), p. 12.
26. See Jay Joseph, 'The 1942 Euthanasia Debate in the American Journal of Psychiatry,' *History of Psychiatry* 16 (2005) and James Q. Whitman, *Hitler's American Model* (Princeton: Princeton University Press, 2017).
27. Hansen, 'Something Rotten in The State of Denmark,' pp. 14–15.
28. See Robert V. Guthrie, *Even the Rat Was White: A Historical View of* Psychology *(New York: Harper & Row, 1976)*.
29. Michael Sherry, *The Rise of American Air Power* (New Haven: Yale University Press, 1987), p. 121.
30. On engineers and Nazism see Jeffrey Herf, *Reactionary Modernism* (Cambridge: Cambridge University Press, 1984).

31. Ute Deichmann, *Biologists Under Hitler* (Cambridge: Harvard University Press, 1996) p. 331.
32. Philip R. Reilly, *The Surgical Solution: A History of Involuntary Sterilization in the United States* (Baltimore: John Hopkins University Press, 1991), p. 101.
33. Ibid, p. 95.
34. John Frow, 'Information as Gift and Commodity' *New Left Review* 219 (September/October 1996), p. 94.
35. Richard Lewontin, *The Doctrine of DNA: Biology as Ideology* (London: Penguin, 1993), p. 72.
36. Margaret Lock, Globalization and the State: Is an Era of Eugenics in the Offing? unpublished paper, 2007, p. 9.
37. Peter and Ginger Ross Breggin, *The War Against Children* (New York: St Martins Press, 1994), p. 62.
38. Richard Bentall, 'Why There Can Never be a Genetic Theory of Schizophrenia' in Steven Rose, ed. *From Brain To Consciousness* (London: Allen Lane, 1998).
39. See Kalina Kamenova, Amir Rashef, and Timothy Caulfield, 'Angelina Jolie's Faulty Gene: Newspaper Coverage of a Celebrity's Preventive Bilateral Mastectomy in Canada, The United States and The United Kingdom.' Genetics in *Medicine* 16 (2013).
40. 'Every scientists knows there is not a straightforward mapping between genotype and phenotype; we know this so well that we don't talk about it. But the general public don't realize it and they use the most dangerous word in genetics, which is the three letter word 'for': a gene for this and a gene for that.' Steve Jones, 'Darwinism and Genes' in Jeremy Stangroom, Ed. *What Scientists Think* (London: Routledge, 2005), pp. 9–10. This begs the question of why there is a widespread public misunderstanding.
41. See Lori Andrews, *The Clone Age: Adventures in the New World of Reproductive Technology* (New York: Henry Holt, 1999)and Wendell Wallach, *A Dangerous Master* (New York: Basic Books, 2015).
42. Julian Borger, 'Who's Testing Our Genes—and Why?' *The Guardian*. 13 September 2000. In the Shriver Center in Massachusetts, for example, physicians reported 582 cases of people who were turned away because of 'flawed' genes.
43. See David Jones, 'The Prospect of Personalized Medicine' and Krimsky, 'Conclusion,' in Krimsky and Gruber, *Genetic Explanations*, p. 279.
44. 'Born into Debt: Gene Linked to Credit-Card Imbalances,' *Scientific American* 12 August 2010.
45. See Jay Joseph, et al., 'The Twin Research Debate in American Criminology,' *Logos: A Journal of Modern Society & Culture* (Spring 2015).

46. The presenter may have had in mind the early denunciation by G. K. Chesterton in his *Eugenics and Other Evils: An Argument Against the Scientifically Organized State* (New York: Cassel & Co, 1922). There he demolished the logic behind a law to institutionalize the 'feeble-minded,' pointing out that 'there is scarcely any human being to which this term has not been conversationally applied by his own friends and relatives on some occasion or other,' and hence what will stop the state from going after anyone it chooses? (p. 16).
47. Andrews, *The Clone Age*, p. 7.
48. See David Cay Johnson, *The Making of Donald Trump*, (New York: Melville House, 2016).
49. Sheldon Krimsky, 'Introduction,' in Sheldon Krimsky and Jeremy Gruber, eds. *Genetic Explanations: Sense and Nonsense* (Cambridge: Harvard University Press, 2013), p. 4.
50. Nicholas Weiler, 'Cultural Differences May Leave Their Mark on DNA,' University of California—*San Francisco Newsletter* 9 January 2017. Accessed at: https://www.ucsf.edu/news/2017/01/405466/cultural-differences-may-leave-their-mark-dna.
51. Krimsky, Conclusion, in Krimsky and Gruber, *Genetic Explanations*, p. 272.
52. Edward Shorter, *A History of Psychiatry: From The Era of The Asylum To the Age of Prozac* (New York: John Wiley & Sons, 1997), p. 246.
53. Speaker, Conference on evolution, society and genetics at ICA in London, 24 January 1998.
54. Callie H. Burtt and Ronald L. Simmons, 'Pulling Back the Curtain on Heritability Studies: Bisocial Criminality in the Postgenomic Era,' *Criminology* 52, 2 (2014), p. 251.
55. Jonathan Leo, The Search for Schizophrenia Genes, *Issues in Science and Technology* (Winter 2016), p. 69.
56. For modern genetics one hardly can improve on the advice of Herbert Muller who flirted with eugenic notions half a century ago before coming to the logical conclusion that we 'first need to organize a cooperative society [where] inequalities due to artificial class distinction, race prejudice, inherited fortunes and privileges are done away with, which will bring us much closer to the ideal eugenic conditions in which practically every individual will have as favourable opportunities for development as every other, and thus have his potentialities recognisable for what they are...then for the first time we shall have an estimation of a man's intelligence from a genetic standpoint.' Herbert J. Muller, *Out of The Night: A Biologist's View of The Future* (London: Gollanz, 1936), p. 104.
57. Leo, 'The Search for Schizophrenia Genes,' p. 69.

Loose Ends: Considerations on the Aftermaths of the Celtic Tiger and the Northern 'Troubles'

> "If you wish to know what the spirit of conquest, religious hatred, combined with all the abuses of aristocracy without any of its advantages, can produce, come to Ireland."
> —Alexis de Tocqueville, 1835[1]

From the imperially imposed destitution rued by aristocratic iconoclasts Tocqueville and Beaumont to the epic financial meltdown imposed by domestic quasi-aristocratic bankers and allied insiders is quite a rocky journey, but one with steady themes: deference to authority, comprador capitulation to external forces, celebration of the conventional, and exclusion or erasure of anyone the least bit critical of elite schemes.[2] By the look of things, the Celtic Tiger, defunct or not, is still digesting its critics. The upshot of the Tiger era was not a presumably desired deepening (after a Rostovian 'take-off' in the 1960s) of a vibrant if mostly foreign manufacturing base and a widening of prosperity but resort instead to conjuring money out of thin air just long enough for the slickest operators to cash in.[3] In retrospect, and even at the time, it is hard to credit the notion that defeat was snatched from the jaws of victory in the developmental quest, a debacle, given who was in charge, was always in the marked cards.[4]

Progress in Ireland is all too aptly signified in the serpent Ouroborus swallowing its own tail, especially in the dispiriting sense of symbolizing a cyclical return.[5] Ireland has been thrust not back to proverbial 'square one' where the citizenry can radically reconsider the socio-economic enterprise and how to go forward from here; instead middleman elites, as McCabe terms them, defiantly pressed the reset button on what should be a thoroughly discredited model. As the 'success narrative' of the Tiger years fades into recriminatory nothingness, one hopes it is true that 'a debate started in earnest as to whether we managed collectively to delude ourselves over the last number of years,' despite a power structure that has not budged one bit.[6] That one can name worse cases, such as Greece, is not comforting.

Fintan O'Toole, Raymond Crotty, Paeder Kirby, Ronnie Munck, Jim Wickham and a host of scholars now arrayed around TASC sounded unheeded early warnings of misshapen development policies and then in the 2000s of frothy financial legerdemain too.[7] Before the bubble burst Bertie Ahern, like Hamlet, dabbled with 'self-slaughter' as a solution, at least for barking mad critics. Fear not for gatekeepers after the crash because no one gets punished for herd behavior in major institutions. The leaders plead they knew no one (who mattered) who raised grave questions about the developmental model or about the financial web of ghostly gossamer on which everything increasingly rested in the noughties. Irish academics too humbly even mock themselves for 'operating at a safe remove from politics' when they were pointing out that the economy rested on unstable ground.[8] The core problem is that just as gender patterns are seen as 'reflecting essentialist and immutable realities,' so too is the world economy.[9] It simply is out there and must be adjusted to. Structure rules all. On that point Celtic Tiger proponents and critics seem agreed. Sod agency, unless it is an industrial development agency fine-tuning the terms of dependence.

Ireland from one end of the island to the other is the classic 'policy taker' (versus 'maker' or 'breaker') so far as the international order of predation is concerned, though there is no absurdity in Irish policy responses that was not manifested in mightier neoliberal powers like the USA and the UK.[10] For decades financiers have been fashioning what is for them a utopian world without risk, which is not capitalism as the textbooks know it but a rigged game, ultimately protected and coddled by sympathetic politicians, judges and administrators within the 'competition state.'[11] Will this preposterous free market fundamentalism ever become too threadbare to take seriously? What more calamitous events will it take? What screams from the bank bail-out experience is the 'emperor's new clothes' observation that those in charge of the world economic system are busy doing their pious best to unravel it.

So ensued bailouts, austerity and reinflation of bubbles in the USA, UK and more widely the EU, in the service of shoring up banking systems that are themselves best described as incorrigible toxic assets.[12] In the Republic, symptomatically, a recent high-spirited volume 'refuses to allow the next generation to accept the incarceration of thought that has captured its predecessor,' rejecting the 'old official Ireland of banking oligarchs, social partnerships, mighty mandarins, and states monopolies'—and then trots out the same old 'lean and mean' neoliberal nostrums.[13] One cannot be blamed for yearning again for 'the greatest growth in income per head over the period 1985–2010,' except that it hasn't sunk in that virtually all of it was bubble-based. It is not only decrepit Bourbons who forget nothing and learn nothing. Institutions close ranks during crises.

After relating a long sour litany of scandals in finance, policing and political bribery in 1980s Ireland, keen investigators lamented that 'institutions from An Garda Siochana to the Roman Catholic Church still operated on the basis that a scandal for the institution was worse than any fidelity to legal or moral standards.'[14] Nothing, as Archbishop McQuaid reportedly said after the liberalizing Second Vatican Council, has changed. Not if he could help it anyway. Not if they can help it now. McCullagh, like Coakley and McCabe, notes 'discursive moments' in late 2008 when a self-serving elite diagnosis succeeded in blaming the entire Irish people, not bankers and speculators, for thinking up an infinitely complicated way to keep a stagnant system afloat on credit and exports. The key here is that you don't really have to fool people into believing a plainly silly story, you just have to fool people into thinking everyone else believes the story, which is much easier and more disheartening for all those who otherwise might mount a challenge.[15]

The origins of this ideational and institutional stasis stem from thwarted revolutionary aspirations, which Foster, among many others, argues with ample if not clinching evidence was never likely in the 1916–1923 epoch.[16] Ernie O'Malley, cited in an essay above, serves as the 'median' Irish rebel, as unencumbered with social change aspirations as any politician or economist. O'Malley, Foster notes, soon joined those who 'rail against the new state for not delivering what they fought for'—so, beyond independence, there was indeed some hitherto inchoate vision of social betterment.[17] O'Malley scorned 'the convictions of purely revolutionary workers who stood outside the nationalist movement and a certain amusement at their arguments.'[18] Yet even this arch-nationalist republican admitted that 'class distinctions would jut out, and our merging into what we were pleased to call "the people" was a figment.'[19] O'Malley also credits the crucial and perhaps indispensable role of worker action for the success of the struggle, so far as it went, just as Kostick argues.[20] It was not historically inevitable that labor 'waited,' but the consequences are immense.

O'Malley was not disposed to think too far ahead, but plenty of others were. Figures like James Connolly or Paedar O'Donnell or George Gilmore are not fairly characterized as 'prisoners of their own concepts,' but were more aware of their constraints than critics seem to be of their own biases. (The Gerty McDowell image fails to 'reverse the gaze' and consider that it is her beach companions who are most locked into a self-stunting swirl, not her.) Paeder O'Donnell's nationalism was the antithesis of bourgeois nationalism, which his opponents appreciated well enough to want to shoot him for the sake of the difference. Translating socialist principles into locally applicable terms is a legitimate activity, which has had its successes elsewhere. The argument by English, Grant and predecessors regarding the 'theoretical inconsistencies of mixing republicanism with socialism' portrays this venture as a kind of crime of intellectual miscegenation (like mixing Marx and Freud, which engendered many fascinating works) and is just as foolish as opposition to any other form of miscegenation.[21]

So what is to be done? Pity the poor developmental state. The formidable task of 'getting it right' regarding the coordination (and/or lucky confluence) of international conditions, domestic coalition formation and suitable institutional structure is an epic work that is never quite done. Neoliberalism imposes daunting, if not impossible, conditions. What were advantageous arrangements yesterday can burden or obstruct one unduly today. There's no resting on laurels because, as O'Riain, and countless preceding scholars observe, development is 'a politically contested process that generates continuous, albeit different, challenges as it unfolds.'[22] Pragmatism, a word people rarely quibble with, was interpreted to best serve the mission, as Albert Reynolds stated in 1989, 'to evolve, and apply policy so as to underpin rather than undermine growth prospects.'[23] The Celtic Tiger carefully eschewed the *dirigiste* element that deepened success for some Asian counterparts. The Irish polity, like Anglo-American counterparts, also was heartily disinclined to redistribute benefits to the less well-connected.[24] High growth—regardless of the 'black hole'—teamed up with rising income inequality, a stinginess regarding welfare and a surge in 'virulent racism' on both sides of the border toward immigrants.[25]

The developmental ideal of 'self-reproducing dynamics' was so elusive because no one really pursued it. After the *Telesis Report* in 1982 sounded the tocsin about overreliance on the multinationals, the Irish Republic refashioned itself into what O'Riain termed a 'developmental network state' whose purported objective was to thread foreign investment more securely into the economy, to cultivate local enterprise and to deepen their connections. Irish growth also was based on a willing coalition that other analysts call neo-corporatism or a cognitively locked social partnership"—espousing what O'Riain nicely terms 'solidarity without equality.'[26] Contrary to business hype, the sources of Ireland's 1990s 'takeoff' lay in foreign investor enticements, public sector spending and a hefty influx of EU structural funds to shore up infrastructure. There indeed is latitude for institutional experiment here and supple state institutions can influence the character of the market they operate in, even though O'Riain comes perilously close in all his work to a social constructivist claim that capitalism only is what states make of it.

The analytical upshot is that the considerable' power of the global economy is not determining—the analysis shows that there is significant room for politics'—a lesson repeatedly noted from Fernando Cardoso in the 1960s stretching to yours truly in the 1990s.[27] Yet the point bears repeating. O'Riann, like other critics, shows how economic success, as understood by its main myopic beneficiaries, undermines the very institutional supports that make the system work in the first place. 'If the institutions of the Celtic Tiger could generate the results they did in face of domestic neoliberal populism and an international order hostile to state and social shaping of economic life, what might they achieve given a more supportive political order?'[28] Good question.

Financialization means making money from money rather than from production (in the absence of sufficient demand and investment opportunities); it is devising, exploiting and gorging on arcane pecuniary devices and getting away with it even when failing.[29] With so much spare cash seeking investible outlets one might imagine that investors would be in a disadvantageous position and be eager to go along with any productive scheme that public authorities propose. Not at all. What Philip Cerny termed the 'competition state' edges itself away from the ordinary populace and places itself at the service of global firms and banks, trusting that everything would work out because there was no alternative.[30]

Kirby finds the Irish experience redolent of a 'competition state with pockets of developmentalism.'[31] Even those pockets look like grist for the next sell-off. The tally sheet on the waves of privatizations and public–private partnerships in the neighboring UK has not been a happy one either, but they go on anyway.[32] One path forward is a dispelling of the stubborn myth that valiant investors, and not state spending, always generate the conditions for productivity and prosperity, as Mazzacato most recently elaborated.[33]

As for the North, obfuscation was indeed crucial to achieving the Good Friday Agreement so that rival political figures could interpret it to their own communities in the most favorable way. Stepping stone to the all-Island Republic or final recognition of the British link? Yet what an analyst alertly calls the republican movement's 'continuation of war by other means' slowly has gained the upper hand over recalcitrant white working class loyalists.[34] Northern Ireland from the continuous peace of 1997 onward has seen indefatigable foot-dragging, dissident republican violence, escalation in house prices, racist sprees by loyalist gangs, proliferation of 'peace walls' and a power-sharing executive without much power to alleviate local matters and, as of this writing, under threat of collapse over conflict between a resistant Sinn Fein and SDLP versus the leading conservative DUP over approving an austerity budget.[35] There is little sign that stringent economic conditions are uniting rather than alienating the communities, especially their working class members. The inequalities that underlay the conflict have not gone away, though the Catholic community made undeniable strides over the course of the conflict. The political establishment in the Irish Republic, with a wary eye as well on constitutional Sinn Fein, is in no more a hurry now than it was earlier to integrate a million plus discontented Loyalists into a single political structure.[36]

Conclusion

The argument that 'state-centric approaches ignore the fact that the national state can only exist within a larger system of states and institutions' is cogent as far as it goes.[37] Even the most conservative scholars of international political economy will agree. The question is, how far? One brilliantly daffy theory I heard spun long ago in an Irish pub was that we all come into life with a mission to move half the distance away from our instinctive natures if we are to be fulfilled, content or even just sane. If you are extroverted, move toward introversion; if introverted, go toward extroversion. Everyone is thus encumbered with a difficult task. This is no less the case for analyzing how international forces affect nation-states through the interpretive (and interest-laden) lenses of domestic groups, at least those who have a say in how the state responds. One task today is generating a movement for an 'alternative political economy'—one that does not privatize profits and socialize losses would do for a start—for which a recent TASC survey indicates immense latent popular support.[38] A related task is finding the economic policy equivalent of Andre Gorz' 'non-reform reforms' for guiding the next phase. From Tocqueville to the present an emphatic 'lack of a moral tie between rich and poor' remains the case and indeed is required for increasingly feral finance capital to expand.[39]

NOTES

1. Emmet Larkin, ed, *Alexis de Toqueville's Journey in Ireland, July–August 1835* (Washington, DC: Catholic University Press of America, 1990), p. 26. Also see Gustav de Beaumont, *Ireland: Social Political and Religious vol 2* (London: J. Botson & Palmer, 1839).
2. On the authoritarian strain in political culture see Diammaid Ferriter, *The Transformation of Ireland 1900–2000* (London: Profile Books, 2005).
3. 'Deepening' entails fastening foreign firms more firmly into local supply networks, generating more Irish-owned industry, public or private, service or manufacturing. See, for example, Tham Siew Yean and Loke. 'Industrial Deepening in Malaysia: Policy Lessons for Developing Countries,' *Asian Development Review* 28, 2 (2011). Guillermo O'Donnell long ago noted that deepening' also can become compatible with dependent industrialization.
4. See Sean O'Riain, 'Snatching Defeat from the Jaws of Victory: Ireland Rediscovers Crisis.' in Perry Share and Mary P. Corcoran, eds. *Ireland of the Illusions: A Sociological Chronicle 2007–2008* (Dublin: Institute of Public Administration, 2010) and his *The Rise and Fall of The Celtic Tiger* (Cambridge: Cambridge University Press, 2013).
5. Carl Jung, *Collected Works*, Vol. 14 (London: Routledge & Kegan Paul, 1968), para 513.
6. Share and Corcoran, eds. *Ireland of the Illusions*, pp. 2, 3.
7. Fintan O'Toole, *After The Ball* (Dublin: New Island, 2003), Denis O'Hearn, *Inside the Celtic Tiger* (London: Pluto Press, 1998), Raymond Crotty, *Ireland in Crisis* (Dover, NH: Brandon, 1985) Ronnie Munck, *The Irish Economy* (London: Pluto Press, 1993), Paul Sweeney, The *Celtic*

Tiger: Ireland's Economic Miracle Explained (Cork: Oak Tree Press, 1998), Paeder Kirby, *The Celtic Tiger in Distress* (Basingstoke: Palgrave, 2002) and *Explaining Ireland's Developmental Economic Growth with Weakening Welfare* (Geneva: Research Institute for Social Development, 2008), James Wickham, 'Dependence and State Structure,' in Otmar Holl, ed, *Small States in Europe and Dependence* (Vienna: Austrian Institute for International Affairs, 1983) Kurt Jacobsen, 'Peripheral Postindustrialization' in James Caparoso, ed. *A Changing International Political Economy* (Boulder: Lynne Rienner, 1987) and *Chasing Progress in the Irish Republic* (Cambridge University Press, 1994). Also, more temperate in tone but no less concerned, see Eoin O'Malley *Industry and Economic Development* (Dublin, Gill and Macmillan, 1989) and Lars Mosjet, *The Irish Economy in a Comparative Institutional Perspective* (Dublin: National and Economic Social Council, 1992).

8. Doncha O'Connell, 'Public Intellectuals' in Mary P. Corcoran and Kevin Lalor, eds. *Reflections on Crisis: The Role of the Public Intellectuals* (Dublin: Royal Irish Academy, 2012), p. 22.
9. Pat O'Connor, 'Reflections on the public intellectuals role in a gendered society' in Ibid. p. 60.
10. On these distinctions see Stephen Krasner, 'U.S. Commercial and Monetary Policy: Unraveling the Paradox of External and Internal Weakness,' In Peter Katzenstein, ed., *Between Power and Plenty* (Madison: University of Wisconsin Press, 1978).
11. See Alexandra Ouroussolf, *Wall Street at War* (Oxford: Polity Press, 2012).
12. Ron Suskind, *Confidence Men* (New York: HarperCollins, 2011).
13. Ed Burke and Ronan Lyons, eds. *Next Generation Ireland* (Dublin: Blackhall Publishing, 2011).
14. Michael Clifford and Shane Coleman, *Scandal Ireland* (Dublin: Hachette Books, 2010), p. 198.
15. See chap. 4.
16. Roy Foster, *Vivid Faces: The Revolutionary Generation in Ireland 1890–1923* (New York: Penguin, 2014), p. 329.
17. Ibid., p. 309.
18. Ernie O'Malley, *On Another Man's Wound* (London Rich & Cowan, 1936), p. 144.
19. Ibid., p. 317. 'We could not see any definite social shape or direction to our efforts … The people had to live the round of the soil and solve its problems of economic and of living relationships, which were more of living than my relation to the fighting effort only.'
20. Conor Kostick, *Revolution in Ireland: Popular Militancy 1917–1923* (Cork: Cork University Press, 2009, 2nd ed.).

21. Adrian Grant, *Irish Socialist Republicanism Republicanism, 1909–1936* (Dublin: Four Courts Press, 2012), p. 223; Richard English, *Radicals and the Republic* (Oxford: Oxford University Press, 1994). Grant allows for adaptability but implies this is somehow a form of cheating.
22. O'Riain, *The Politics of High Tech Growth* (Cambridge: Cambridge University Press, 2004), p. 125.
23. Cited in Michael Boss, 'The Collapse of the "Celtic Tiger" Narrative,' *Nordic Studies* 10 (2011), p. 120.
24. Eileeen Connolly, 'The Institutionalization of Anti-Poverty and Social Exclusion Policy in Irish Social Partnership,' *Working Papers in International Studies, Centre for International Studies, Dublin City University*, 2006. p. 2.
25. O'Riann, *Politics of High Tech Growth*, p. 63. Also Christine Kinealy, *War and Peace: Ireland since the 1960s* (London: Reaktion Books, 2010), p. 317.
26. Mary Murphy, 'Ideas, Interests and Institutions: Explaining Irish Social Security Policy' *Research Working Paper 08/08, Combat Poverty Agency* September 2008.
27. O'Riain, *Politics of High Tech Growth*, p. 222.
28. ibid, p. 11.
29. See Tijo Salverda, 'Who Does the State Work For?' *Real-World Economics Review* Issue 71, 28 (May 2015). http://www.paecon.net/PAEReview/issue71/Salverda71.pdf.
30. Philip Cerny, 'Paradoxes of the Competition State: The Dynamics of Political Globalization' *Government and Opposition*, 32, 2 (1997).
31. Paeder Kirby, 'The Competition State - Lessons for Ireland,' *Limerick Papers in Politics and Public Administration*, No. 1 (2009), p. 19.
32. 'The Treasury estimated the lifetime costs of Labour-era deals at 215 billion pounds, paying for deals with a capital value of between 55 and 65 billion pounds.' Polly Toynbee and David Walker, *The Verdict: Did Labour Change Britain?* (London: Granta Books, 2013), p. 117.
33. Mariana Mazzucato, *The Entrepreneurial State: Debunking Public Versus Private Sector Myths* (London: Anthem Press, 2013), p. 193. On the 'Sussex school' of technology and economics from which her analysis hails, see Kurt Jacobsen 'Microchips and Public Policy: The Political Economy of High Technology,' *British Journal of Political Science* October 1992.
34. Kevin Bean, 'The Politics of Fear? Provisionalism, Loyalism and the "New Politics" of Northern Ireland,' in James W McCauley and Graham Spenser, eds., *Loyalism after the Good Friday Agreement* (London: Macmillan, 2011), pp. 61, 62.

35. 'Northern Ireland crisis talks fail to resolve standoff over welfare reforms.' *The Guardian* 2 June 2015.
36. See John Coakley, ed. *Changing Shades of Orange and Green* (Dublin: University College Dublin Press, 2002); David McKittrick and David McVea, *Making Sense of The Troubles* (Belfast: Blackstaff Press, 2000), and Jonathan Tonge, *The New Northern Irish Politics?*(Basingstoke: Palgrave Macmillan, 2005).
37. Smith and Kutz-Flamenbaum, 'Prisoners of our Concepts: Liberating the Study of Social Movements.' Simon Teune, ed. *The Transnational Condition: Protest Dynamics in an Entangled Europe* (New York: Berghahn Books, 2010) 211.
38. Think Tank for Action on Social Change (TASC) *The Solidarity Factor* November 2014.
39. *Tocqueville in Ireland*, p. 43.

Conclusion: Algren, Academe and Conformity

Conformity sounds like a condition one only would find debated earnestly on a *Mad Men* episode, a throwback to a bygone era of calculated timidity, of learning to sell oneself on the social scene, of cookie-cutting oneself to expectations in a tight job market, of ... Hang on, yes, conformity is back, though less sincerely so than in the scared straight 1950s. People conform for all the familiar reasons. One doesn't notice because they act like everyone else. In many milieus being a conspicuous oddball or dissident can still get you hurt, fired, ridiculed or shunned. Protective coloration, not ripeness, is all.

The advantages of 'going along to get along' are dangled. The proving ground in a shrinking middle-class culture is a smooth transition from the campus to the leaner, meaner work place. Once upon a time passing this marathon test with flying colors resulted in bigger paydays, delicious opportunities, approval of similar self-seeking peers and affirmation that you are on the fast track. You even get lauded as a rascally daredevil for performing perfectly tepid acts. They got it covered, those guardians of the status quo, in any time, any culture, any place. Christopher Lasch, as mentioned earlier, skewered cold warriors in the 1960s for their 'infatuation with consensus.'[1] Many devotees of 'The God That Failed,' soon to form the molten core of the neoconservatives, were more 'attracted to Marxism in the first place as an elitist and antidemocratic ideology than as a means of analysis which provided not answers, but the beginnings of a critical theory of society.' How can one begin to lampoon those overwrought international relations journal editors today who fastidiously ban from their periodical any research containing WikiLeaks material, none of which has proved untrue?[2]

Over the last few decades, 'straight' people diligently rigged the economy, deranged the legal system and purchased the favor of enough pliant members of Congress so as to deny goodies to anyone except bank moguls and crony capitalists. Every ounce of one's energy and ingenuity propels productivity whose monetary rewards flow to the distant top.[3] This radical rearrangement didn't happen overnight. The best that any postmodern employee can yearn for is to run in place. It hardly comes as a surprise that in academia many readers misread the sociological implications of Thomas Kuhn's most famous work as proving that truth is a majority vote of a scientific community.[4] Conform or quit.

Is conformity innate? Is there a gene for it? The social cues are too powerful for a crucial test ever to be performed that reliably separates cultural from material influences. So youngsters growing up in a post-postindustrial society ache to break into cliques ranging from private clubs to secret college societies to 'epistemic communities' so as to gain an invaluable edge in a race they dare not question. Ivy Leaguers swarmed into Wall Street jobs where they lay their pedigrees at the feet of a suspendered Mammon, managed to sabotage the Western economy, looted it, made the average citizen pay for it and called it progress.[5] Nonetheless, staple-faced Goth bar denizens, no less than the fashionistas in the posh Manhattan bar, are about as nonconformist as a school of tropical fish.

Why it's positively unhealthy to misbehave. Richard Kraft-Ebbing in 1892 concocted the glorious diagnosis 'political and reformatory insanity' to label wayward souls who dared to exhibit 'an inclination to differ from the mass opinion.' The incubation period is long, often reaching back to childhood,' the eminent researcher solemnly estimated.[6] Science, such as it is, marches on. Still, it's difficult to hold a pose for long—the hypocritical Victorians spawned the rancorous Freud—so ruptures are inevitable.

Must You Conform? is the title of a gloomy tome that I plucked from a library shelf in Champaign-Urbana long ago.[7] That the question needed to be asked said a lot about the period. The University of Illinois then was the largest 'Greek' (fraternity and sorority) campus in the USA. Teens competed to impress Cro-Magnon committees and then assiduously to make the right contacts: networking, as it is so sanitarily termed today. Paul Goodman in *Growing Up Absurd* fretted about a 'dangerous conformity' hardening into a toxic fixture of life.[8] Even billionaire J. Paul

Getty, of all people, deplored conformity as a trait that 'can do the Free World's cause more harm than a dozen Nikita Khrushchevs.'[9] In its heyday *Mad Magazine*, a zany lifeline of critical sanity for many disturbed (by the world) kids, thrived on ridiculing the mania to conform. All this shifted, outwardly, in the late 1960s when crew cut frat rats sprouted Sergeant Pepper mustaches and long hair as they hastened to catch up with what most regarded as the latest fashion. Certainly, in that dispiriting case, John Lennon was on the mark to blurt bitterly that on balance in the 1960s 'Nothing happened except we all dressed up.'[10]

The neo-medieval era of *in loco parentis*, dress codes and looking alike is long gone. Now gaze upon rainbow hair, nose rings, ornate tattoos and puncture marks. But those wily marketers always outflank us, issuing artfully opaque slogans about the 'hip transgressive,' 'urban chic' and so on.[11] Still, some things were agreeably different in those days of yore. Out of savings from summer construction jobs I paid nearly all expenses at a flagship state university. Couldn't happen now. That generation wasn't shackled by the indenturing debts of today's students and so a latitude to experiment scared apprehensive 'squares' who, as Tennessee Williams well knew, 'hate anything not in their book.' Check the Nixon tape transcripts and find Tricky Dick and his soon-to-be-penitentiaried pals plotting to raze the sources of affordable university education in order to smash youth movements. How can you question anything when the creeps in control keep you deep in hock?[12]

'Rusty wasn't a bright boy,' Lieutenant William Calley's high school principal approvingly remarked, 'but he did what he was told.' Obedience was the saving grace of mediocre but willing executioners at My Lai. Nick Turse's recent Vietnam book affirms what any unblinkered student of that war already knew, that atrocities were commonplace and cover-ups were the norm.[13] Conformists, not misfits, are needed to commit mass atrocities. (To an editor's request for an article on a multiple murderer, to be entitled 'Crime of the Century' Algren spat, 'I don't want to go to Vietnam.'[14] As Andrew Bacevich, a welcome defector, comments, the military 'did not look kindly on nonconformity. Climbing the ladder of success required a curbing of maverick tendencies; you needed to be a team player.'[15] Colin Powell, yet to answer for his likely role in covering up My Lai, spoke of the 'pragmatics' required in getting ahead, as if ambition excused any and all indecencies accompanying it. Yet Americans always have displayed a deep streak of conformity, a collective longing to be rugged individualists all in the same backwards baseball cap way. Tocqueville witheringly wrote that he 'knew of no country in which there is so little independence of mind and real freedom of discussion as in America.'[16]

In the early 1950s in a slim manuscript *Nonconformity: Writing on Writing*, Nelson Algren, fresh from a National Book award for his gritty volume that started as a war novel but transfigured into the gutter-level tragedy of a card sharp junkie, delivered a jeremiad about conformity greasing the skids of American society into the paranoiac McCarthy era. What conformists yearned for 'was an eternally elusive secure zone in which to live what authorities ordain as a normal life,' Algren seethed. Yet life is 'never lived that way, though many people persuade themselves to the contrary.'[17] Good writers apprise us of what we forgot or never noticed or deliberately ignored. Life in the 1950s *Father Knows Best* mode was abnormal, a televised fiction, such that this blithe, candy-coated facade was worth peeling away in dyspeptic retrospective films later on, such as *Pleasantville, Blue Velvet and A Boy and His Dog*. Why did audiences root for Jim Carrey to shatter his intricately ordered artificial 'life' in *The Truman Show*? Many taboos then vanished or are on the wane today for having since been stubbornly and strongly confronted.

At the 1950 National Book Award ceremony Algren, who had signed a *New York Times* letter 'Speak up for freedom,' and chaired the Chicago Committee to Secure Justice in the Rosenberg case, was a marked man, high on the FBI's list and that of every pseudo-patriotic private snoop. (Peruse KeyWiki, a rightwing website ratting out anyone mad enough to commit senselessly progressive and humane acts). Reactionaries cherish their lists, from the 'Hollywood Ten' to␣ProporNot, tracking who's been naughty and who's not been nice enough to them. Algren's blistering thoughts on conformity first saw light in the Chicago Daily News in 1952.[18] Doubleday commissioned a book on the subject but declined to publish it in 1953, the same year the FBI yanked Algren's passport.[19] In *Nonconformity* Algren appraised the impact of this true 'big chill' upon writers, but every intimidated or complacent American was his intended audience too.

Algren commences with F. Scott Fitzgerald's bathetic 'struggle to write with profundity and at the same time live like a millionaire'—a dizzying doomed acrobatic act. Fitzgerald was left 'wondering and blinking, as he contemplated his Savoy Hotel bill, whether one could be both a good writer and a good person.' Algren feared that American writers were slipping and sliding into the 'inert whirlpool of egotism that is world of the average businessman.' Overly cautious writers, Algren accused, were abandoning the 'problem of the heart in conflict with itself which alone can make good writing.' A new batch of beady-eyed scribes sees 'the way things are going, the main things are not problems of the heart but to keep one's nose clean.' As one scans mainstream book review pages today one learns that Algren's complaint still carries a lot of power.

Algren was a meticulous chronicler of the 10% or so scrabbling at the rock bottom of the social scale 'where everyone has to win every round just to stay alive.' Algren acquired some of the rude *savoir-faire* of the streets, but only so much. 'I was a fairly good mark, not too good a mark,' Algren recalls about his costly mingling with junkies and hustlers.[20] Algren's lamentation on conformity resonated with kindred critics such as Erich Fromm. 'The average individual does not permit himself to be aware of thoughts or feelings that are incompatible with the patterns of his culture, and hence he is forced to repress them,' Fromm observed, perhaps a tad too clinically. 'To that degree to which a person—because of his own intellectual and spiritual development—feels his solidarity with humanity, can he tolerate social ostracism, and vice versa.' Fromm's next sentence, though, captured Algren himself: 'The ability to act according to one's conscience depends on the degree to which one has transcended the limits of one's society and has become a citizen of the world.' Presto—the incorrigible nonconformist. Poor house, here I come.

Algren revisits the profoundly emetic spectacles of director Elias Kazan, actor Jose Ferrer and playwright Maxwell Anderson on bended knees before the House Committee on Un-American Activities. Algren warns those likewise tempted to genuflect to pea-brained bullies that 'he knows enough of the heart that it cannot conform,' not without exacting a very high price.[21] Are there any extenuating circumstances ? Algren cited Finley Peter Dunne's fictitious worldly wise barkeeper Mr. Dooley about 'turning on the gas [light] in the darkest heart you'd find they had a 'good raison for th' worst things it done' which include 'needin' th' money.' While Algren had a renowned soft spot for 'lonesome monsters,' the profit motive by itself was never a valid alibi.[22] Sociopathic traits were no alibi either. Glance at Hervey Cleckley's *The Mask of Sanity*, written at the time, and you'll find prophetic descriptions of the psychopathology of a Dick Cheney, Donald Trump and any Wall Street honcho you care to name.[23]

Nonconformity, posthumously published in 1998, was composed during the Korean War or near enough, about 'five years after we have begun to rearm.'[24] Algren rhetorically asks regarding the military-industrial complex: Are we more secure for 'putting a hot-car thief in charge of a parking lot?' No nation even comes close to the US level of carefully misnomered 'defense' and 'homeland security' expenditures. Iran today terrifies our policy makers. Really? Algren mauled 'long-remaindered intellectuals on short leashes' who obligingly burble that things are 'worse in Russia, as if it helps.' Things are worse in Greece and Spain right now. Feel better? And Greece is coming to a neighborhood near you if aficionados of austerity continue to get their cynical way. Contemporary 'intellectuals on short leashes' infest news programs: George and David and Cokie and the rest of the glossy chattering corporate cheerleaders. A forerunner of theirs in the 1950s, Norman Podhoretz, whose book *Making It* celebrates himself as an envious outsider aching to become a WASP establishment minion, assaulted Algren for his 'boozy sentimentality.' Scorn from affluent pipsqueak quarters is normal.

Algren praises Theodore Dreiser, H. L. Mencken, Thorstein Veblen, Lincoln Steffens and Sinclair Lewis. Our singular American genius Mark Twain towers among even that fine company. Algren skewers popular novelists who yearn 'to give pleasure to the reading public' and craftily plead that they have 'no right to impose [their] views on race and religion.' So, Algren shrewdly deduces, 'if it isn't the writer's [or, I would add, social scientist's] task to relate mankind to the things of the earth, it must be his job to keep them unrelated.' Repelled by the businessman's creed that 'no values are greater than thrift, self-preservation, and piety,' Algren speaks witheringly of the tinselly show, of a 'neon wilderness' dominated by whitewashed high-rise sepulchers brimming with effervescent schemers. He accused the middle class of adoring 'personal comfort as an end in itself' which 'is, in essence, a denial of life.'[25] He detested ingrown literary cliques, pulling themselves up the ladder by each other's Gucci bootstraps. 'When [a writer] sees scarcely anyone except other writers,' says Algren, 'he is ready for New York' and what Algren terms 'bellhop writing'—writing to order. 'No book was ever worth writing that wasn't done with the attitude that 'This ain't what you rung for, Jack—but its what you're damned well getting.'

Fitzgerald put 'one little drop of something—not blood, not a tear, not my seed, but me more intimately than these, in every story.' What Algren looked for in writing was not just pity but 'vindictiveness' of a certain kind. (For Algren the moralist it didn't count if the cause you champion is only your own interests.) 'A certain ruthlessness and a sense of alienation from society is as essential to creative writing as it is to armed robbery'—summed in the frank furious urge 'to get even.'[26] Of course, Algren concedes, he most likely won't get even but it's worth trying. 'The artist must approach his work in the sane frame of mind in which the criminal commits his deed.' In this moneychanger's paradise 'it's easier to make people mean than to make them kind [and] society is organized so meanly that man cannot help but perpetrate villainies.' (Consider Algren's pulverizingly poetic *Chicago: City On The Make.*) Joe Bageant wrote in the same spirit about crushed and choleric denizens in small towns and in rural America.[27] 'Americans everywhere face gunfire better than guilt.'[28] Moral courage may not be in shorter supply than physical courage, but it certainly gets less publicity and approval. Maybe it's why we hear so little of Algren these days.

No one is entirely immune to the lure of the bright lights blazing around a refined cutthroat system of getting and spending. 'From the coolest zoot-suit cat getting leaping drunk on straight gin to the gentlest suburban matron getting discreetly tipsy on Alexanders, the feeling is that of having too much of something not really needed, and nothing at all of something desperately needed. They both want to live and neither knows how,' Algren writes, and 'that is the trap.' As for most therapists, we may ask, 'Doctor, what's my problem?' And the doctor cannot speak the truth [because] to stiff-arm a customer with the alarm that his trouble is something as simple as cowardice, or as hopeless as a spiritual void, would be only to lose that [fee] to a competitor with a more flattering tale to tell.' Few resist the advantage of 'being on the side of the house.' As for the other end of the scale where junkies and down-and-outs dwell, when authorities 'bear down they make our risk bigger, and the cost goes higher ... So the junkies got to come up with more gold than ever, and the only one place to get it. Off the square.' So much for our supposedly straight-laced war on drugs.

'We presume the accused to be guilty by the act of having been accused'—all the better to strike them with sneaky drones or imprison them via stage-managed Star Chambers. McCarthyism stank of 'the same sickness as that of Salem' where we 'exorcize our devils by destroying the dissenters or odd fish of the tribe.' The syndrome that we 'boast about our strength yet display our fear' never quite dissipated in a nation that elected Donald Trump, even if as the joker in the pack of candidates officially on offer.

Nor have the 'smokescreens with which we ingeniously conceal our true condition from ourselves' dispersed. And 'our assumption of happiness through mechanical ingenuity is nonetheless tragic for being naïve.'[29] It has taken a generation or two to soak for that one to sink in. Ultimately, 'when we get more houses than we can live in, more cars than we can ride in, more food than we can eat ourselves, the only way of getting richer is by cutting off those who don't have enough,' diagnosed Algren. One didn't need a crystal ball, or even Thomas Piketty's recent book, to discern what the 1% were up to.[30]

Algren was no saint in a threadbare cassock but he stuck, however crankily, to his vocation. Perhaps he might have treated his women, including Simone De Beauvoir, a tad better. The streetwise author got his pockets picked with the greatest of ease by average Hollywood hucksters. Algren, a poker addict, could not resist trying to 'fill the inside straight,' a mentality any worthwhile writer knows and needs, though not at the card table.[31] In all the arts an inveterate will to gamble is the supreme asset, and it remains the case in our *Mahagonny* world where no motive other than gain is deemed entirely sane. Conformists play the percentages, and rational choice proponents adore those who do. Hence, in the social sciences, from behaviorism in psychology to rational choice in political science, we recurrently encounter a 'doctrine of causality which, with respect to human conduct, requires at the outset the categorical exclusion of conscious experience,' Matson surmises.[32] Consciousness—the capacity for critical self-reflection—introduces disorder, and authoritarians in whatever field want none of that.

Societies, as some sullen wit aptly remarked, honor their conformists when they are alive and their troublemakers when they are dead. Yet no one remembers the conformists, the sycophants or those who in Kuhn's sense 'mop up' in, or rigidly color within the lines of, a dominant paradigm, except exactly as the mediocrities they were. What Algrendetected in Irish playwright Brendan Behan's chubby face reflected his own venturesome soul: Behan, he wrote, 'deploys defiance while concealing pity' and so 'his intellectual belief in the class struggle is modified by his emotional conviction that the only class is Mankind.'[33] Literature is fundamentally a rebel's trade because, Algren urged, it 'is made on any occasion when a challenge is made to the legal apparatus by a conscience in touch with humanity.' Any trade can be a rebel's trade, even and especially the social sciences. As Lasch long ago argued, there is no need for intellectuals to 'deprive themselves of the real influence they could have as [people] who refuse to judge the validity of ideas by the requirements of national power or any other entrenched interest.'[34] A 'conscience in touch with humanity' is what must animate their crafts too in order for them to count.

NOTES

1. Christopher Lasch, 'The Cultural Cold War: A Short History of the Congress for Cultural Freedom' in Barton J. Bernstein, ed. *Towards a New Past: Dissenting Essays in American History* (New York: Vintage, 1969), pp. 323, 338. Also see Peter Steinfels, *The Neoconservatives* (New York: Simon & Schuster, 1979).
2. The finicky journal is *International Studies Quarterly*. See *The WikiLeaks Files* (London: Verso, 2015), pp. 10–11.
3. 'Recovery in US is lifting Profits, But not Adding Jobs.' *New York Times* 3 March 2013.
4. See Wes Sharrock and Rupert Read, *Kuhn: Philosopher of Scientific Revolutions* (Oxford: Polity Press, 2002), pp. 223–226.
5. See Karen Ho, *Liquidated: An Ethnography of Wall Street* (Durham: Duke University, 2009).
6. Thomas Roder et al., *Psychiatrists—The Men Behind Hitler* (LA: Freedom Publishers, 1995), p. 23.
7. Robert Lindner, *Must You Conform?* (New York: Rinehart, 1956).
8. Paul Goodman, *Growing Up Absurd: Problems of Youth in the Organized System* (Random House, 1960), p. 80.
9. Quoted in Erich Fromm, *May Man Prevail?* (London: George Allen & Unwin, 1962), p. 79, fn18.
10. 'The same bastards are in control,' Lennon continued. 'The same people are running everything.' Quoted in John Lahr, *Automatic Vaudeville: Essays on Star Turns* (London: Methuen, 1985), p. 109.
11. Elizabeth Wilson, *Bohemians: The Glamorous Outsiders* (London: IB Tauris, 2000), p. 233.
12. See the 1971 Lewis Powell memo, a 'call-to-arms for corporations' according to Bill Moyers, which predicted or, indeed, served as a template for establishment strategy for the next half a century so as to suppress voices lower on the social ladder. http://reclaimdemocracy.org/powell_memo_lewis/ Also see Michel J. Crozier, Samuel Huntington, Joji Watanuki, eds. *The Crisis of Democracy* (New York: New York University Press, 1975).
13. Nick Turse, *Kill Anything That Moves: The Real American War in Vietnam* (New York: Metropolitan Books, 2013).

14. Nelson Algren, *Algren at Sea: Notes from A Sea Diary & Who Lost an American?* (New York: Seven Stories Press, 2008), p. 332.
15. Andrew Bacevich, 'The Unmaking of a Company Man' accessed at http://www.commondreams.org/view/2010/08/26-6.
16. Alexis de Tocqueville *Democracy in America, Volume 1* (New York: Aeterna, 2011), p. 208.
17. H. E. F. O'Donohue, *Conversations with Nelson Algren* (New York: Hill and Wang, 1964), p. 22.
18. Algren, *Nonconformity*, p. 99.
19. Bettina Drew, *Nelson Algren: A Life on the Wild Side* (Austin: University of Texas Press, 1991), p. 237. See also Mary Wisniewski, *Algren: A Life* (Chicago: Chicago Press Review, 2016).
20. 'Nelson Algren Interview' *Paris Review* (Winter 1955), p. 6.
21. Algren, *Nonconformity*, p. 4.
22. 'The stories that follow have the common hope that ever man, no matter how lonesome nor what a monster, is deserving of understanding by us other lonesome monsters.' Nelson Algren, *Nelson Algren's own Book of Lonesome Monsters* (New York: Lancer Books, 1962).
23. Hervey Cleckley, *The Mask Of Sanity: An Attempt to Clarify some Issues about the So-Called Psychopathic Personality* (St Louis: Mosby, 1955).
24. Algren, *Nonconformity*, p. 10.
25. Algren, *Nonconformity*, p. 20.
26. Algren, *Nonconformity*, p. 34.
27. Joe Bageant, *Deer Hunting with Jesus: Dispatches from America's Class War* (New York: Crown, 2007) and *Rainbow Pie: A Redneck Memoir* (New York: Scribe Publications, 2011).
28. Nelson Algren, *Chicago: City on the Make* (Garden City: Doubleday, 1951), p. 95.
29. Algren, *Nonconformity*, p. 76.
30. Thomas Piketty, *Capital in the 21st Century* (Cambridge: Harvard Belknap Press, 2014).
31. Drew, *Nelson Algren*, p. 257.
32. Floyd Matson, *The Broken Image*, p. 37.
33. Algren, *Algren at Sea*, p. 57.
34. Lasch, 'The Cultural Cold War,' p. 356.

INDEX

A
Afghanistan, 10, 92, 111, 112, 131, 134, 137
Agency, 15, 47, 57, 79, 152, 172, 208
Algeria, 110, 113, 116, 118, 128
American Political Science Association (APSA), 17
American Political Science Review (APSR), 22
American Psychiatric Association (APA), 151
Anarchy, 52, 53, 75, 150
Anthropology, 63
Appeasement, 77, 81–83, 154, 165
Argentina, 89
Articulation, 56, 59, 60, 62
Athens, 99
Austerity, 19, 209, 212, 222
Austria, 214
Authoritarian personality, 54

B
Bailouts, 209
Balance of power, 6
Bay of pigs, 86

Behavioral revolution, 33
Behaviorism, 2, 224
Belgium, 83
Bosnia, 78
Brunei, 89

C
Cambodia, 83, 88, 161
Caribbean, 82
Casablanca (film 1942), 5
Central Intelligence Agency (CIA), 83, 88, 89, 93, 109, 113, 116–118, 130, 166
Chile, 87
China, 81, 113, 189
Civil Operations and Revolutionary Development Support (CORDS), 110
Civil rights, 78, 132
Civilian casualties, 7, 86
COINTELPRO, 161
Cold war, 2, 57, 80, 83, 130, 175
Collaboration, 6, 7, 24, 75, 160
Collective action, 19
Columbia, 20, 112

Conformity, 159, 175, 199, 217–221
Constructivism
  conventional, 4, 9, 42, 44, 50, 54–57, 61
  critical, 9, 53, 54, 56
Contexts, 3, 9, 30, 42, 49, 56, 59, 61, 150
Counterinsurgency (COIN), 4, 10, 109–112, 114, 115, 119, 122, 125, 130–133, 136, 165
Cuba Missile crisis, 57, 172
Culture, 4, 5, 18, 47–49, 59, 176, 217, 221
Cynicism, 9, 84, 96, 160

D
Dachau, 46
Darwinism, 204
Deception, 74–76, 83, 86, 88, 91, 95, 164
Decolonization, 111
Democracy, 17, 20, 22, 27, 32, 61, 74, 81, 83, 87, 125, 126, 135, 157, 176
Development policy, 10, 47
Diagnostic and Statistical Manual, 188
Dien Bien Phu, 169
Domino theory, 150, 166
Downing Street memo, 93
Drug trafficking, 80

E
Economics, 2, 8, 10, 18–20, 57
El Salvador, 111, 115, 128, 129, 136, 137
Ellis Island, 190
Environment, 45, 49, 58, 94, 135, 156–158, 188, 197–199
Epistemic communities, 218
Ether, 30
Eugenics, 2, 188–195, 197–199, 201

European Union, 108

F
Feeble-mindedness, 193, 194
Financialization, 211
Foreign aid, 74
Frankfurt school, 3, 43, 54, 157, 159
Freud, Sigmund, 5, 10, 149–152, 155–159, 163, 164, 172, 173, 175, 177, 210

G
Gandhi, Mohandas, 159
Genetic engineering, 10, 187, 189, 196, 198
Germany, 6, 7, 47
Globalization, 13, 215
Good Friday Agreement, 212
Gramsci, Antonio, 9, 41, 42, 44, 49, 53, 57, 58, 60
Grand strategy, 81, 131
Guerrillas, 112, 117, 119, 120, 124, 136

H
Hamlet Evaluation System (HES), 119, 123
Harlem renaissance, 174
Heredity, 188, 193
Hollywood, 220, 224
Huk rebellion, 134
Human Genome Project, 196
Hypocrisy, 74, 78, 94

I
Idealism, 62, 80
Ideas, 1, 9, 42, 44, 46, 49–52, 60, 175, 225

Identity, 23, 47, 52, 54–57, 61, 162, 163, 196
Ideology, 1, 48, 54, 60, 79, 165, 195, 217
India, 22, 128, 130, 189
Indian wars, 133
Indonesia, 114
Institutionalists, 43
Intelligence agencies, 8, 75, 76, 91, 93
Iran, 85, 89, 90, 222
Iran-Contra affair, 106
Iraq, 10, 17, 57, 77, 85, 92, 111, 117, 130, 131, 136, 137, 163, 169, 171
Ireland, Republic of, 22, 58, 129, 207
Irish Republican Army (IRA), 129
Israel, 89, 163, 188

K
Kenya, 128
Keynesianism, 50, 55
Korea, 81, 89
Kuhn, Thomas, 3, 17, 28–30, 218, 224
Kuwait, 83

L
Land reform, 125
Laos, 83, 86, 88, 161
Lebanon, 89, 168

M
Malaya, 118, 119, 143, 147
Manic-depression, 189
Maquis, 7
Marine corps, 9, 113, 139, 141
Marxism, 3, 43, 51, 63, 157, 217
Maslow, Abraham, 1

Mathematical models, 2, 8, 18, 26
McCarthyism, 44, 65, 81, 223
Media, 34, 75, 78, 84, 89, 92, 95, 99, 103, 189, 196, 197
Methodological conservativism, 29
Methodological pluralism, 11
Militarism, 69, 77
Military-industrial complex, 165, 222
Munich agreement (1938), 78, 154, 165
"Munich complex", 176
My Lai massacre, 61, 110, 115, 158, 165

N
Narcissistic personality disorder, 165
National Book Award, 220
National Institute of Health, 196
Nationalism, 6, 8, 122, 210
National Security Council, 89, 90
Nazism, 6, 203
Neoconservatives, 225
Neoliberalism, 34, 177, 210
Neurosis, 156, 175
New American Century (documents), 87, 169, 177
Newton, Isaac, 8, 36
Nicaragua, 89
Niger, 92
9/11, 74, 80, 84, 91, 111, 169, 176
Normality, 29, 30, 194, 199, 222
Northern Ireland, 121, 129, 212, 216
Nuclear weapons, 74, 97, 180
Nuremburg trials, 195

O
Oil, 90, 136, 153
Operation Duck Hook, 87
Operation Mongoose, 80

P

Pacification, 111, 116, 118–125, 127, 128, 133, 136, 143, 166, 167
Palestine Liberation Organization (PLO), 163
Paradigms, 3, 29, 62, 71
Paranoia, 2, 155, 159, 167, 182
Parsimony, 4, 33, 79, 80, 165
Patriot Act, 17, 80, 92
Peace movements, 87, 88
Pentagon Papers, 126, 166, 168
Perestroika (political science), 3, 8, 20, 22–27, 31, 34–36, 39
Peru, 112
Philippines, 14, 133, 134, 144, 148
Phoenix program, 115, 120, 121, 136
Physics, 30, 31, 93
Poland, 102
Policy entrepreneurs, 52
Political correctness, 58
Political psychology, 2, 149
Positivism, 4, 41
Poverty, 191
Projection, 23, 154–156
ProporNot, 220
Psychoanalysis, 2, 10, 43, 149–152, 154, 155, 157, 158, 160–162, 164, 165, 170–175, 177–182
Psychology, 2, 38, 46, 63, 150, 156, 158, 160, 165, 171, 172, 174, 175, 178, 179, 184, 189, 203, 224
Psychopathology, 170, 221
Public opinion, 1, 3, 78, 82, 83, 87, 90–93, 95
Puritanism, 192

R

Racism, 195
RAND, 2, 115, 118, 119, 122
Rational choice, 4, 6, 8, 9, 18, 19, 21–23, 27–29, 31–33, 46–48, 62, 122, 135, 156, 161, 224
Rationality, 2–5, 45, 62, 84, 150, 152
Realism, 4, 46, 62, 78–80, 84, 85, 94, 96, 100, 108
Realpolitik, 9, 75, 77, 78, 80, 91, 95, 156, 169, 170
Reductionism, 2, 152, 188
Relationism, 3, 11
Relativism, 30
Republicanism (Irish), 210, 215
Resistance, 5–9, 22, 87, 114, 116, 127, 129, 132, 134, 135, 137, 155, 176, 178, 187, 201
Roman Catholicism, 209
Russia, 116, 222

S

Saudi Arabia, 89
Scandinavia, 49
Schizophrenia, 189, 197, 200, 201
Science, 1–5, 8, 9, 17, 18, 20, 21, 24–30, 32, 33, 44, 46, 49, 52, 63, 149, 151, 152, 160, 172, 187, 190, 193, 195, 198, 200, 218, 224
Scientism, 2, 199
Sociology of knowledge, 1, 5, 60, 64
South Africa, 59, 71, 90, 188
South East Asia, 113
Soviet Union, 19, 157
Sparta, 150
Sterilization, 193–195, 201, 204
Strategic hamlet program, 115
Subjectivity, 47, 155, 158, 161, 175
Superego, 149, 158, 164, 181

T

Technology, 2, 98, 152, 195, 197, 202, 205, 215
Tet offensive, 124, 166
Thermidore, 25
Torture, 6, 115, 121
Tuskegee experiments, 196

U
Unconscious, The, 2, 3, 5, 10, 151, 155, 163, 171, 176, 177, 192
United Kingdom, 204

V
Vichy (France), 5–8
Vienna circle, 3
Vietnam, 9, 22, 48, 57, 61, 80, 85–88, 90, 108–111, 113, 115, 116, 119, 121–125, 128, 130, 132, 133, 137, 151, 165–170, 172, 219
Vietnam syndrome, 61, 77, 92, 154, 165

W
Wall Street, 24, 93, 218, 221
Watergate, 161
Weapons of mass destruction (WMD), 92, 153, 170
Welfare state, 55, 176
Wittgenstein, Ludwig, 4
World Trade Organization (WTO), 52

The manufacturer's authorised representative in the EU is Springer Nature Customer Service Centre GmbH, Europaplatz 3, 69115 Heidelberg, Germany. If you have any concerns regarding our products, please contact ProductSafety@springernature.com

Printed and bound by CPI Group (UK) Ltd, Croydon, CR0 4YY

23/03/2026

02076662-0004